BORN AGAIN TO SERVE

Victor Paul Wierwille

BORN AGAIN TO SERVE

Dorothea Kipp Wierwille

American Christian Press
The Way International
New Knoxville, Ohio 45871

International Standard Book Number 0-910068-79-8
Library of Congress Catalog Card Number: 96-60712
American Christian Press
The Way International
New Knoxville, Ohio 45871
©1996 by The Way International
All rights reserved
First Edition 1996. Second Printing 1997
Printed in the United States of America

*For historical purposes, care has been taken to preserve the spelling
and punctuation of the original sources.*

*To the glory of God
and to the believers who stood faithfully
with Dr. Victor Paul Wierwille during these
formative years of his ministry as well as
those who are standing with us today.*

Hebrews 12:1

Contents

Preface / 1

Acknowledgments / 3

Family History / 4

Family Crest / 6

Childhood / 7

Life on the Farm / 12

High School Years / 16

Early Influences / 18

Mission House College / 23

Our Wedding / 27

Graduate Schools / 30

First Congregation / 33

Moving to Van Wert / 45

E. Stanley Jones / 48

Rufus Moseley / 52

Perry Hayden / 55

Glenn Clark / 56

Rhoda Becker / 59

Doctor of Theology Degree / 67

Hobbies / 68

The Power of Prayer / 74

E. W. Kenyon / 76

Foreign Missions / 77

Receiving the Holy Spirit / 78

Starr Daily / 82

Tenth Anniversary / 84

Mary's Healing / 87

B. G. Leonard / 90

Albert Cliffe / 94

Bishop K. C. Pillai / 96

Power for Abundant Living / 99

E. W. Bullinger / 102

Seeds of The Way Corps / 105

Preparation to Go Abroad / 107

England / 119

Welcome to India / 125

Bible Lands / 175

Europe / 189

Return to the U.S.A. / 202

George M. Lamsa / 212

International Outreach / 214

A New Headquarters / 219

Nurturing Growth / 221

A Permanent Headquarters / 232

Remodeling at the Farm / 248

The Diamond Club / 254

John Noble / 263

Moving Day / 264

Books by Victor Paul Wierwille / 269

About the Author / 271

Preface

The idea of writing my husband's biography didn't originate with me. I was asked to do it. Previously when a biography was mentioned, I had thought I would be able to contribute to one. I was very aware that no one else could accurately relate Dr. Wierwille's life without my input. He and I were raised in the same community and lived much of our lives together. I felt I knew his life better than anyone else and therefore could reconstruct it most fully and authentically. Thus when I was asked to write a biography of Dr. Wierwille, I became thankful to God for the privilege.

I chose to begin this book with the historical background of the Wierwille family, giving the context into which Dr. Wierwille was born. The biography then continues through his school years, his two pastorates, the radio broadcast ministry, our seven-month foreign teaching tour, his resignation from the denomination, the launching of The Way Ministry on an independent basis, and our moving The Way Headquarters to New Knoxville, Ohio. In other words, this book covers Dr. Wierwille's life from 1916 to 1961. I plan to continue his life's story from 1961 to 1985 in a second volume.

In considering how to tell Dr. Wierwille's life story, I certainly didn't want to interpret or analyze him or compare him to any Bible saint. I set out to chronicle his actions and his own words—to let them speak for him. Of course I, as the author, had to decide what to include in the story and what to leave out, otherwise this work would be way too long.

It is very important to me to give an overall scope of the life of Dr. Wierwille: his work, his interests, and his relationships with family, friends, and others who influenced him. I have worked diligently for accuracy. I have searched the historical files of The Way to be certain of quotations, events, places, and dates. If any of the facts in this volume are different from previously published ones, I believe the ones in this book to be more accurate because the Historical Department and I have diligently checked and rechecked them. I do not want to have written a string of remembrances which have blurred with time and thus represent the past haphazardly.

You will see as you proceed through the book that it is what I would term a "multimedia biography." The Way Historical Department has helped me find photographs, programs, newspaper and magazine clippings, legal documents, deeds, minutes of meetings, mass letter mailings, and personal letters. I have inserted them right in the text to try to help you, the reader, gain a fuller impression of what I'm trying to communicate. These multimedia give the volume an informality and, at the same time, add dimension to better understanding the life of Dr. Wierwille.

It is my heartfelt desire for our people, whether they knew Dr. Wierwille or not, to have a clear index into him as a person: what he was like, what he did, how he became what he was. I want people to see that as he studied and researched, he progressively learned in a step-by-step manner. I want people to understand how Dr. Wierwille searched for knowledge of God and His Word from a host of people, people who loved God and had insight which helped enlarge his scope of understanding and practice. I want people to see his zeal in presenting the accuracy of the Word and then in providing a way for others to become leaders prepared to teach God's Word. I want to give vitality to the name of a person who now is awaiting the return of our lord. My hope is that this life's account will inspire believers to love and trust God more fervently as they grow in believing action to become more committed to whatever it is that God is working within them and to stay faithful to their callings.

Acknowledgments

First of all, I wish to thank the Board of Trustees of The Way International—Rev. L. Craig Martindale, Dr. Donald Wierwille, and Mr. Howard Allen—for asking me to do this work and for their wholehearted support of this project.

My sincere appreciation goes to Dr. Wierwille's sisters, Lydia and Sevilla, who have answered some of my questions, especially questions about the early years; to all five of my dear children who have taken a great interest in this project by prayerfully upholding it; and to my daughter Karen Wierwille Martin for her enthusiasm and encouragement in my getting started on this work. She has been my partner in believing as I was writing, she helped greatly in choosing the multimedia that are being used, and she was my assistant in polishing the manuscript.

I am grateful to The Way Historical Department, Way Publications, Word Processing, and Printing Services. So many people have shown great interest in this book and have held it in their prayers while I was putting it together. These I also thank. It has been my joy to serve together with each person mentioned in *Born Again to Serve*.

Family History

★ *Vierville-sur-Mer, France*
◉ *Ladbergen, Germany*

The Wierwille family ancestry can be traced as far back as the 1300s to a small town in northern France called *Vierville-sur-Mer,* translated "Wierwille by the Sea." These Viervilles were Huguenots, a group of French Protestants who staunchly resisted Roman Catholic attempts to dominate the religious and social life of France. In the sixteenth and seventeenth centuries, many Huguenots left France to escape religious persecution, the Viervilles among them.

The Viervilles fanned out and fled to either Germany, England, or Switzerland. The oldest extant record of their being in Germany is a tax record in the district of Tecklenberg in 1543. The next documented location of the Vierville family is found in Ladbergen, Westphalia, in the 1680s.

In adapting to their relocation from France to Germany, the Viervilles altered the spelling of their name in order to maintain a consistent pronunciation. Since a French *V* is pronounced like a German *W*, the German spelling became *Wierwille.*

Some of the Wierwilles from Ladbergen became early participants in a large German movement to immigrate to the United States for religious, political, and economic freedom. The ship that brought Johann Heinrich Wierwille, Dr. Wierwille's great-grandfather, and his family to the United States was registered at Port Baltimore, Maryland, on January 1, 1839. Church records document the presence of Dr. Wierwille's ancestors in the New Knoxville, Ohio, area in 1841.

A four-generation Wierwille genealogy beginning with Johann Heinrich, who immigrated to the United States in 1839

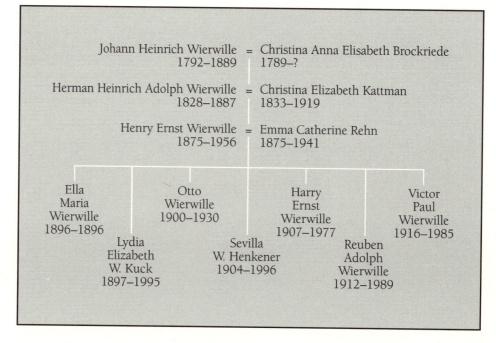

Dr. Wierwille's grandfather, Herman Heinrich Adolph Wierwille, also known as Adam Wierwille, purchased his New Knoxville farm in three parcels: October 1, 1846—53.31 acres, public land sold during the presidency of James K. Polk; June 1, 1848—40 acres, public land sold during the presidency of James K. Polk; and July 1, 1850—53.85 acres, public land sold during the presidency of Zachary Taylor.

Some, but not all, of the 147 acres originally purchased by Adam Wierwille was redistributed with other local acreage by the time Henry Ernst, Adam's son, inherited the land, still 147 acres. Then Henry Ernst willed the same land he had inherited to his three sons, Harry Ernst, Reuben Adolph, and Victor Paul, the same land that was deeded to The Way International in 1957.

Family Crest

The Wierwille family crest, which originated in northern France during the 1300s, was found by Dr. Wierwille in 1978 when he visited the Château de Creully near Vierville-sur-Mer.

Dr. Wierwille slightly adapted the coat of arms by replacing three sea gulls with three doves. Otherwise, the design has remained the same for nearly seven hundred years, representing a family dedicated to God, freedom, and integrity.

The crest bears six distinct horizontal stripes—three blue and three silver. Blue, the color of the sky, represents God's canopy over the earth. It symbolizes fidelity, faithfulness, careful and exact observance of duty, and adherence to truth. Silver is one of the earth's precious metals and often represents treasure. Here it symbolizes God's people, who hold His treasure (holy spirit) in earthen vessels.

A red fascia (band) runs diagonally across the crest, binding the stripes together. The color red represents both life and death since it is the color of blood, which contains the life of the flesh.

The doves on the center blue stripe represent God's gift of holy spirit. There are three because the number three signifies completeness. With God's gift of holy spirit given on the day of Pentecost, man can once again be complete, having body, soul, and spirit. The presence of God's spirit within the Wierwille family members is a key to their living victoriously from generation to generation until the return of Jesus Christ.

Château de Creully as it now looks

Childhood

Victor Paul was born to Ernst and Emma Wierwille on December 31, 1916, in the same farmhouse his forefathers had built. He was born the last of seven children: Ella Maria (born in July 1896, lived only two months and twenty-seven days), Lydia (1897), Otto (1900), Sevilla (1904), Harry Ernst (1907), Reuben (1912), and Victor (1916). Although Victor appeared to be a healthy newborn, his mother noticed after a short time that he was not developing as he should. Emma prayed for her baby, as her manner was. The doctor couldn't seem to find a cause for Victor's problem; in those days people just called it "short growth." Ernst and Emma, in seeking help for their baby, called the revered minister of their church, the Reverend L. H. Kunst, to come and water baptize him. This was the best thing they knew to do, and they acted accordingly. God's grace took care of the rest. After being baptized, Victor recovered very quickly.

Victor Paul Wierwille

Dorothea Sarah Kipp

As was the tradition, Victor's name was placed immediately after his baptism on the church's "cradle roll," which hung in the Sunday school department. As of a child's third birthday, the child was permitted to attend Sunday school, and the cradle roll card became the child's property.

Babies were always brought to church. In the New Knoxville community, Sunday school and Sunday morning church services were seldom missed by any of the families; it was truly the central focus of the community's life. The mothers with babies and young children sat in a designated area of the church. Victor's mother, who impressed me as an indulgent lady in comparison to my mother, always brought a purse

The Wierwille family, 1922

filled with soda crackers to entertain Victor and the other children seated near them.

When it came time for a family picture, Victor needed some extra encouragement to stand up and face the camera. His countenance shows his feelings. Victor was six years old when this picture was taken.

Back row (l. to r.): Lydia, Harry, Otto, Sevilla. Front row: Ernst, Reuben, Victor, Emma

In September of 1922 at the age of five and a half, Victor entered public school at a little one-room brick schoolhouse known as "Stork's School," which was about a mile's walk from the Wierwille farm. There he studied and played for six years.

After sixth grade, he was bused with the other children of that part of Van Buren Township, Shelby County, into the village of New Knoxville to New Knoxville School where he completed the next six years, receiving his high school diploma in May 1934.

The Wierwille family loved music. They looked forward to spending Saturday evenings in their music room, gathered around a piano or

The current appearance of what originally was Woodland School, or as it was popularly called, "Stork's School," after a teacher

Victor's second-grade report card

pump organ, with Dad Wierwille leading the singing of hymns. If neither Lydia nor Sevilla were around to play the organ or piano, Dad would get out his tuning fork to assist him in getting a hymn pitched correctly.

By age thirteen Victor regularly listened to a music radio program over station WLW in Cincinnati, featuring a singer named Bradley Kincaid. At that time Victor's father bought him a twenty-dollar guitar, and Victor began teaching himself to play the guitar so that he could sing and play the country-western songs of his musical hero. "Bradley Kincaid had the greatest influence in my learning music," Victor occasionally remarked.

After teaching himself to strum and sing, Victor was frequently invited to perform at box socials. Box socials were social events for the families whose children were attending various one-room schoolhouses. At these occasions there would be a program of entertainment, and then the food boxes were auctioned and sold to the highest bidders. The boxes were attractively decorated, and food was put in them by young girls of datable age. With no one supposedly knowing who packed the individual boxes, the young men would bid and buy them and then have the pleasure of eating the contents with the girls who had prepared them.

Shortly after being given his guitar, Victor and two other friends formed a musical group composed of a pianist, an accordionist, and, of course, a guitar player, Victor. These three were invited to perform one summer weekend at radio station WOWO in Fort Wayne, Indiana. That was the first time Victor asked me to go somewhere with him. His invitation was due partly to my being a good friend of Lillian Kuck, the pianist of the group.

By the age of thirteen or fourteen, the youth of our church would have already attended catechism for three years, during which time they memorized many hymns and scripture verses and were instructed in morals and values, reinforcing much of what had been taught previously both at home and from the pulpit. Catechism was a more personal and direct method to teach the Bible, hymns, and church doctrine to the youth of the congregation.

The final year of catechism was taught by the pastor himself rather than his assistant. That last year's instruction was considered most important, so the students went to catechism class on Wednesday afternoon after school as well as on Saturday mornings. Then after successfully completing catechism, we young people were confirmed, a major event in our lives, and we became members of the church.

Confirmation group photo, spring 1931. Rev. Kunst is in the center; Victor is second from the right in the front row.

Being confirmed and becoming a church member made us eligible to sing in the church choir. And so Vic, as we many times called him, became a member of the choir, joining his brother Reuben and his father, who sang in the church choir for over forty years. Victor confessed that one reason he had enjoyed the choir was that he could quit his farm work early on Wednesday evenings so that Reuben, Dad, and he could get to choir practice.

On Saturday afternoons at exactly 4:00 the New Knoxville church bell always rang, reminding everyone in town and on the neighboring farms to get ready for Sunday, a day of rest from the usual farm work other than taking care of the basic needs of the animals. Saturdays were busy days for the girls, as they were assigned to polish shoes and see that all the Sunday clothes were ready to wear and the baking done. Saturday night was bath night in preparation for dressing up for church the next day. So when the church bell was heard at 4:00 on Saturday afternoons, the community hurried to finish chores and get ready for a church-oriented Sunday morning and, usually, Sunday evening as well. Sunday afternoons were characteristically spent visiting relatives, friends, and neighbors.

Life on the Farm

The Wierwille farm, circa 1920

On September 10, 1923, while brother Otto and his wife, Edna, were living with Dad and Mom Wierwille in the farmhouse, a daughter, Virginia Rose, was born to them. She became a beautiful and sweet little housemate for Victor who, as her uncle, was seven years old when she was born. At the age of three Virginia Rose suddenly became sick with diphtheria and fell asleep. Her death was a very sad experience in the life of the impressionable ten-year-old Victor.

Her body was laid in state in the living room of the Wierwille home. Because of the diphtheria quarantine, the family had to have a private memorial service. Otto asked Victor to sing "Whispering Hope" at the service. "I know I sang because no one else was permitted to come," Victor observed. Afterward, Otto gave him a silver dollar and a hug and thanked him for singing. This blessed Victor very much. Seven years later this brother, Otto, was killed in a car accident in Lima, Ohio. He left behind a widow and an infant son, Charles.

Work never stops on a farm. After the fall harvest each year, Dad Wierwille and his sons would go to the woods for several days to prune out branches and cut up the fallen or dead trees which weren't good for lumber but could be used for firewood. The entire community was diligent to keep their farms and woods neat and orderly. After the fallen trees and branches were cut up, the twigs were burned; but the larger pieces of wood were chopped, split, and stacked to dry. This wood would then be good for burning in the wood-burning stoves after a year of aging. The split timber was hauled from the woods to the woodshed, which stood close to the house. (The one chore the brothers always complained about was carrying wood from the woodshed to the woodbox in the house.) That same, original woodshed was moved a few years ago to The Way Woods. Before we moved the old woodshed, it had been used in camps and summer schools since 1962 for housing women. Therefore it had been lovingly known as "The Nest." It was used for housing during the Rock of Ages.

Another major fall and winter job was fixing farm machinery and greasing the plowshares and cultivators to keep them from rusting during the cold winter months. Since the children were in school five days a week, they could help with this work only on Saturdays.

In late spring when it was time to cultivate the new young corn growth, sometimes the plants became covered with small clods of soil by the cultivator. Young Victor frequently followed after the plow and threw the clods off the young plants with a stick. So, on this 147-acre farmland in Van Buren Township in Shelby County, Ohio, Victor was quite involved in helping his father and his one brother, Reuben, with the field work, as well as taking care of chores with the farm animals: horses, cows, chickens, pigs, dogs, and cats.

Before the hot days of summer commenced, the Wierwille family would begin cooking and eating their meals in the summer kitchen. Because cooking at that time was done with wood-burning ranges or kerosene stoves, the stoves not only cooked the food, but gave off considerable heat in the kitchen as well. So to keep the main house cool during the heat of the year,

The Wierwille farmhouse, 1908. (l. to r.): A hired hand, Grandma Christina, Lydia, Sevilla, Emma, Otto, and Ernst

the Wierwilles had a summer kitchen. This was a pleasant change from the routine of the rest of the year, a practice helpful before the advent of insulated electric stoves and air-conditioning.

In the teens and twenties, gypsies traveled through this locality of New Knoxville. They traveled in groups and frequently parked their buggies and surreys along the road by the lumber mill near Vic's one-room schoolhouse. The schoolchildren were afraid of them because of the rumors that gypsies practiced witchcraft and kidnapped children. Thus the teacher made the students stay in the schoolhouse until the travelers moved on after pumping water from the schoolhouse well.

Also in those days there were a few "tramps" who walked along the roads. These vagabonds soon learned where hospitality was extended and made regular stops for food and shelter for a night at those homes. The vagabonds Victor remembered as frequenting the Wierwille home were two men called George May and Joe Suess. The dogs didn't like George, so he would have to defend himself with his satchels as he walked up the lane to the house. George was a happy guy who had a big appetite. He was known to eat everything on the table, even the butter out of the dish. When George stopped by, Mom Wierwille would speak in German, instructing the family to be sure to take their food quickly as she brought it to the table. Joe Suess wasn't quite so voracious. Joe was a quiet and very appreciative person. His back was totally bent, so he had to turn his head to the side to see the road ahead. Victor said how blessed he always was to see his mother take care of those tramps, as they were called, as she had such a big, wonderful heart. He said, "I think the great love I have for people comes from Mother. The discipline comes from Dad."

Ernst and Emma, Victor's father and mother, circa 1930

Mom Wierwille was known for being outgoing and helpful. Whenever her grandchildren came to visit, she always reached for the tin soda-cracker box or the cookie jar as soon as they came in the house. She would follow up with a glass of milk or water before they could ask. She was just such a caring, thoughtful person.

During my high school days and into my years of nurses' training, I was invited to the Wierwille home many times for Sunday noon dinner. Mother Emma always seemed to have a full cupboard of pies, cakes, and freshly baked bread. Along with that, she would also have jello with fruit, mainly bananas topped with whipped cream, for dessert. No wonder the family never ate out. Even when they went to the county fair or on a day trip somewhere, they packed their meals at home.

High School Years

Since Victor didn't like to ride the bus to high school, he rode into town in bad weather with the neighbor boy in his horse and buggy, and in nice weather he rode his bicycle. During his sophomore year, Victor and Reuben were given a motorcycle to share by their father, and thus began Victor's lifelong romance with motorcycles. As a high schooler, Victor became quite versatile and even did trick riding, such as standing on the motorcycle seat while sailing through town. The old

Double A Restaurant proprietor, Adolph Henschen, recalled seeing Victor performing in this way on several occasions.

Since his older brother Reuben had been quite a school prankster, Victor was a marked young man when he got to high school and was blamed for many mischievous antics that sometimes went on, like cutting the class bell wires and bringing rabbits and birds into the school. At one point the school superintendent severely punished Victor by paddling him and expelling him from school for a week. In fact, he told Victor he didn't care if he ever came back. Victor, in anger, made up his mind that he would never return.

Victor later said, "Being the fall of the year, my father consoled himself with the thought that my dismissal was not without its benefits because it was corn-cutting time and I could be used in the fields." However, sister Sevilla reasoned with him and begged him to go back to school, which, when he finally calmed down, he agreed to do. On his birthday in 1980, Vic again admitted, "Sevilla must be thanked—she kept me going to school."

As a young man, Vic loved sports and played basketball throughout high school. When it came time to think seriously about what he wanted to do with his life, he considered being a lawyer or a physician or a preacher. One reason, no doubt the major reason, Victor thought about becoming a physician was that I was already in training to become a nurse. Obviously, he eventually chose to become a preacher. His father urged him

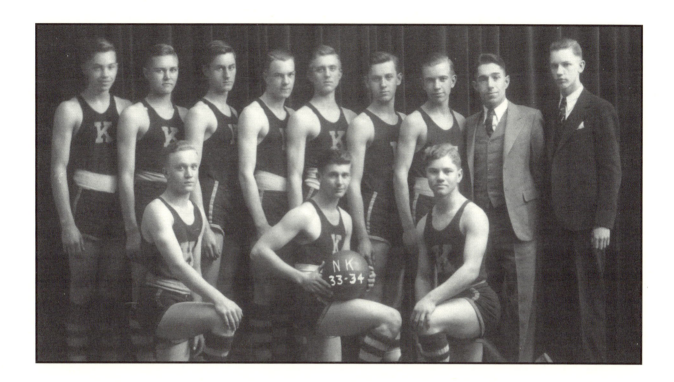

The high school basketball team. Victor is in the middle of the back row.

strongly to stay on the farm, but his mother's prayers prevailed for him to be a great teacher of God's Word.

Though Victor did not go into farming as his father had hoped, Dad Wierwille's word did carry clout. Vic had had a great record in high school basketball and was offered a basketball scholarship by The Ohio State University. But Dad Wierwille had the final word when he announced, "We have supported Mission House College in Wisconsin with our church money, and that's where you'll go to college." End of subject.

It was tradition in these German families for the youngest son to stay on the farm, farming the land and taking care of his parents until they died. At that time the youngest son would inherit the farm while the other children in the family would be compensated in the parents' will with money and other effects. So it was in the Wierwille family.

Since Adam (1828–1887) predeceased his father, Johann (1792–1889), Adam's wife, Christina (1833–1919), inherited the land. Christina then willed the farm to her youngest son, Henry Ernst Wierwille (1875–1956), and his wife, Emma (1875–1941), Victor's parents. When Dad Wierwille died, he broke the "youngest son tradition." Since Victor Paul was the youngest son of his generation and had broken the custom by choosing not to farm, he and his two brothers Harry and Reuben jointly inherited the family farm.

Victor's high school graduation portrait, 1934

17

Early Influences

This photo was taken on "The Great Day of Dedication," August 19, 1894, of the German Reformed Church in New Knoxville.

The New Knoxville Centennial Souvenir book of 1938 informs us that "the beginning of the First Reformed Church dates back to the early 1830s. Religious gatherings of the early pioneers were held in their homes, the embryo of the church today. The first regular resident minister served the congregation from 1840 to 1843."

At a fall mission festival when Victor was about nine or ten years old, a guest minister, Dr. Lohman, was shaking hands with people at the end of the service. When Vic's turn came to shake hands, Dr. Lohman looked at him and gently inquired, "And what do you want to be when you grow up?" Victor quickly replied, "I want to be a man of God, just like you." In retrospect, the family often retold this anecdote.

Interesting to note was the custom at the New Knoxville church of using Sunday morning offerings for mission work. And then at "mission festivals" every year in September, another special offering was collected for missions. If church members wanted to give money for the local church's needs, like the pastor's salary and church building maintenance, they had to take their money directly to a special fund at the bank, which had been established in 1910. Pledged money for the local church's operation was not collected at church.

Dr. L. H. Kunst, the most revered person in our community, stood with conviction as a clergyman for God's Word. His example had a tremendous influence on Victor's life. One noteworthy example of Dr. Kunst's taking a stand for his convictions pertained to the building in New Knoxville in the 1920s of a dance hall, which the young people of the village desperately wanted. They had purchased land and were ready to begin building. On the Sunday morning prior to ground breaking, Dr. Kunst in his sermon told his congregation not only that they didn't need the dance hall, but also that they would have to build it over his dead body. Because of such a strong statement from the most respected person in their community, the dance hall was never built.

Later in life, when Dr. Kunst was living in retirement with his daughter in Philadelphia, Victor and I visited him there for a few hours. Before we left him, he encouraged Victor by saying, "Ach, Victor, you just preach de Vord, just preach de Vord, no matter vat anyone says." His English was still spoken with a German accent; his voice, as always, was firm and sure.

Promptness, detail-mindedness, orderliness, and good stewardship were qualities instilled in Victor from his birth. Victor's father, Ernst, had a tendency to be both stern and impatient. He moved with a quick step, was always very punctual, and could be impulsive. If something came to his mind to do, his wife, Emma, had to be ready to "shift her gears"; frequently his impulses were to go visit someone. Dr. Wierwille recalled his father in his earlier years chewing tobacco and reading his Bible as his evening ritual.

For the twenty-five or thirty years that I knew Ernst Wierwille, he, as a consumer, always bought whatever was considered "the best" and "the biggest." When he bought a family car, it was the nicest. When he bought a tractor, he bought the latest. In 1913 he bought his first automobile, a Maxwell.

Before the motorized farm equipment was invented, the horses, of course, were a very necessary part of field work. Here again, it was not just any horse that Dad Wierwille bought and used. His horses had to be purebreds. Victor several times related how his father went to the New York Harbor to pick up a horse which he had ordered from France. Then he rode in the boxcar with that horse back to Ohio. Dad Wierwille chose the strong Percheron breed for the workhorses, breeding up colts

Victor on a Percheron, circa 1930

with them and winning several blue ribbons and a Grand Champion at the Ohio State Fair.

Dad Wierwille's mother, Grandma Christina Wierwille, lived with Ernst and his family, surviving her husband by thirty-two years. Ernst was the youngest son in the family, so he stayed on the "home farm." The code of behavior at that time was that his parent, Grandma Christina, was responsible for the business of the farm as long as she lived. So whenever anything was bought, the aging parent still had to pay because she held the money which the proceeds of the farm provided. Dr. Wierwille related seeing Grandma Christina go to her dresser, lay out a farmer's red handkerchief, and take out gold pieces from the drawer. Counting as she placed the gold pieces on the handkerchief, she would then tie it up and give it to Dad Wierwille for the agreed-to purchase.

Grandma Christina Kattman Wierwille, 1833–1919

When her husband died in 1887, Christina took charge of the farm. She was a good organizer, and Dr. Wierwille told how she personally arranged to take their cream and eggs to the railroad station in Botkins and send them by train all the way to Cleveland. There she had someone meet the train and take the produce to the Cleveland market where it brought a far better price than it would have gotten locally. Also, "she 'ruled the roost.' She was a very strong, intense woman," Dr. Wierwille remembered. "Grandma was tough and made all of us work. And my mother never complained about her."

Dr. Wierwille remembered his grandmother as always having one drawer in her dresser with candy in it. She was generous in handing it out to the children. The candy was kept in the drawer at the top of the same dresser that had gold pieces in a lower drawer—a versatile dresser indeed.

In the mornings after everyone had finished eating breakfast, Grandma Christina read to the family in German out of *Unsere tägliches Brot (Our Daily Bread),* a daily devotional booklet. She lived with Dad Wierwille and his family until the day she died in 1919. The day before she died, she hitched up her own horse to a carriage, refusing help from anyone, to go to the doctor.

Life on the farm was pretty much self-supporting, with much of the food grown at home. About all that was ever bought from the grocery was flour, sugar, Post Toasties, rice, bananas, jello, and spices. Hogs, pigs, chickens, cows, and during hunting season, wild game (squirrel, rabbit, and pheasants) were all available meats for the table. Of course, produce of eggs, milk, and butter was plentiful. A large garden was planted every spring, with lovely flowers grown in one area of it. The vegetables commonly grown were peas, green beans, red beets, tomatoes, lettuce, onions, cabbage, and potatoes. Homegrown fruits were cherries, apples, pears, plums, raspberries, and grapes. Many of these fruits and vegetables were canned in glass jars and stored for the following winter's use.

One of Victor's youthful assignments was to help cut up cabbage for sauerkraut, a traditional German dish. Sauerkraut was made in a large ten-gallon crock and stored in the cellar. The cellar was a small room, about eighteen feet square, under the house with an outside stairway and with the type of cellar door that children could slide down when it was closed.

Onions, apples, and potatoes were also stored in the cellar, where they would keep cool but not freeze. It was a cool place in the summertime and kept produce from freezing in the wintertime— an elementary but practical refrigeration system.

Butchering day was a great day on which neighbors helped each other from before sunrise until after sunset at a designated neighbor's house. Typically three or four hogs would be butchered in one day. In the days following butchering day, the women were busy preserving the various cuts in several ways. In addition, a family usually bought a quarter or a half of beef from some person in the community who had butchered beef, as one family couldn't use the entire beef at one time. The beef needed to be canned, cold-packed in glass jars, and cooked for three hours in a hot water bath to be a treat to eat later. Another method for preserving meat before modern refrigeration was hanging it in smoke in the farm smokehouse to be cured.

Before electricity came to the New Knoxville area, the households used oil lamps, followed by carbide lamps. In 1920 a single-phase electrical line was brought to the area. At that time Dad Wierwille asked the neighbors to band together and negotiate with the Dayton Power and

Light Company to supply the area farmers with electricity. The Dayton Power and Light Company then extended a three-mile electrical line with sixty poles under the supervision of the apprentice training program. (Not until 1972 was this original electrical line changed from single-phase to three-phase for covering the added demands of The Way International.)

With the coming of electricity came many new things such as electric lights, refrigeration, and the radio. Radio station KDKA from Pittsburgh had begun broadcasting programs on the evening of November 2, 1920, with the returns of the Harding-Cox presidential election. This occasion is generally considered as marking the beginning of broadcasting in its modern form.

In 1930 Rev. Charles E. Fuller began his "Old-Fashioned Revival Hour," broadcasting from Long Beach, California. Also at that time, Rev. Cadel from the Cadel Tabernacle in Indianapolis, Indiana, was heard every morning in the barn while we farm families did our milking and other chores.

The newfangled telephone had been brought into the area already in 1905. It didn't take many years for each family in the community to make use of this convenience, though at first everyone was on a party line. The Wierwille family's first telephone number was 13–23, which meant that the party line was line 23, and 13 was the Wierwille number. One long ring followed by three short ones meant the Wierwilles were getting a call.

This type of living characterized the cultural circumstances in which Victor and I grew up.

Mission House College

Dr. Wierwille recalled years later, "The year that I left for college was the year that hog cholera struck and we lost almost every hog. The family was hurting financially. Dad had to go someplace to borrow money so that I could go to Mission House College for my freshman year." This, however, was a very temporary situation from which the family soon recovered.

Victor had a strong basketball record throughout college. As a forward, he lettered for four years and led the team twice in scoring. One year he was among ten all-conference players selected at the forward position by the vote of the tri-state coaches. His coach said about Victor, "He was not a big man as far as basketball players go, but he was a furious player." On May 18, 1965, Vic was honored at the spring athletic banquet at the college (now known as Lakeland College, Sheboygan, Wisconsin). He was the sixteenth athlete to be elected to his alma mater's Hall of Fame.

Besides basketball in college, Vic also played football, was a broad jumper, high jumper, and sprinter in track, and found time to play the infield and pitch on the baseball team. In short, he loved to participate in sports.

One of the many ways Vic kept himself socially busy during his college years was by being active in revitalizing the fraternity Mu Lambda Sigma. This fraternity's purpose, the charter said, was threefold: spirituality, scholarship, and fraternity. It provided a definite stimulus to greater scholastic achievement and added interest in extracurricular activities of the school. The motto of Mu Lambda Sigma was "God first, my fellowman second, and I am willing to be third," a concept Victor believed in and promoted his entire life. He became the fraternity president his junior year, and Dr. Bauer, his revered philosophy professor, was the fraternity's sponsor.

During the college and especially seminary days, Vic and some of the other seminarians would get into discussions about the Bible and its teachings. "The pros and cons of water baptism" probably headed the list of often-discussed issues. Since neither side could conclusively prove its position, they stayed with the traditional teaching and practice—and kept wondering about it.

Three college friends: Victor, Bill Wild, and Harry Bredeweg

A sentimental note Victor wrote on June 26, 1938, near his graduation day

> Three years ago we [Harry Bredeweg, Bill Wild, and Victor Wierwille] became good friends when Bill and I were rooming together. Last year we had a big five, this year a small ten: Cricket, Hefty, Durst, Jake, Schild, Dave, Johnny, Bill, Bredy, and Vic-- and yet in between floated the Big Three (Bill, Bredy, and Vic) -- possibly the biggest three friends that ever lived. It was wise not to speak badly of either one of the three when one was in hearing distance, for we were one for all and all for one. We worked more and yet played more and had more fun than you could imagine being complied [sic] in three years.

It also bears mentioning that the professors at the Mission House College did not believe Jesus Christ was born at Christmastime; but their attitude was, What difference does it make? So they continued to adhere to tradition.

I believe that most of the men who entered the pre-seminary and seminary studies when Victor did really had their hearts set on helping people and wanting to learn and teach God's Word. And so it was with Victor. His problem was that he never could make the Bible "fit," to use his word. He always was keenly aware of its apparent contradictions so far as he understood it. But he constantly was looking for greater understanding.

During the early years in college, Vic became a prolific reader and gave much credit to his professors who had helped him form a system of study. In theology, the greatest impression was made on him by Mission House's Dr. Louis C. Hessert in systematic theology and ethics. Victor noted, "Dr. Hessert was a man who loved and encouraged me, and I shall always respect his great ability in academics. He gave me a diligence for the systematic accuracy of the Word of God and a thirst for knowledge in ethics." Later, in January 1951, Dr. Hessert was our guest teacher at St. Peter's Church in Van Wert for the Universal Week of Prayer conducted throughout the entire nation among all denominations.

Another man who influenced Victor in his college years was Dr. Ernst. Dr. Wierwille stated, "Dr. Karl Ernst introduced me to exegetical theology and Hebrew. Being a good friend of Dr. Karl Barth of Switzerland, Dr. Ernst presented Dr. Barth's theological positions in my classes, so I felt well acquainted with Dr. Barth when I finally met him many years later in Basel, Switzerland.

"Both Dr. Hessert and Dr. Ernst encouraged me to consider the possibility of doing postgraduate work and to someday become a professor at a theological seminary. They wanted me to go to Princeton Theological Seminary in hopes that I would pursue either exegetical theology or systematics. It must have been disappointing to them when I chose practical theology, then taught by Princeton's Dr. Andrew Blackwood. The latter inspired me in practical theology, religious education, and the related subjects."

At Mission House, Victor especially loved his classes in philosophy with Dr. Joseph Bauer. Later, in choosing courses at the University of Chicago Divinity School, Dr. Weiman there told Victor that he couldn't teach him any more in philosophy than he already knew because his teacher at Mission House College, Dr. Bauer, was the ultimate in this field!

It must have been Dr. Bauer who was the inspiration for Victor to put together a collection of thoughts during his college years which he called *Little Lights Along the Way*. In 1937, in a letter written to his family, Victor suggested that a book written by Tarshish, *Little Journeys with the Lamp Lighter*, had given him his idea. The following quote from that letter sheds insight into his writing *Little Lights Along the Way*:

> *The Way, of course, is Jesus Christ taken from his statement in the New Testament. I said "Little Candles" because in life little things mean more than the big things, for big things do not happen very often. Most generally the little things in life either make a man or break him. In spite of their smallness, they are great. Candles, of course, signify a small light, but a great many small lights produce a lighted "way."*

Among his entries written in *Little Lights Along the Way* are these:

Not to decide is to decide against.

Life often leaves men with wrecked ideals.

What does it profit if I know how to study and converse but do not know what's right?

We are very often ascetic individuals—we willingly evade and stand in the background just to see others doing what we should.

Never do the wrong the first time, because it may be the second time when it will have established itself as being right.

The "what and why" of wrong is always told, but how to eradicate it is very seldom mentioned.

Each profits by the other; one cannot stand alone.

Let me experience life that I may know myself.

These are a few entries selected from Vic's collection written at the age of twenty.

Our Wedding

Our official wedding photo on July 2, 1937

Victor and I had dated sporadically throughout our high school years and during his first three years of college in Wisconsin. Victor came to visit me in Cincinnati at the Deaconess Hospital whenever he returned home to Ohio on vacations. Then in May 1937, when I was finishing nursing school and after he had completed his junior year at Mission House College, he asked me to marry him. I was very agreeable to his proposal, and I accepted his fraternity pin as a gesture of our engagement.

About six weeks later we eloped and were married on July 2, 1937. Since Victor was twenty (I was twenty-one), we could not get a marriage license in the state of Ohio without having one of his parents sign for him. So we arranged to go to Kentucky where we could freely get a license. We called Rev. Tormoehlen at the Zion Evangelical and Reformed Church in Owensboro, Kentucky, and planned the ceremony. Victor's friend from college, Harry Bredeweg, and the minister's wife, Mrs. Tormoehlen, were our witnesses.

Later that summer Victor and I traveled by motorcycle to Sheboygan, Wisconsin, taking with us his little American toy terrier, known as The Kid. Vic liked The Kid so much that he even used to put him inside his jacket and sneak him into the movies. In a college letter dated October 10, 1934, addressed to his brother Reuben and sister-in-law Mary, Victor wrote, "Say, you know, I could have sold him [The Kid] for one hundred dollars the other week. You could not buy that dog for three times that much, for he just can't be bought."

Looking back and thinking about The Kid is so amusing to me. After his formal education years, Victor got larger hunting dogs and he occasionally mentioned how annoying he thought small dogs were.

Before we left for Wisconsin, I had arranged with the Memorial Hospital in Sheboygan to join their nursing staff. Upon arrival I rented a room within walking distance of the hospital while Victor again moved back into the dormitory at Mission House College, ten miles away, out in the Wisconsin countryside.

We felt that there were two reasons to keep our marriage a secret. For one reason, Vic could continue playing college basketball, since that privilege might be taken away from him if it were known he was married. Another reason was a rule that pre-seminary students were not permitted to get married before completing their seminary training. But by December of his senior year, Vic was securely positioned on the basketball team and felt safe that he would be allowed to complete the season. He was excited about our marriage of six months and wanted to let friends and family know, so at the December break in 1937, we went home to New Knoxville and announced our marriage to our parents. Vic's parents accepted me wholeheartedly. My parents were not exactly excited about the news, but they were loving nevertheless.

My nurse's photo, May 1937

Pre-seminary and seminary students always were assigned a minister advisor while they were in school. The advisor was to be helpful in overseeing and guiding the student. Vic's advisor was Rev. Nathan Vitz in New Bremen, Ohio. So at this time in December 1937 Vic wrote to Rev. Vitz, telling him about our marriage. We received a note back from him wishing us well and stating that he hoped everything was "honorable."

VICTOR WIERWILLE AND DOROTHEA KIPP ANNOUNCE MARRIAGE OF LAST JULY 2

1937

It was announced at a birthday celebration held in honor of Victor Paul Wierwille that Miss Dorothea Kipp, daughter of Mr. and Mrs. Edward Kipp and Mr. Wierwille, son of Mr. and Mrs. Ernst Wierwille, both of New Knoxville, had been united in the holy bonds of matrimony on July 2, 1937.

The wedding was solemnized by the Rev. Tormohlen of the Zion Evangelical and Reformed church of Owensboro, Ky.

Harry Bredeweg, of Linton, Ind., an intimate friend of the bridegroom, was the sole attendant. The ceremony took place in the church. After the wedding the bride and bridegroom accompanied Mr. Bredeweg to Linton where they remained for a few days.

Mrs. Wierwille is a graduate of the Deaconess Hospital School of Nursing, Cincinnati, O., and is now affiliated with the Memorial hospital nursing staff in Sheboygan, Wis. Mr. Wierwille is a senior in college at the Mission House, Sheboygan.

Friends extend best wishes to the couple.

Graduate Schools

On May 29, 1938, Victor received the Bachelor of Arts degree at the Mission House College, Plymouth, Wisconsin. The following summers of 1938, '39, and '40, Vic attended the University of Chicago Divinity School while continuing his seminary studies at Mission House Seminary during the regular fall, winter, and spring school terms.

A graduation photo of Harry and Imogene Bredeweg, Victor and me

Victor is third from the left with Vernon Opperman behind him and Harry Bredeweg second from the right.

We spent special weekends and vacation days during these three years of seminary in the home of friends, the Jabergs, whose acquaintance Vic had made in Sheboygan in the years before our marriage. Rev. and Mrs. Jaberg welcomed us so warmly that we called theirs our second home. Still I felt uneasy about accepting their kind invitations so frequently. When I mentioned this to Victor, he said that we would in the future offer the same hospitality to others as the Jabergs had extended to us.

On occasion Rev. Jaberg also asked Victor to preach in the pulpit of his church, Ebenezer Evangelical and Reformed Church. I recall that on August 27, 1939, Vic preached on the topic "Strength in Weakness." From youth on, the central idea is to be strong. Vic preached, "The attitude of our complete heart-life has become weak, and we have tried to cover up our unbelief, our internal laxity, with an external greatness. Thus, what is strength? In Isaiah 30:15 we read, '. . . in confidence shall be your strength. . .'; faith in God shall be your strength. Psalms 18:32 and 33 tell us, '*It is* God that girdeth me with strength, and maketh my way perfect. . . and setteth me upon my high places.'

"We are not happy because we have found a way of dodging life's tragedies and difficulties, but because we have obtained the secret of triumphing over them. There are countless situations in which the power of Christian faith is manifest, not by the way it gives us deliverance, but by the manner in which it enables us to transcend these evils and be superior to them."

In June 1940 I left my nursing job in Sheboygan and went back to my parents' home at New Knoxville to get ready for the birth of our wonderful first child, Don, which event took place on Sunday, August 11. Vic was in Chicago for summer school. He came home on short notice when I went into labor and remained with me for a day after Don's birth. He then went back to Chicago to finish summer school.

Later that August of 1940, all three of us traveled on old U.S. 30 to New Jersey so that Vic could begin studying for his Master of Theology degree at Princeton Theological Seminary. He believed he could learn much at Princeton, especially from Dr. Blackwood in practical theology. Dr. Blackwood later told Vic that his was the finest theological

library of any student who had ever graduated from Princeton Theological Seminary.

On Saturdays before Princeton University's home football games Vic would usually sell programs; this allowed him to see the games free of charge. During our year in New Jersey I took nursing jobs when Vic was available to baby-sit. Later that year my sister Deloris came to help us with little Don.

Vic's family was so supportive of us. The year we were at Princeton, Dad Wierwille, Lydia, Harry, Reuben, and Reuben's wife Mary came to celebrate Vic's birthday on the last day of 1940. It was a wonderful visit. But upon returning to New Knoxville, they found Mother Wierwille very ill with pneumonia. Vic and I prayed daily for her healing. Then one day in mid-January when we were praying, Vic felt that we should go home to see her. So we got into our old Dodge, which used almost as much oil as gas, and for the first time took the newly opened Pennsylvania Turnpike back to Ohio, making our trip much faster than we ever before dreamed possible.

On the cold January evening when we arrived, Mother Wierwille was resting in bed at sister Lydia's home. She wanted to hold six-month-old Don but was too weak to do so for very long. The three of us stayed only a short while, expecting to return the next morning to visit again. We spent the night at my parents' home nearby. Early the next morning we received a phone call breaking the news to us that Mother Wierwille had fallen asleep. She had been such a tremendously loving and prayerful person; we knew we would miss her very much. She was sixty-six years old.

After the memorial service, we returned to Princeton, where Victor finished his course work and wrote his master's thesis, "Peter As An Evangelistic Preacher," which completed the requirements for his Master of Theology degree.

On May 13, 1941, Vic, along with twenty other Princeton seminarians, received that degree. We then returned to New Knoxville for a few days, en route once more to the Mission House College and Seminary, where Vic formally received his Bachelor of Theology degree, which he had actually completed the work for at the end of the summer of 1940. His diploma is dated September 1, 1940.

Receiving his Bachelor of Theology degree at the same time with Vic was a young man named Vernon Opperman. Vernon and Vic had been in school together from the first grade at that little brick schoolhouse outside New Knoxville, Ohio, until graduation from seminary, outside Sheboygan, Wisconsin—good friends already for nineteen years. Vic was now twenty-four years old.

First Congregation

*I*n June 1941 Victor was ordained into the Christian ministry in the Evangelical and Reformed Church in New Knoxville, Ohio, his home church since birth.

Prior to his ordination, Victor had corresponded with the church synod of the Evangelical and Reformed denomination asking about churches in Ohio in need of pastors. One of the responses came from a Mr. Cleon White of Payne, Ohio. So, shortly after his ordination, Victor preached a "trial sermon" in Payne, his dad and brother Harry coming for the occasion. The congregation was "on trial" with the pastor-candidate, and the candidate was "on trial" with the congregation. According to church procedure, after a trial sermon the congregation would have the choice of giving the minister a "call" if they were in favor of his becoming their pastor or a rejection if they were not favorably disposed toward him. The congregation would then confirm the "call" in writing. Next, if pursued, the candidate would accept or reject the call. Victor, now officially "Reverend Wierwille," accepted the call to the Payne church and was installed there on July 6, 1941, as minister for St. Jacob's Evangelical and Reformed Church.

Since St. Jacob's did not have a parsonage and no house was available to rent in Payne, Rev. Wierwille and I, with one-year-old Don, moved in for a few weeks with a wonderful aged lady and spiritual mainstay of the church, Mrs. Henschen. Soon we found an empty farmhouse about three miles out of town, a most pleasant place during warm weather, up on a hill where we got the benefit of cool breezes at night. Before the weather got too cold (there was no means to heat that house; only a wood-burning stove in the kitchen), a rental house about three blocks from the church became available. This house had central heat, and Rev. Wierwille had a very nice room at the front of the house for his office.

Double Ordination

A most unusual event took place in First Church, New Knoxville, O., on Sunday evening, June 29, when two sons of the congregation, Vernon Opperman and Victor Wierwille, were ordained to the Christian ministry by the committee of Northwest Ohio Synod, composed of Revs. D. A. Bode, D.D., T. G. Papsdorf and George Kehl, and Elders Henry Deerhake and William Elshoff. Rev. Clarence Schmidt, also a son of the congregation and pastor of Immanuel Church, Town Herman, Wis., preached the ordination sermon. A large congregation was present, and all rejoiced in this sending of more laborers into the great harvest field.

These young brethren had grown up together and had attended the same schools for 20 years. The last 7 years were spent in the Mission House College and Seminary. Mr. Wierwille had also studied in Chicago University and in Princeton Seminary. Thirty-four young men and two young women of this congregation have, in previous years, been ordained to active Christian service in the ministry or deaconess work. There are now 38 stars on our congregational service flag, for which we thank God unceasingly. Twenty-eight of our young women have become wives of pastors, and, in this capacity, they have spread the noble influence of New Knoxville. The former pastors deserve many thanks for their untiring efforts and prayers so that, as Dr. O. B. Moor wrote in the splendid centennial history, "the stream of ministers might flow on unceasingly."

Our newly ordained ministers had both received their call to the ministry under the pastorate of Dr. L. H. Kunst; they regretted greatly that he could not be present at these services. The present pastor has tried to take his place and be a "father" to his congregational sons.

On Sunday evening, July 6, the Rev. Victor Wierwille was installed as pastor of St. Jacob's Church, Payne, O., by the committee of Northwest Ohio Synod composed of Rev. Otto H. Scherry, Dr. D. A. Bode and Elder Grey King. There was a good attendance, a fine interest and a spirit of thankfulness that, after a vacancy of two years, this flock has again secured a shepherd. May God bless this happy relationship.

Rev. Victor Opperman has accepted a call to Hope Church, Suphur Spring, O.

May the great Head of the Church awaken others to serve in His vineyard!

Rev. Wierwille's first pastorate, 1941–1944

At an elders' meeting before coming to this church in Payne, Rev. Wierwille had been informed that he would not be allowed to preach on money, to which he agreed. Money is always a sensitive issue, especially for those who have little or none. And this church had none, Rev. Wierwille noted. Although the congregation had regularly been involved in many kinds of fund-raising programs, they still hadn't been able to pay their bills. Rev. Wierwille therefore had them cancel all their fund-raising programs except one event, the "Election Day Soup Sale," because the townspeople anticipated this tradition, enjoying the food and fellowship when citizens came out to vote.

The congregation literally had no funds; they had not even paid the previous minister his salary for his final few months with them, a debt owed for over two years. Several years before, the congregation had sold the church's large parsonage for its cash value, but that money was long gone. Rev. Wierwille strongly believed that the congregation needed to be taught to tithe in order for God to bless them.

October was the month designated by the denomination to teach on giving. That October, Rev. Wierwille prepared and taught on the Biblical principle of tithing. After the Sunday morning service, the consistory, the governing board of the congregation, called a meeting with Rev. Wierwille and reminded him that he had promised not to preach on money. His answer was, "I never mentioned money once; I said 'tithe' and 'giving'."

The next Sunday he continued to teach on tithing, as were his plans. After that instruction on giving, the congregation saw an immediate turnaround, and the church gradually got back on its feet financially.

Rev. Wierwille loved to teach and to preach. His teachings were practical from the very beginning of his ministry. I remember a few early sermons that really stood out to me. "The Marathon Runner" was based on Hebrews 12:1: "Wherefore seeing we also are compassed about with so great a cloud of witnesses, let us lay aside every weight, and the sin which doth so easily beset *us*, and let us run with patience the race that is set before us." The picture Rev. Wierwille painted was of being a winner in the "race" of life, laying aside every weight and envisioning the ankles with wings to travel fast and far.

Another sermon was based on the blessed man from Psalm 1, which says, "Blessed *is* the man that walketh not in the counsel of the ungodly, nor standeth in the way of sinners, nor sitteth in the seat of the scornful." These three positions depict various degrees of existing without blessings. But the blessed man is the person who has his delight "in the law of the Lord," and meditates in the law of the Lord day and night.

"The Payne days," Rev. Wierwille later recalled, "were days of looking within my heart, my own life, and seeing, 'What can I do to help people more? What can I do to build the truth of God's Word and the love of God in people's hearts and lives?' It was a time of spiritual inventory of my own life."

My routine after Sunday morning services was to drive home with little Don and get dinner started while Rev. Wierwille stayed to visit with the people or to have a meeting with the consistory. Our Sunday morning routine on December 7, 1941, went as usual. I arrived home after church, turned on the radio, and heard of the terrible disaster at Pearl Harbor. How shocking! It was—and still is—unforgettable. Rev. Wierwille remembered his thoughts: "I debated that day what I as a minister should do. What do I do with my country at war? Do I enlist? I decided I'd do a greater service to my country by staying at home and serving as a minister here."

During our first six months in Payne, Rev. Wierwille saw to it that all the back salary was paid to the former minister, paying it out of our own salary. By the spring of 1942 the congregation was financially able to build a modern six-room parsonage on the adjoining lot to the church: three bedrooms, two bathrooms, a small kitchen, a long living room across the front of the house with a drop-leaf dining table at the end near the kitchen, and a complete basement. Our church began to prosper because the people were heeding God's Word according to what they had been taught.

On Saturday, April 11, 1942, our family again was blessed when our lovely, sweet little baby girl, Karen, was born.

In June that year we moved into the new parsonage, which we dedicated on July 12 along with new hymnals for the church. The members and friends of the congregation had contributed more than twenty-one hundred dollars within the first seven months after the house was completed to make possible the house and hymnals, and our total indebtedness was around fifteen hundred dollars. On the first Sunday in February 1943, a special collection was received in order to pay off the mortgage on the parsonage. And on March 7 we held a special mortgage-burning service.

After our move into the new parsonage, Rev. Wierwille found a room a block away from the church, formerly a dentist's office, which he rented and made into his office/study. Not a particularly patient young minister, he got pretty discouraged by not knowing how to handle various challenges within the congregation. At one time he told me that he was ready to quit the ministry if he didn't learn how to handle these seemingly helpless situations. Something seemed to be lacking in answer to prayers.

"I'd had the best education money could buy; but with all that I knew, I just could not help people. I was discouraged the first year in the ministry, 1941–42. I thought, 'Had my dad spent all that money to educate a fool?' I prayed a great deal about it. Even then I was discouraged with my life. The principles of the ministry bothered me. The shallowness bothered me."

The annual Paulding County Sunday School Convention was held Friday evening, September 5, and Sunday afternoon and evening, September 7, 1941, at our church in Payne. These three meetings were set "to worship, receive inspiration for daily living, and acquire information about the unique place religious education holds in the proper training for your son or daughter and its importance for your own spiritual growth."

At this same time Rev. Wierwille introduced a Bible study and teacher-training course which he taught. The purpose was to "bring to hand every element required to build up knowledge, acquaint you with methods, and supply inspiration for dealing with the problems that confront teachers and workers."

Rev. Wierwille's outreach beyond the congregation then began on July 23, 1942, with a column called "Religion in the Weekly" in the local weekly newspaper, *The Payne Reflector*. He wrote, "The aim in this is a column written for your enjoyment, edification and growth in matters pertaining to the spiritual advancement of your personality." He expected to see some results, so he closed his first article with this statement: "We are anxious to hear from you and your response will help to determine the value of this column to your own life and the well-being of your community."

During this period Rev. Wierwille was doing much searching. We talked things over usually after going to bed since he was busy all day long. One night he asked me, "Do you think you have the holy spirit?" After a little hesitation I said, "Yes, I believe I do." He asked, "What's your proof?" Well, I couldn't think of any proof except that I loved God very much. We talked about who we thought might be good enough to go to heaven. We mentioned people who were very loving.

"God has a place in our church for an hour a week. 'This is how far we'll go and no further, even if it is God's Word.' That seems to be the general attitude of our people." Rev. Wierwille was thinking out loud.

Ever since our arrival in Payne, Rev. Wierwille had been looking around for fellowship—checking for meetings, Christian publishing companies, and camps in the area. The Higley Press in Butler, Indiana, came to our attention, which then led us to the Winona Lake Conference Grounds. Rev. Wierwille invited Rev. Arthur E. Bloomfield from the Winona Lake Conference to teach at the Payne church. He spoke on "All about the Rapture" and "The Great Outline of Prophecy." The time spoken of in the Book of Revelation was another area Rev. Wierwille was researching. We realized much later that this book of the Bible was not written *to* us, but only *for* us—for our learning.

RELIGION in the WEEKLY

Rev. V. P. Wierwille

The Canary and the Cat

Would you leave your canary in care of the cat? Whether or not you own a canary or a cat, you know that is not the thing to do. You would not leave your valuable papers, priceless keepsakes and jewelry unguarded in your home. You are aware of the folly of risking loss through fire and theft so you make such provisions as seem wise. Are you as thoughtful about the greatest treasure you possess?

Are you leaving your canary in care of the cat? Your soul in care of the devil? Your soul is worth more than all the accumulated riches of the world. Yet how many of you would not trade your soul, and do so, for a little of that riches? It is insane folly to go through life with your more valuable asset inadequately protected.

If your soul is in the care of the Lord Jesus it is safe and secure in the NOW and in the HEREAFTER. A cat will kill a canary, a thief will steal treasure and the devil will deceive and destroy the soul. Nothing but eternal loss can be expected by leaving your soul in the devil's care.

As for Jesus, "He hath poured out His soul unto death; and he was numbered with the transgressors; and he bore the sin of Mary, and made intercession for the transgressors."

ST. JACOB'S EVG. & REF. CHURCH
Sunday
Church School   9:30 A. M.
Divine Worship   10:30 A. M.
The Chimes Hour   12:00 noon.

Rosalind Rinker

Rev. Wierwille visited the Higley Press frequently for fellowship with the people there. In later years he said, "If you want to improve in a sport, play with someone better than you"; so he also fellowshipped with people from whom he might learn. "Robert Higley, having learned of my academic background and my ability of researching certain subjects, asked me to be a contributing editor for the *Christian Action* magazine [which the Higley Press published]. This opportunity I gladly accepted, and the venture proved fruitful." It was also at this press that Rev. Wierwille met Rosalind Rinker, a former missionary to China and Korea, now devoting her time conducting Christian Action evangelistic meetings. Rev. Wierwille brought Rosalind to our home near the end of the summer. We met with her privately, along with two high school girls who helped Rev. Wierwille by cleaning his office and doing some typing for him after school every day. Rosalind taught us, among other things, that we needed to read the Bible rather than read around it. This idea seemed somewhat radical to a highly read, highly educated young man. She then further suggested, "Why don't you search for the greatest of all things in life which would teach Christian believers the *how* of a really victorious life?" He took her advice and began studying the Word more diligently.

The contacts we made at Higley Press and the Winona Lake Conference were central to our spiritual growth. There we heard dynamic speakers at the Christian Action Conferences, such as R. G. Le Tourneau, a very progressive businessman who literally believed God's promises of prosperity in tithing, and Homer Rodeheaver, who had at one time been soloist for the famous evangelist Billy Sunday. Homer Rodeheaver was a great promoter of outstanding Christian music, singing with a great voice or playing a trumpet as he led tremendous audience singing.

Another evangelist who had inspired Rev. Wierwille with his great musical ability was Rev. Charles Fuller. Rev. Wierwille had stated, "I listened to Charlie Fuller's radio program, 'The Old-Fashioned Revival Hour,' every Sunday morning before I went to church or to my office. He inspired me so with his music. He was an evangelist who had great charisma, great ability, and one of the first preachers involved in radio. Rev. Fuller was such a humble man and wanted to bless people. Why *wouldn't* the spirit of God work within him? It did."

Rev. Wierwille and I grew with our little congregation as we visited and became more personally acquainted with them: meeting their families, their children in college, understanding family relationships and backgrounds. Rev. Wierwille always spoke of our church as "The church with the open door and the open Bible."

Thinking that he wasn't kept busy enough or fruitful enough in his own estimation, Rev. Wierwille began germinating the idea of producing a radio broadcast in which young people from our church and other community churches would entertain with Christian music and he would teach. In preparation for broadcasting, Rev. Wierwille wrote short sermons regularly, writing about things that he had learned from various situations of his life. Soon Higley Press published some of these as articles.

Later he completed writing *Victory Through Christ,* his first book, which was published in 1945 by the Wilkinson Press in Van Wert, Ohio.

VICTORY THROUGH CHRIST

By
VICTOR PAUL WIERWILLE

The word **Victory** is on the lips and in the minds and hearts of people all over the world.

As a nation we are looking for **Victory.** As a Church we are looking for **Victory.** As individuals we are looking for **Victory.**

The big question is, will this VICTORY be genuine? This question is answered in these meditations.

Victory without Jesus Christ is defeat, and not victory at all in the final analysis.

Before there can be "Victory Over," which there must be if we wish to live harmoniously with ourselves, our neighbors, and our God, there must be "Victory in." THE VICTORY OF CHRIST IN THE SELF.

Genuine Victory, no matter where achieved, can only be lasting when it is VICTORY THROUGH CHRIST.

CONTENTS

I	VICTORY OVER WORLDLINESS
II	VICTORY OVER UNBELIEF
III	VICTORY OVER SELFISHNESS
IV	VICTORY OVER INDIFFERENCE
V	VICTORY OVER TEMPTATION
VI	VICTORY OVER PRIDE
VII	VICTORY OVER ANGER
VIII	VICTORY OVER TONGUE
IX	VICTORY OVER MOODS
X	VICTORY OVER FEAR
XI	VICTORY OVER TROUBLE
XII	VICTORY OVER SIN
XIII	VICTORY OVER DEATH
XIV	VICTORY OVER DEFEAT

ABOUT THE BOOK

The special concern of these meditations is to honestly face some of the problems that arise in the life and in the thoughts of our Christian young people. Such problems as are here treated may also haunt more mature believers.

The author of these meditations builds upon the firm foundation of God's blessed Word. He seeks to view his own experiences and the experiences of others in the light of this holy revelation of God. He speaks out of his own experience as a minister of the Gospel. In association with the young people he finds them asking some perplexing questions about the Christian religion, which these meditations seek to answer.

A prayerful and a thoughtful study of the thoughts presented will enrich the life of all sincere readers. His thoughts will stimulate thought and by God's grace strengthen faith and clarify understanding.—Dr. L. C. Hessert.

It was an inspiring book of fourteen chapters, a compilation of radio addresses to young people. He dedicated this book to his father.

Rev. Wierwille stated in the foreword of this book, "Our communities are overrun with people whose very faces portray their defeat. Their wills are dead, their consciences are dull, their hearts are barren, and they are spiritually sick. . . . The emptiness and loneliness of their lives is covered up by the spending of self in worldly pleasure. . . . Dr. Louis C. Hessert, Professor of Systematic Theology at Mission House Seminary, Plymouth, Wisconsin, . . . has given me through conversation and discussion a vastly deeper conception of all that is involved in personal victory."

Dr. Hessert wrote the preface to Rev. Wierwille's book, saying, "A prayerful and a thoughtful study of the thoughts presented will enrich the life of all sincere readers."

The book is brief, vivid, and edifying, containing many flashes of spiritual insight. "Victory Over Defeat," the final chapter, shows how "one word has made a life; one word has ruined a life. But the mightiest of all the single words ever uttered is the word that fell from the dying lips of one who was seemingly engulfed in defeat, but whose cross has answered 'the hopes and fears of all the years'—Finished! . . . . Our salvation is finished through Him; our defeats are turned into victories."

In May of 1943 Rev. Wierwille was asked to give the baccalaureate sermon for the graduating class of Payne High School. He chose as his topic "He Was Expendable," teaching how Jesus Christ was considered expendable by the mob. "The Christ who made you and our nation what it is, gave us our rich heritage because he was expendable. 'Though he was rich, yet he became poor, that you by his poverty might be rich' [II Corinthians 8:9]. Jesus said, 'I lay down my life, that I might take it again. No man taketh it from me, but I lay it down of myself' [John 10:17, 18]."

During this time, with the United States being consumed in World War II, the draft for the military service of our country was stepped up and some of our church members were personally affected. It happened that two boys of draftable age were first cousins. When only one of the cousins was drafted, the family became divided by strife. The immediate family whose son was drafted became angry, isolating themselves to the extent of no longer coming to the services on Sunday. Rev. Wierwille tried to counsel with the mother and father, the latter an elder of our church. He wanted the parents to take an honest look at the situation. Rev. Wierwille admonished them not to become hard-hearted and let that rule their lives. He explained to them how their obstinance could endanger their son's life. (We seemed to understand at this time how attitudes influence effects.)

After a very long time, possibly even a year, the family suddenly showed up in church one Sunday morning. After Rev. Wierwille had preached and given the benediction, the father quickly stood and began to speak before anyone could leave. Rev. Wierwille didn't interrupt. What a tense moment. The man began, "Well, we've heard another good sermon." After that, we all relaxed a little. He then apologized to everyone there for his not having participated at church for such a long time, and he expressed a desire that he and his family would again share in our wonderful fellowship. This change of heart, publicly announced, was definitely an impressive answer to prayer.

Beginning with a radio broadcast on Saturday, October 3, 1942, Rev. Wierwille and his assembled youth group performed their first live radio production. Rev. Wierwille certainly didn't realize at the time that this program would launch a ministry which would change the lives of thousands. His first radio program was designed to teach principles of the abundant life "through musical performances and scriptural messages." Dr. Wierwille later said, "I felt we had to do something to bless the people, and a radio broadcast might arouse some excitement and serve as outreach." The personal impact of such regular teaching and preaching, Dr. Wierwille explained, "was that it got me back to digging the Word. . . . That broadcast and the Sunday morning service made me, *made me,* go to the Word for two or three new teachings a week. It got me into the Word, got me growing in it, and kept me fluid.

"We were pioneers in using young people for our performances," he continued. "All of the other religious programs used adults. But I thought if we started with young people, it would grow into something and the adults might catch on."

The first broadcast of Vesper Chimes; October 3, 1942. I am on the far right.

Continuing until September 7, 1943, for eleven months, Rev. Wierwille, myself, and our singing young people drove with two cars every Saturday to the radio station in Lima, a distance of approximately fifty miles, to produce our Christian broadcasts. By September of 1943 we had acquired the technology to broadcast directly from the church. This broadcast, transmitted over Lima's station WLOK, was called "Vesper Chimes." Shortly thereafter we renamed it "The Chimes Hour Youth Caravan" since the broadcast time had been changed from Saturday evenings to twelve noon on Sundays. The program was financially supported by interested listeners.

Since the Payne church never had Sunday evening services except on special occasions, Rev. Wierwille and The Chimes Hour had the goodwill of the consistory to go out on Sunday evenings to other churches and groups to present a program which consisted of Christian music and teaching God's Word. One invitation for such a presentation was extended to us by a small church in Van Wert which sent a middle-aged couple to make arrangements with us for an engagement. It was January 1943 when Rev. Wierwille preached at St. Peter's Evangelical and Reformed Church in Van Wert for the first time. We certainly never suspected at the time that this church would become our next pastorate.

During the spring of 1944, the Van Wert church had asked Rev. Wierwille to hold a communion service on Resurrection Sunday evening. Because Rev. Wierwille was always making sure that the setup was correct, he went early to see that everything was in order. Among other things, he asked the elders, "Do you have the wine for communion?" They said, "We didn't know if you wanted grape juice or wine." Rev. Wierwille answered, "We want wine." So one of the older gentlemen said, "You come with me and we'll get it from my house cellar." So Rev. Wierwille went with him, and there were the wine barrels all around his cellar wall. The gentleman said, "Now you taste the wines, and the one you like best we'll take." Rev. Wierwille remarked later that if he had followed that suggestion he wouldn't have been able to have been in charge of the communion service.

Rev. Wierwille said the following of his days in Payne:

After all this activity and reaching out to learn more, I must know to satisfy my inner yearning. And so I stood in my newly rented office and prayed to the Father. "Father, teach me the Word; teach me the Word." He told me as plain as day that if I would study the Word, He would teach me the Word like He had not been able to teach it to anybody since the first century. And, of course, at that time I thought, "Now that's a dandy. Boy, if

I learned this Word of God, everybody will listen to me. The whole church will be blessed; my denomination will grow by leaps and bounds because we'll have the Word of God." And I thought that was terrific. But during the process of that revelation, I said, "Father, how will I know that this is You and that You'll really teach it to me?" Because I had worked the Word in commentaries and the rest of it, and I couldn't understand it, couldn't get it to fit.

And the sun was shining brightly. It was in the fall of the year. Gorgeous. There wasn't a cloud in the sky. And just on the inside of me it seemed to say, "Well, just say to the Father, 'Well, if it'll just snow right now, you'll just know that this is God talking to you.'" 'Cause you see, I'd never had much experience with God's talking to me. And this business of His saying to me, just as audibly as I am speaking to you, that He'd teach me the Word if I'd teach it, sort of shook me. I'd been expecting to hear from heaven for a long time, but I hadn't heard that way before. Oh, my ears were perhaps clogged up. Since that time I've heard a lot of things from Him.

And I said, "Lord, to know that this is true, I'd like to see it snow." And I opened my eyes, and it was pitch-dark, almost pitch-black outside, and the snow was falling so thick. I have never seen it fall that thick since that day.

And I sat in that little office, and I cried like a baby. Because I guess it was about my time to cry because I'd grown up but I didn't know the Word. And from that day on since He promised He'd teach me the Word, I have tried with all my heart to learn this Word.

Rev. Wierwille never told anyone of this experience until much later when he was teaching The Way Corps. It was a most astounding phenomenon which he kept to himself.

Victor and Harry working at their hobby in Michigan

During our ministry in Payne, almost every Monday afternoon until brother Harry was called to the army, Rev. Wierwille and I visited him at his furniture factory in Spencerville. We seemed to need the refreshing that we found in spending time with him. Rev. Wierwille's family came to Payne often to visit us, and usually they brought us produce from the farm, which was always very welcome and appreciated.

By early 1944 we could sense that our days in Payne were coming to a close. Rev. Wierwille felt he had spiritually led that congregation as far as they wanted to go. So in June we made a move, a distance of approximately twenty miles, to St. Peter's Evangelical and Reformed Church in Van Wert, Ohio. It was difficult for the Payne church members to understand that we would exchange a church of approximately 120 members for the 16 on the Van Wert church's active membership list. This made our last weeks at Payne awkward and very, very uncomfortable.

Moving to Van Wert

In the middle of June 1944 our family of four, soon to be five, moved to a small yet adequate parsonage at 109 South Harrison Street, Van Wert, Ohio. Dr. Wierwille reflected fifteen years later, "That is where the research and teaching ministry really took root."

Van Wert was located on one of the crossroads of America. U.S. Route 127 ran north and south from Canada to Florida, and U.S. Route 30, called the Lincoln Highway, reached from the East Coast to the West Coast. St. Peter's Church was located on U.S. Route 30 so that travelers could conveniently stop to worship on Sundays.

The congregation at St. Peter's Evangelical and Reformed Church made many improvements in both the church building and the parsonage before we moved there. Remodeling in the parsonage consisted of installing one and a half bathrooms, a large utility room, kitchen cabinets, and various light fixtures. Then the walls and floors were redecorated. When we moved in, everything felt so nice and clean, and we soon felt very much at home living there.

The church building also had had new light fixtures installed, the walls and ceiling redone, and a new center aisle carpet laid. A small room on the second floor that had been used for "dumping grounds," as

The Van Wert church as it looked in July 1944, except for the basement which was added later

The St. Peter's Parsonage

Dr. Wierwille called it, was refurbished as a children's Sunday school room. The roofs of both the parsonage and church building were reshingled and the exteriors repainted. We still continued to use two potbellied coal stoves to heat the sanctuary. (The stovepipes would sometimes get so red-hot, reaching almost to the twenty-foot-high ceiling, that the neighbor lady would call us thinking that the church might be on fire, as she saw red through the "iced" windows.) We bought a "base burner," a hard-coal stove, to heat the parsonage. Every year we continued to make small improvements, such as a new curb walk, new floor covering in the parsonage kitchen, and new communion table appointments consisting of two single brass candlestick holders and a small brass cross.

A few weeks after our move, on July 9, Rev. D. A. Bode came from our home church in New Knoxville, Ohio, to install Rev. Wierwille as pastor in the little Van Wert church. Again, as he had in Payne, Rev. Wierwille called this church, "The church with the open door and the open Bible."

The next morning, after Rev. Wierwille was installed, on July 10 our family was blessed when our second beautiful daughter, Mary Ellen, was born.

The work of the broadcast continued after the summer months as usual. We, while in Payne, had had a close association with St. Peter's Church by occasionally having Sunday evening services there before the move. We continued the broadcast over the Lima station with some of the Payne youth staying involved and with some Van Wert youth being added.

These young people came on Sunday mornings well before the noon broadcast time, as each had an assignment in setting up for the broadcast before the final run-through of the program. The actual setup couldn't be done, however, until the Sunday morning services were concluded.

Sundays continued to be busy days for Rev. Wierwille, with a Sunday morning service, a broadcast at noon, and then an evening service or a Chimes Hour performance. The radio broadcast was never a means of replacing the church, but a supplement to the church in bringing the gospel of Jesus Christ's deliverance to many otherwise unreached persons. "As we continued to increase our effective ministry, the researching of the Word became more important because of the keys to the greatness and the accuracy of His Word that began to slowly unfold through the years at Van Wert. The more I worked the Bible, the more I began to see that the greatness of God's power lay in the Holy Spirit field."

An early Chimes Hour group. Rev. Wierwille is on the far right.

E. Stanley Jones

The E. Stanley Jones Ashram with Rufus Moseley and Stanley Jones in the middle of the front row in suits and Rev. Wierwille in the back row, center right

Rev. Wierwille had made plans to go to the E. Stanley Jones Ashram (as he called his religious retreats) at Salisbury, North Carolina, the latter part of that July 1944. Since there was gas rationing because of World War II, rides had to be shared. So Rev. Wierwille rode with three other people from northwestern Ohio to North Carolina.

Later Rev. Wierwille said of E. Stanley Jones, "I considered him a wonderful friend. I learned a great deal from him and I liked him very much. But I began to grow and develop not only to enjoy intellectualism, but also the heart and love which I picked up from Rufus Moseley, Starr Daily, and Glenn Clark."

Once when I heard Brother Stanley (as he was many times lovingly referred to) speak, he was advising young people not to be ordained into the Christian ministry if they felt blessed to keep out of it. If their heart was for going into the ministry, then they needed to do it.

Ernst and Emma Wierwille's wedding photo, 1944

On October 4, 1944, Dr. Wierwille officiated at the second marriage of his father, who by then had been a widower for three and a half years. When sister Lydia saw that her father was determined to marry again, she went ahead and picked out the lady, a widow, for him. The new stepmother had as loving a heart as the mother had had. Incidentally, both women were named Emma and the stepmother's name was Wierwille by her previous marriage, although not directly related to Dad Wierwille.

From October 1 to 8, 1944, a Christian Action Conference was held in the Van Wert church in collaboration with the Higley Press. The Chimes Hour, at this time composed of young people from ten different churches in the Van Wert community, presented the music. In addition to Rev. Wierwille, Rev. Edward Adams of the Higley Press and Mr. H. E. Wiswell, editor of *Christian Action* magazine, were the speakers; and Mrs. J. W. Bower conducted a daily class in methods of child evangelism. This was an education and outreach method to win people to Christ and to get more people involved in the work of the ministry.

Just before New Year's Day 1945, after all the holiday festivities were finished at the church, I became sick with rheumatic fever. Rev. Wierwille's father went to every health-related person he could think of to help find a cure for me, but it took four very long, agonizing months for me to get well. Miss Gertrude Mittermeir, a schoolteacher from Upper Sandusky, Ohio, one of the four people who had shared a ride with Rev. Wierwille to the E. Stanley Jones Ashram in North Carolina in July, came to visit me on several weekends. Rev. Wierwille had learned about her knowledge of spiritual healing from her sharing with him on that North Carolina trip. She told me about Glenn Clark's book *How to Find Health through Prayer*. This was our first personal introduction to a more concrete knowledge of God's will concerning health and healing. Gertrude said that she learned from Glenn Clark the principle we could apply, namely that God had not given us our three young children for someone else to raise. That sounded reasonable to me. At that time, however, we had to place the three children in a couple of our church members' homes. Mary, at six months, stayed with Bill and Pearl Becker. And Karen, at two, and Don, at four, were taken care of by Paul and Edna Kreischer and their high-school-age son, Roger.

Rev. Wierwille and I had agreed to move to St. Peter's Church in 1944 for a $100-a-month salary. There was one family in the congregation who frequently invited us to dinner and always paid our milk bill. (At this time a milk delivery van brought milk to our porch several times a week.) Rev. Wierwille's family supported us with produce from their farm garden and eggs, as well as by financially contributing to the radio ministry. At one time I asked my husband, "How long does your family have to continue to support us? I was believing God to support us, as we had prayed." He explained, "Well, God is inspiring my family to do so." With this response, my heart and conscience were relieved of a burden I had carried for quite a while.

In May 1945 we held a youth conference at our church, having gotten the idea from our young people who had attended such a conference at Taylor University in Upland, Indiana. We invited Rolland and Mildred Rice, returned missionaries from China whom Rev. Wierwille had met at that Taylor University conference, representatives of the Oriental Missionary Society, to be our guest speakers. Mr. Rice was an instructor in the Peking Bible Seminary.

As a result of Mr. Rice's inspirational teachings, some of our young people felt moved to prepare for full-time Christian service. Because several of these young people needed financial aid in order to study for the work ahead of them, we set up a fund called the Student Aid Foundation, which was supported by gifts from people listening to our radio broadcasts. Among the students helped by the Student Aid Foundation was Coramae Walter (now Coramae Peters), who then enrolled in Taylor University for that September 1945 semester.

Coramae Walter

St. Peter's had never had an "altar call" in its history, though Rev. Wierwille had seriously considered it. An altar call is a method used in many evangelical churches of inviting anyone who wants to accept Jesus Christ as lord in his life, or anyone who wants to make another commitment of some kind, to come forward at the end of the meeting for prayer. Rev. Wierwille wanted to try an altar call, but he did not want to upset the older people or get them stirred up by doing something new and unusual. New methods in a church are usually handled with great sensitivity. So before a Sunday evening meeting when Rev. Wierwille was praying with the young people, he determined that the time was right to have the altar call. At the end of the service during the time of the altar call, one of the parents went up to the railing where her daughter was kneeling and took her out of the church. Since our Sunday evening services were what one could call "experimental," the mother trusted the Sunday morning ritual and continued to attend those services regularly, but she never did return to the evening services.

Rev. Wierwille, ever since his seminary years, had gone to meetings anywhere in the United States where he thought he might learn more about God and His Word and learn more about how to present His Word more effectively to the spiritually hungry. He went to Christian conventions, revival meetings, Pentecostal conferences, healing meetings, and family camps. If places were near enough, he would take our family and other interested people. All of us went to meetings in Indiana, Michigan, and Ohio whenever we knew of them, believing we'd learn something, which we always did.

Two of the people I haven't yet mentioned from whom we were learning at that time were Dr. Frank Laubach, with the practice of the one-on-one principle in learning, and John Gaynor Banks, who organized the fellowship of St. Luke in the study and practice of Christian healing in the Episcopal Church.

In 1946 many of us went to healing meetings of William Branham. During the point of the services when Rev. Branham ministered healing, Rev. Wierwille, as part of the clergy, was standing on stage with him, observing what was going on. Rev. Branham received revelation by getting "goose bumps" showing on the back of his hand. Rev. Wierwille taught many times since then that this manifestation to Rev. Branham was phenomenon and is not promised in God's Word to happen. This was an early example to teach us the truth that God can go beyond His Word but He cannot do less than His Word. I say "us" because Dr. Wierwille always immediately taught what he learned.

During a leave of absence in June and July of 1946, Rev. Wierwille was invited to and taught at the Gordon Divinity School in Boston, Massachusetts, for its summer term. He served as a professor in the homiletics department, enjoying his students there.

Rufus Moseley

One of the main speakers of the 1944 Ashram in North Carolina was a spirit-filled man whom I mentioned previously, Rufus Moseley. Brother Rufus, as everyone called him, a retired professor by that time, literally jumped for joy as he taught, making reference and sometimes calling one foot "glory" and the other "hallelujah." This flamboyant expressiveness seemed at first very repulsive to Rev. Wierwille; but as he continued to listen to Brother Rufus's teaching and appreciate his enthusiasm, he received great spiritual knowledge that he could easily put into practice. Rufus expressed so much of God's love.

In May 1946 Rev. Wierwille invited Brother Rufus to speak at our church. Brother Rufus was a graduate of Peabody University, attended Harvard several summers, spent a spring session at Heidelberg University in Germany, and attended the University of Chicago. He had taught history and philosophy at Mercer University in Macon, Georgia, from 1894 to 1900. In his retirement he taught many times at various camps.

His teachings were so simple yet so dynamic. "When we are born from above through faith that causes us to receive Him, we are born of His nature, of His love, of His Word, of His seed, and are given power to become like Him." Also, "We're made for the highest and nothing short of His best for us, and our best for Him, for all can satisfy us. . . . So centralize on Jesus and his way of life as perfect union, perfect love, and perfect joyous obedience and you get these and you get everything." He wrote in his book *Perfect Everything,* "Many are tempted to believe that everything man needs is within himself, that all he needs to know are the laws of mind . . . and no need for a personal God or savior. . . . We must be wise enough to be taught and led by the Holy Spirit."

Rufus knelt with Rev. Wierwille in the church in Van Wert at two different times and prayed for Rev. Wierwille to manifest holy spirit by speaking in tongues. Brother Rufus did not understand how to receive holy spirit into manifestation and could not, therefore, teach anyone; but he certainly was filled with it. He told Rev. Wierwille that he didn't know why he couldn't help him to receive but that someday someone would be able to help him manifest holy spirit.

Brother Rufus's greatest contribution to our ministry was his love for Rev. Wierwille and his encouragement of Rev. Wierwille's search for "power from on high." Though Rufus Moseley was unable to lead Rev. Wierwille into speaking in tongues, he accurately told Rev. Wierwille, "Whenever you receive the fullness of the holy spirit, you will really be able to help others receive; because you have quested, you will have understanding."

Rev. Wierwille mentioned that he had borrowed this statement from Brother Rufus: "Tell the truth and you can forget about it. Tell a lie and you better remember it."

Our church members, with excitement for what they were learning, began sharing with their relatives and friends what Rev. Wierwille had taught them about the Word of God. One of the church elders witnessed to and brought a young married couple to our services by the names of Sam and Dorothy Ralston. Sam and Dorothy, both very smart and hardworking, owned a large farm. One spring one of Sam's wheat fields looked so unpromising that he called the county agent to get some ideas about what to do with it. The county agent suggested turning the field over and planting a different crop. By this time Sam had more knowledge and confidence in God's Word, and he didn't feel he should lose his investment, so he called Rev. Wierwille to come to his field and pray for it. After they prayed, Sam just thanked God for blessing his land every time he passed by. When it was time to harvest, the yield from that field exceeded the others!

When we left the Van Wert church in 1957, Sam was truly puzzled. He really never understood why it was necessary for us to leave; he very much wanted us to stay at St. Peters. Their daughter, Kathy, was a member of the Third Way Corps, his wife, Dorothy, was one of our best Sunday school teachers, and Sam and Dorothy still come to our services on Sunday evenings. They have been faithful and supportive for many, many years.

Another family who came as a young married couple to attend our church during our early years in Van Wert and are still supportive of our ministry, attending our services almost every Sunday, are Dan and Marilyn Friedly. As a second-generation nurseryman, Dan cultivated an evergreen nursery. So he and Marilyn have helped us greatly as we beautified our grounds at the home of The Way International. Together they are artists in the field of landscaping. Their son Danny was a Third Way Corps graduate.

As Rev. Wierwille was always looking for ways and means to help others, he tried to instill this desire in the members of the congregation as well. One of the Sunday school classes was inspired to call themselves the "ARTHO" class, the acronym for "**a**lways **r**eady **t**o **h**elp **o**thers."

Dr. Wierwille one time observed about his early years in Van Wert, "For three years I didn't have a sick person in my congregation. I never made a hospital call in three years except to see newborn babies. I used to have a standing joke about how there weren't enough people in the congregation for them to get sick or to die."

News traveled about Rev. Wierwille's deliverance messages, so various people contacted him when they had special or desperate needs. Rev. Wierwille wholeheartedly wanted to help people by God's power. He told one story about trying to help an alcoholic who came into the church service one Sunday morning. Though he was eager to help, his technique was counterproductive. When Rev. Wierwille saw this alcoholic sitting in the congregation, he decided to forego preaching his prepared sermon and instead preached on the evils of alcohol and alcoholism. After the service was over and Rev. Wierwille, as was his custom, shook hands with the churchgoers at the door, the alcoholic spoke some telling words to Rev. Wierwille. He said, "I already knew all the evils of alcoholism. You didn't need to tell me what I know about better than you do. I came to get deliverance this morning, but all you did was put me farther under." Rev. Wierwille immediately went to his office nearby and prayed for forgiveness, vowing never again to preach a negative sermon.

Perry Hayden

In his search for Christians with a dynamic knowledge of God, Rev. Wierwille somehow heard of Perry Hayden, a Quaker miller from Tecumseh, Michigan, who was inspired by a message in his Quaker church and set out to illustrate some of the Bible lessons in "tithing," "rebirth," and "returns on what you sow." As quickly as arrangements could be made, Rev. Wierwille invited Perry to come from Michigan to visit our church and tell us about his experiment.

Perry's research began a few years before this, when he sowed one cubic inch of wheat. After harvesting the increase the next summer, he took out one-tenth of that harvest as a tithe, according to Malachi 3:10, and gave it to the church; he planted the nine-tenths of what he called dynamic kernels the next fall. He repeated the process each year until by the fifth planting, that nine-tenths grew to the point of needing 230 acres of land! At that point he didn't own enough land to carry the experiment further, so he solicited and received Henry Ford's assistance in furnishing land to continue his experiment, which was still going on when Perry was our guest. The following statistics from a newspaper article tell Perry Hayden's story as he demonstrated the promise of God through his planting/harvesting experiment.

An Experiment of Tithing

First Harvest, July 9, 1941—yield 1 quart (from 1 cubic inch of seed).
The tithe was 2.284 ounces.

Second Harvest, July 4, 1942—yield 70 lbs.
The tithe was 7 lbs.

Third Harvest, July 10, 1943—yield 16 bushels.
The tithe was 1.6 bushels.

Fourth Harvest, July 8, 1944 (planting required 14 acres).
The tithe was 3.7 bushels.

Fifth Harvest, July 1945 (planting required 230 acres).
The tithe was 715.9 bushels.

Sixth Harvest, July 1946 (planting required 4,443 acres for the 5,000 bushels of dynamic kernels planted).
The expected yield from this sowing was 13,852.4 bushels.

If continued into the seventh year, they estimated that they would need the entire state of Indiana for planting. This was an experiment to see God's promise in concretion. God opened up the windows of heaven and poured out the blessing that was not able to be received. With all of the land accessible to Perry Hayden and Henry Ford, the increase was too great to carry the experiment any further.

Glenn Clark

Having attended the Camp Farthest Out in the summer of 1945 at Lake Koronis in Minnesota, Rev. Wierwille invited the camp's founder, Glenn Clark, to come to speak and teach us in 1946. We had first heard of Glenn Clark when Rev. Wierwille went to the E. Stanley Jones Ashram in July 1944. Glenn Clark was formerly an English teacher and track coach at Macalester College in St. Paul, Minnesota. For about fifteen years his college English students had excelled and won many national writing competitions. In coaching he insisted that the athletes he coached be considerate of each other and carry no bitterness for one another or else these players would be benched. "That's what makes a winning team," Glenn said many times. Teamwork with love and without animosity and jealousy were fundamental issues with him. Glenn himself seemed totally devoid of jealousy in any form.

Because of his dream of "going farther out spiritually," Glenn developed the concept of the Camps Farthest Out. His first experimental camp was held at Camp Koronis in Minnesota, in 1931. Glenn wrote, "When calls began coming from other states begging me to start a Camp Farthest Out in their neighborhoods, I was surprised for I considered myself the world's worst orator. When people explained they didn't come for oratory, they came for manna, I began to comb the country over for men who could bring them manna in a better form than I."

In 1948 we took a group of our Youth Caravan to enjoy the two-week camp, again at Lake Koronis. They called the experience "a little part of heaven." Another remark was, "The biggest thrill of my life perhaps was the experience of discovering true Christian love."

One of our believers, Pat Haggerty, interviewed Glenn Clark's daughter Marion on April 9, 1982. Marion stated, "Strains of new ideas other than those of the churches were admitted to the camps. My father was not a minister, so he neither had to defend the existing church nor was he called on to defend a falling away of the church."

Prayer had been the beginning and the ending of camps. There was a new vitality in prayer times; there was a greater expectancy in our praying. Glenn felt that prayer involved one's using the whole physical body, so in his camp program he included "creative writing," as well as "rhythms" (motion to music), "so you get your whole body in alignment with prayer."

We thought Glenn Clark's Camps Farthest Out was the best design in camps that we had ever seen. And so we have used many of the C.F.O. principles and activities in The Way Family Camps at Camp Gunnison—The Way Family Ranch in Colorado.

A very impressive and moving experience at one of Glenn Clark's Camps Farthest Out in Minnesota occurred when Rev. Wierwille was present. It involved a miracle of healing from a polio epidemic in the surrounding areas of Minnesota. The disease was so rampant in the vicinity of the camp that it would take a miracle to halt its spread. Rev. Wierwille commented, "Glenn, who had a wonderful spiritual sensitivity, believed, and rightly so, that fear was the cause of the especially large outbreak of the disease. While our group at camp was thinking about what could be done, we prayed and sang a song which was fantastically touching and uplifting." Glenn Clark had taught on God's great deliverance and then came out with the hymn "Unafraid." This hymn had been born in "occupied China" when both Chinese and foreigners began to sing it there. It has been said that the soldiers were marching to it and the students sang it as they went to school. This same hymn was sung at the C.F.O. camp in an action to stop the polio epidemic in Minnesota. These are the words of that powerful chorus:

I will not be afraid.
I will not be afraid.
I will look upward,
And travel onward,
And not be afraid.

His arms are underneath me.
His hand upholds me,
His love enfolds me,
So I'm not afraid.

His Word will stand forever.
His truth it shall be
My shield and buckler,
So I'm not afraid.

So we go singing onward.
We're pressing upward,
We're marching Homeward
To Him, unafraid.

Dr. Wierwille always believed that Glenn Clark's inspiration to use this hymn was the reason the polio epidemic in that area of Minnesota in 1945 was stanched.

One year there were over seventy C.F.O. camp sessions in the United States and several in other parts of the world. Their success was especially remarkable and only possible because the camps were based on the highest form of expressive effort of large groups of people working in harmony. Glenn Clark predicted that "henceforth the Camps Farthest Out movement will be a world movement. They will be called C.F.O.: Christ for Others, a kingdom of God movement of good tidings that is destined to spread throughout the world." Glenn was a fountain of ideas, wanting his camps to be available to a wide public at the least possible cost. He loved the people he helped, and his mind was filled with the Word of God. In the epigraph of his autobiography, *A Man's Reach,* Glenn quotes the poet Robert Browning: "Ah, but a man's reach should exceed his grasp, or what's a heaven for?" In other words, a man should reach beyond his own capabilities so that God in Christ in us is needed to help achieve one's goals.

Glenn began a College Farthest Out to teach students the greatness of their lives and walks with God. All the branches of learning would be correlated and their principles and laws integrated around a philosophy of life based on absolute faith in the reality of God. Can't you see how those principles would be most attractive and draw Rev. Wierwille's heart! Rev. Wierwille taught in the first of three summer sessions of the College Farthest Out held at Maple Plain, Minnesota. Two other terms were also taught in a wing of State Teachers College at Livingston, Alabama.

Again Rev. Wierwille not only invited and shared our guest Glenn Clark with our church and radio group, but with the Van Wert public as well. The American Lutheran Church opened their doors to the meeting so that the entire community could be blessed by coming to hear Glenn's message.

Glenn was present for Rev. Wierwille's thirtieth birthday and teased him that now he would be allowed to teach, following the life of Jesus Christ who began his public ministry at the age of thirty.

Rhoda Becker

In late September 1947 we experienced a great and lasting thrust to the ministry when Rhoda Becker (now Rhoda Wierwille) came to work with Rev. Wierwille as his personal secretary as well as the minister of music for the radio broadcast. Beside these two major responsibilities, Rhoda also directed the church choir and was the church pianist.

Rhoda had begun playing the piano for church services, Bible conferences, and evangelistic meetings when she was fifteen. At Moody Bible Institute in Chicago she had majored in piano and took advanced studies in choral technique, harmony, and related subjects. Versed in the Fred Waring technique of choral work, as well as having had extensive training in child evangelism, she was from the outset an understanding helper in the ministry and became like a member of our family, always so willing and eager to serve. After being with us for a while, she was encouraged by some of our people to go elsewhere where she could make two or three times the salary she was getting in Van Wert. She responded to them, "I want to stay because of the fire of the Word of God that is inside of Rev. Wierwille."

Rev. Wierwille wrote the following in a letter addressed to radio friends: "This October letter to you is an appeal for prayer. I am not appealing for money. Such a commodity is not the first necessity. I appeal for prayer. When a deep and wide stream of prayer is flowing it will carry a sufficient cargo for all needs. 'My God shall supply all your need'." Rev. Wierwille spoke with deep conviction about the power of prayer after learning from Glenn Clark and seeing the results of his prayers.

On October 2, a group of people involved with The Chimes Hour met to discuss its finances. Brother Harry spoke very earnestly as to how through deeper consecration of self and possessions, through prayer and tithing, we could not only as individuals but as The Chimes Hour group become a great power for good and for the salvation of souls.

October 30, 1947, the articles of incorporation under the laws of the state of Ohio became official for the broadcast as a nonprofit religious organization with a full Board of Directors consisting of twelve members and designed "For the furtherance of the gospel of the kingdom of God to young and old alike both through radio and public appearances." This was thought to be a means of putting the broadcast, The Chimes Hour Youth Caravan, Inc., on a more enduring foundation, broadening its field of endeavor and providing a helpful tool in explaining to interested people what the purpose of our ministry was.

CONSTITUTION OF
THE CHIMES HOUR YOUTH CARAVAN INC.

PART 1

1. The name of the body organized under this constitution is
THE CHIMES HOUR YOUTH CARAVAN
INCORPORATED

DOCTRINE

2. The Apostles' Creed summarizes the faith of this organization. The Bible is the primary rule of faith and practice. John 3:16 and I Corinthians 13:13 are the primary Scriptures of the organization.

THE CHIMES HOUR
BY LAWS

1. The purpose of this organization is to present religious radio broadcast, to send religious messages in printed form, and such other further rights and matters incidental thereto.

2. The Board of Directors shall be in number according to the determination of the president. They shall be elected and re-elected yearly. All nominations for the Board of Directors shall be made by the president.

3. The president shall be the presiding officer at all meetings, speaker for the broadcast, and in general and particular in charge of the organization.

4. The regular yearly meeting of the board shall be held the second Sunday of the month of June. All other meetings shall be called by the president at his discretion.

5. At the June meeting all nominations for the Board of Directors shall be submitted by the president for election or re-election.

Articles of Incorporation

—OF—

The Chimes Hour Youth Caravan, Incorporated.

The undersigned, a majority of whom are citizens of the United States, desiring to form a corporation, not for profit, under the General Corporation Act of Ohio, do hereby certify:

FIRST. The name of said corporation shall be **The Chimes Hour Youth Caravan, Incorporated**

SECOND. The place in this State where the principal office of the corporation is to be located is **City of Van Wert**, **Van Wert** County.

THIRD. The purpose or purposes for which said corporation is formed are:

For the furtherance of the gospel of Jesus Christ by radio, or by personal appearance.

FOURTH. The following persons shall serve said corporation as trustees until the first annual meeting or other meeting called to elect trustees. GIVE STREET AND POSTOFFICE ADDRESS

Victor Paul Wierwille, 109 South Harrison St., Van Wert, Ohio

Dorothea Wierwille, 109 South Harrison St., Van Wert, Ohio

Lawrence G. Lee, West Jackson Street, Van Wert, Ohio

IN WITNESS WHEREOF, We have hereunto subscribed our names, this 28th day of October, 19 47.

Victor Paul Wierwille
Dorothea Wierwille
Lawrence G. Lee
INCORPORATORS.

N. B. Articles will be returned unless accompanied by form designating statutory agent. See G. C. 8623-129.

The Articles of Incorporation, first page only

The articles of incorporation were signed by Victor Paul Wierwille, Lawrence Lee, and myself. Lawrence Lee was a young businessman in Van Wert who had become very interested in the possibilities of our Christian outreach.

On November 9, we held the first official meeting of The Chimes Hour Youth Caravan, Inc., Board of Directors. In actuality, the Board of Directors were self-volunteered from the radio ministry area. After they volunteered, in following the bylaws, the president nominated them and they were "elected," so to speak. The purpose of the board was to bring in new ideas and to propagate the ministry of The Chimes Hour Youth Caravan in their own communities. "We must believe God for bigger things tomorrow than today" was Rev. Wierwille's exhortation. The Board of Directors met once a year unless the president found it necessary to call extra meetings.

In that same fall of 1947 a handsome young man by the name of Dick Konkle was witnessed to by a member of our men's quartet. Dick believed what he heard and came to the next rehearsal of the Youth Caravan. He just took in every word. Dick told us how he noted there the tremendous love for God, for His Word, for the group, and that he sensed no jealousy in the group. He said, "I didn't know much. I had only been a Christian for about two months, so I asked Rev. Wierwille many simple questions."

Dick Konkle

When Rev. Wierwille met Dick and noted his interest in God's Word, he began coaching Dick to be the announcer for the broadcast programs. That had been one of our needs. Dick had an excellent radio voice and he developed a real love for announcing and, especially, for reading poems. Dick became a lifelong friend of Rev. Wierwille's. Every fall for many years they went hunting together.

Also in 1947 we began publishing *The Way: The Chimes Hour Young People's Publication.* As a monthly publication, the writings by the young people associated with the radio broadcast were intended to promote more clearly the purpose and aim of The Chimes Hour. "The first aim is to further the work of our Lord; the second is to make Christianity more real to you and us by sharing of our Christian experiences and those of others. It is to be written and edited entirely from a Christian point of view based on the Word of God."

Paid for from broadcast revenues, the first five issues were sent out to interested listeners who wrote to us. After that, ten more issues were published which various businesses or individuals funded. These were acknowledged with a note on the back cover.

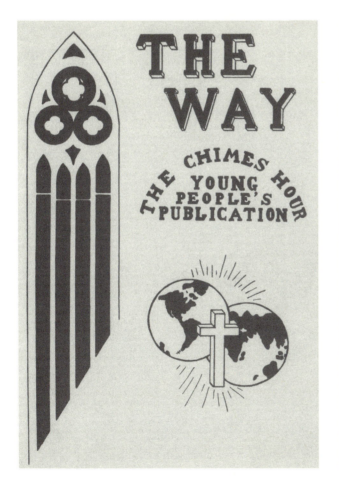
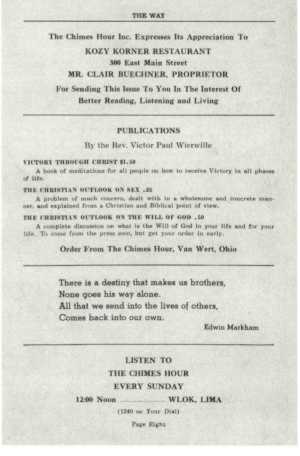

Rev. Wierwille found such ways so that both the giver and the gift were blessed. In the October issue we advertised three publications.

63

PUBLICATIONS
By the Rev. Victor Paul Wierwille

VICTORY THROUGH CHRIST $1.50
A book of meditations for all people on how to receive
Victory in all phases of life.

THE CHRISTIAN OUTLOOK ON SEX .25
A problem of much concern, dealt with in a wholesome
and concrete manner, and explained from a Christian and
Biblical point of view.

THE CHRISTIAN OUTLOOK ON THE WILL OF GOD .50
A complete discussion on what is the Will of God in your life
and for your life. To come from the press soon, but get your
order in early.

Order From The Chimes Hour, Van Wert, Ohio

The Chimes Hour Youth Caravan, circa 1948

Audio technicians at work transmitting from the church to the Lima radio station

On September 1, 1948, Dr. Wierwille began to broadcast every morning as well as on Sunday at noon over station WIMA (formerly WLOK), Lima, Ohio. He said, "As the heartbeat of the Caravan is love, the power beat is prayer." Around this same time, a guest of ours, Dr. Schweinfurth, the executive secretary of the Commission of Evangelism of the national board of directors of the Evangelical and Reformed Church, made the statement, "The Youth Caravan is the most alive spiritual young people's group I have ever seen. Such talent and consecration is seldom found among young people or even adults."

Besides broadcasting during this time, the Youth Caravan also made public appearances out of town each month on the first and fifth Sunday evenings, with the third Sunday evening at home in our church. On March 16, 1947, we had been especially excited to have the Evangelical and Reformed Church choir from New Knoxville along with our former high school music teacher-director, Ferd Eversman, come to Van Wert and join the Youth Caravan in concert. To reciprocate, our Youth Caravan gave a concert at the New Knoxville church on March 13, 1949.

Your Friend and Radio Pastor

"For All People By Young People"

Every Sunday

12:00 Noon
(1240 On Your Dial)

Dear Radio Friend: Again you are receiving THE WAY. This paper this month is a review of 1947-48. I know it will be a joy to read and look through.

On July 5th. Mrs. Wierwille, the three children and I will be leaving for Pikes Peak Seminary, Manitou Springs, Colo. where I will finish my work for the doctors degree. My assistant Adrian Kipp will give the meditations on the broadcast and the young people will design the programs and present them throughout the month of July. We will be off of the air in August. This will be a real task for them since I will be gone, but I know you will stand by the young folks and will support them with your prayers and your gifts all the while I am gone. The summer months are always trying.

          Your Friend and Radio Pastor,
          Victor Paul Wierwille

A note to our friends from the Board of Directors and auditors: We audited the books of the Chimes Hour and found them in balance and good order.

Donations received from June 1, 1947 to May 31, 1948 $4,246.82
Expenses for the same period of time......   4,463.17
Expenses were greater then receipts for the past year by......   216.35

Most of the greater expense is due to the sending of two full time pledged Christian workers to college. Last year we had only one. Of the six years of the radio work we have a total debt of $1,195.68 which is borrowed money and on some of it we have to pay interest. This debt should not be and if everyone that is interested in this Christian work would give according to the way the Lord has blessed them with health and material things then this debt could be paid for in a day and we could go ahead and still do greater and finer work for the Lord. Remember that everyone on this program donates their time and talent with the exception of Rhoda Becker our minister of music who receives $25.00 per week which you will have to admit is a low wage now a days to meet the living costs. "Lay not up for yourselves treasures on earth, where moth and rust doth corrupt, and where thieves break through and steal: But lay up for yourselves treasures in heaven, where neither moth nor rust doth corrupt, and where thieves do not break through nor steal, for where your treasure is there will your heart be also." Matthew 6:19-20.
          The Board and the auditors...

Doctor of Theology Degree

On July 5, 1948, our family of five began a trip in our new 1948 Chevrolet, given to us by the Wierwille family, to Manitou Springs, Colorado. Rev. Wierwille had been taking correspondence work with Pikes Peak Bible Seminary and Burton College and writing his doctoral dissertation on "Peter the Preacher." By being in attendance at the seminary in Colorado, he was completing his requirements for a Doctor of Theology degree. Students there came from India and China as well as various parts of the United States.

Along with taking course work, Rev. Wierwille also taught two classes: "Radio Preaching Techniques" and "Peter the Preacher." On Wednesday, July 28, 1948, he was awarded the Doctor of Theology degree by Pikes Peak Seminary in a ceremony at the Community Congregational Church in Manitou Springs. Immediately after his graduation, the five of us left for Minnesota for the Camp Farthest Out at Lake Koronis. It was a most tremendous and exceptional summer to have our young family experience both occasions.

Dr. Wierwille on the right, at Pikes Peak Seminary. Dr. Stuart Hydanus, who later taught at one of our camps, is on the left. And Dr. Ellis Lininger, the president of the seminary and an educator whom Dr. Wierwille highly revered, is second from the left.

Hobbies

Ever since childhood, Dr. Wierwille had two hobbies: hunting and fishing. He loved to hunt, and every fall of the year he would arrange with various friends to go hunting with him. In the late forties he began obtaining and training hunting dogs. Don sometimes went with his father. Since his dad was away so much, Don said that to go hunting with his dad was just like Christmas to other boys.

During these years Dr. Wierwille would also go fishing, as that was another sport he enjoyed. Uncle Harry would rent a cottage up in Michigan, and we would go as a family with Harry and Reuben and their wives.

In other years we also went on a week's vacation to a lake with my sister and her husband, Dee and Dick Fischbach. Dick remembered when the fish weren't biting how Dr. Wierwille would lay down his pole and pull a New Testament out of his pocket and talk about making the Word "fit" as he looked up some scriptures. The Fischbachs had a fishing bait business at Grand Lake St. Marys, and we claimed their home as our "cottage by the sea" because of the many Monday evenings that we went there to relax.

As our three children were growing up, and when Don was eight years old, Uncle Harry thought they needed a pony to learn to be responsible for and to enjoy. So Uncle Harry bought the three of them a Shetland pony, Ginger, along with some pony paraphernalia. There was a small barn conveniently located across the street and down the alley from the church where we could keep her. Ginger was very tame and gentle with the children, and we did many activities, both playing and working, with her. One activity combining both play and work was Dr. Wierwille's idea of blessing the neighbors in the wintertime by clearing the snow off their sidewalks. He had a triangular snowplow made which would cover the width of the walks. When it snowed, he would hitch up the pony to the snowplow, and she would clear the snowy sidewalks of our neighboring blocks while Dr. Wierwille and Don, with others hitching rides, sat on a makeshift seat on the snowplow.

Dr. Wierwille observed, "While most people regard snow as a necessary evil giving them some unnecessary exercise, there must be some purpose or good in it. When we can see the good, we learn to appreciate God's eternal design." Almost thirty-five hundred years ago a man under the guidance of God wrote: "Hast thou entered into the treasures of the snow?" (Job 38:22). Today we know that snow is an agent of help instead of a hindrance. Besides dissolving into water, snow also brings certain nitrates to enrich the soil.

When Don became a few years older, he took over the snowplowing by himself. On early snowy mornings, he and Ginger cleared the sidewalks, at least to the local hospital, past the Roman Catholic Church, and back to our house so people could walk to work more easily. November 29, 1950, the Van Wert daily newspaper, *The Times Bulletin*, had an article in it about Dr. Wierwille and Ginger with the snowplow. They wrote: "Dr. V. P. Wierwille, pastor of the Evangelical and Reformed Church, apparently enjoys the snow. He clears the sidewalk with his pony and sled scraper around the entire block when the snow isn't too deep for the pony to pull. He says that he, the pony and especially the children who 'help' him enjoy the job."

The consistory members of our congregation had over a period of time become interested in building a basement under the church and installing a central heating system which would also service the parsonage, as it was located on the lot adjacent to the church building. However, after much talk, no action resulted. After a meeting of the congregation on July 3, 1949, when the decision was made to have our own church members do as much of the work as possible, action began to occur. An old ditchdigger named Amil Schaffner, a member of our church, showed up early one Monday morning with a team of horses and a dirt scoop. He removed the boards off the bottom back of the church building and began scooping out dirt from underneath the church. Other members joined him and the more serious work began. Because our people were doing much of the labor in their spare time, progress was slow. But, keeping our eye on the goal, two years later, on September 23, 1951, this new basement, approximately forty feet by eighty feet, was dedicated. It was paid for by the members' tithes and offerings, the total cost being twenty thousand dollars.

Digging out the church basement

Two and a half years later, at the beginning of 1954, we installed new hardwood floors and new, more comfortable pews in the church sanctuary. We also had enough money to burn the mortgage for the church basement. In retrospect, I am amazed how we progressed in getting such a large program going in such humble facilities that we had used for years.

Dr. Wierwille envisioned a mural on the backstage wall in the new basement of the church as a central point of interest and beauty, since the rest of the basement space was designed to be so practical for

Sunday school and teaching space. In Ohio City, a small town a few miles south of Van Wert, he located and asked the artist Rev. Lester Ragon to paint the mural for us. The mural was called *The Hope of the World,* a picture originally painted by Harold Copping. This painting represents all the children of the world with Christ as the central figure—The Hope of the World. The faces of the children reflect their intense interest in what the master is saying. The mural ended up being twenty-two feet long and seven feet high. On either side of the reproduced picture, Rev. Ragon added some picturesque country scenes of his own conception. The flora and fauna in the painting are mentioned in the Bible, and the four seasons are depicted in the landscape, winter being alluded to by a bit of snow on the peak of a mountain in the background.

    The painting was so beautiful that Dr. Wierwille many times expressed how much he wished that Rev. Ragon had painted it on canvas rather than on a wall so that he could have transported the painting around and blessed more people by doing so. The vision of Word Over the World through the medium of artwork was always an important concept to him.

In 1950 we discussed launching a summer camp program to help "get the Word to others." We drew up plans, considering physical facilities such as tents, kitchen equipment, and help. Our goal for attendance was set at fifty people. Dr. Wierwille outlined the following curriculum:

6:45	Rising
7:30	Breakfast
8:00 – 9:00	Bible Hour (later called "The Word Speaks")
9:00 – 10:00	Rhythms (later called "Devotion with Motion")
10:00 – 11:00	Science and the Bible
11:00 – 12:00	Art
12:15	Dinner
1:00 – 4:00	Swimming and Recreation
4:30	Prayer groups ("Hour of Power")
5:30	Supper
6:30	Singing
7:00	Evangelistic Hour

The seed of our desire to have a camp was planted at this time, but it was not yet time to harvest. This camp was put off due to lack of staff and the need for more time to prepare for such an undertaking.

"How to get the Word out" also inspired our buying a church bus, intended to bring children or anyone else wishing to attend Sunday school and/or church services. Plans for the free bus were completed, and on October 8, 1950, this service first became available. The bus schedule had been announced in the newspaper, showing both the bus route and times of pickup.

> **Ride to Sunday School**
> # ON OUR FREE BUS
> —to—
> # EVANGELICAL and REFORMED CHURCH
> Corner Main and Harrison Sts.
>
> To accomodate children and adults wishing to attend our Sunday School we furnish free bus service each Sunday. Following is the schedule of pickup stops Sunday morning:
>
> 1. Jennings Road 8:45
> 2. Wayne and Greenewald 8:46
> 3. Wayne and route 30 8:48
> 4. Sycamore and Chestnut 8:50
> 5. Race and Third 8:52
> 6. Market and Third 8:54
> 7. Waterworks Park 8:56
> 8. Bonnewitz and Jefferson 8:58
> 9. College and Monroe 9:00
> 10. Allingham and Blaine 9:02
> 11. Kear Road and Shaffer 9:04
> 12. Shaffer and Cable 9:06
> 13. Shaffer and 30 9:08
> 14. Sibley at Woodland 9:10
> 15. Sibley at Leeson 9:12
> 16. High at State 9:14
> 17. Congress at Shannon 9:16
> 18. Haley at Airport 9:18
> 19. Summit at Park 9:20
> 20. Harrison at Spencer 9:22
>
> The return trip to above locations will start immediately after the Sunday School Hour at 10:30.
>
> All children and adults not attending any Sunday School regularly, are invited to take advantage of this transportation service. Further information may be obtained by calling the Church office, Phone 2827.

That month of October we again had Rev. Arthur E. Bloomfield from The School of Prophecy, Winona Lake, Indiana, teach us in Van Wert about Biblical prophecies, as we had him teach previously at St. Jacob's in Payne. Dr. Wierwille diligently sought information in every field of the Word of God and invited people from whom he thought he and his congregation might learn.

It was also this fall of the year when one of our quartet members witnessed to a young teacher named Malvin George at the Mendon, Ohio, high school. The member asked Mal, "Do you like quartet music?" Mal answered, "Sure!" He immediately received the invitation to The Chimes Hour broadcast the next Sunday. This was a life-changing occasion for Mal George. The next week he was at rehearsal and joined the group. His fiancée, Janice Dreyer, was a student at The Ohio State University at this time. In March 1951 Mal and Jan were married and together have been a great asset ever since to this ministry, even to the day of this writing.

The Power of Prayer

We learned so much at Glenn Clark's Camps Farthest Out. Our lives were most noticeably changed as we found out more about the power of prayer. One of our earliest experiences with the power of prayer in the area of healing was with an automobile repairman who had been admitted to the Van Wert County Hospital after suffering a major heart attack. When the hospital attendants asked him, as he was being admitted, which doctor he wanted called, he replied that he wanted "Dr. Wierwille." The patient continued to insist he wanted no one but Dr. Wierwille. The hospital attendants proceeded to call a medical doctor who was already in the building, as well as Dr. Wierwille.

The physician had just completed his examination of the heart attack victim when Dr. Wierwille met him at the door of the hospital room. The doctor acknowledged Dr. Wierwille and observed, "If your prayers don't do any more than my medicine, he'll be dead shortly." Dr. Wierwille went in, put his head into the patient's oxygen tent, and asked him what he wanted. The man cursed weakly, "Of course, [cussword], I want you to pray for me. What do you think I called you for?" he gasped.

This man worked every day including Sundays in his auto shop. When The Chimes Hour Youth Caravan program came on the radio at noon, he would always yell at the other mechanics in his garage, swearing first, as was his custom: "Shut up, I want to listen to Wierwille."

When the physician met Dr. Wierwille the next day, he told him that his medicine had worked better than he had expected. Shortly afterward, this man fully recovered. We believers knew that the man's healing was an answer to prayer; the man himself had known that he needed God to heal him. A couple of years after his healing, the man moved out of town and we lost track of him.

Another early answer to prayer for healing was the deliverance of Florence Scheidt, an elderly member of our church who had a thorough knowledge of the history of the Evangelical and Reformed Church. She was such an eccentric person, dressing in what previously had been her mother's clothes, never buying anything new to wear, though what she wore she wore very proudly. To illustrate how unique this woman was, the elders of the church in Van Wert had warned Dr. Wierwille before he ever accepted the call to this congregation that he would get along with everyone else in the congregation except Florence Scheidt. Rev. Wierwille accepted this as a challenge and made up his mind that he definitely would get along with her. One of the reasons Florence seemed hard to deal with was that she was hard-of-hearing. So Rev. Wierwille made it a point to visit her before all official meetings and inform her of the agenda. After this,

Dr. Wierwille with Florence Scheidt and Clara Webber

Florence became a real asset at the meetings, as she had a sharp, perceptive mind.

In the early 1950s Florence got cancer and had to have surgery. A week after surgery she was dismissed from the hospital. But since she had no one to take care of her, we invited her to stay at our home to be attended to and recuperate. Florence had such confidence in Dr. Wierwille that when he prayed for her, she expected and received her complete recovery. She went home from our home after five days, fully healed.

Another example of answered prayer for healing occurred one day while we were at the Van Wert County Fair. An urgent call came for Dr. Wierwille from a young mother who was a member of our congregation. Her young son had caught his finger in the gears of their water pump, and his finger was being held on to his hand by a sliver of skin tissue. Dr. Wierwille went to the hospital, where the surgeon said the finger had to be amputated, which it virtually was already. Dr. Wierwille asked the mother what she wanted the doctor to do. She said she wanted the finger sewed back on. So Dr. Wierwille instructed him to sew it on, which the doctor reluctantly did, saying he could take it off later. Dr. Wierwille prayed that the boy's finger would be knit back into place, and the finger indeed grew back together and functioned perfectly.

E. W. Kenyon

E. W. Kenyon (1857–1948) was another man whose dynamic writings had a great impact on Dr. Wierwille's life. Kenyon was a man who had a great thirst for a knowledge of God. And what he learned, he was diligent to pass on to others.

As a young boy, Kenyon felt the call to the Christian ministry. Although he had to go to work in the carpet mills as a weaver at the age of fifteen, every spare minute he could find was devoted to study of the Bible. He founded The New Covenant Baptist Church in Seattle, and for many years his morning broadcast, "Kenyon's Church of the Air," was an inspiration and a blessing to thousands. Dr. Wierwille came across some of his books by way of a lady on our Board of Directors whose mother had been very blessed as a member of Kenyon's church. Again, by studying Kenyon's writings, Dr. Wierwille was able to teach more of the accuracy of God's Word.

Kenyon's one fixed goal was: "Study to shew thyself approved unto God, a workman that needeth not to be ashamed, rightly dividing the word of truth" (II Timothy 2:15). Dr. Wierwille enthusiastically promoted Kenyon's writings: *The Blood Covenant, The Two Kinds of Faith, The Two Kinds of Knowledge, Identification,* and *Jesus the Healer,* to mention some of them. These were valuable sources of inspiration for himself personally and in his teaching ministry.

Foreign Missions

From April 1 to 14 in 1951, Dr. Wierwille visited our denomination's mission work in Honduras, Central America, by invitation of Miss Bertha Scheidt, a missionary from our Van Wert church and a cousin of Florence Scheidt, previously spoken of. Dr. Wierwille took with him to Honduras letters of goodwill to extend to all the workers on the mission field from the president of the Northwest Ohio Synod, of which our church was a member, plus a special letter from the executive secretary of International Missions of the Evangelical and Reformed Church. Members of our church sent many gifts, as well as letters of greetings. With great anticipation Dr. Wierwille prepared for his first on-location exposure to foreign missions, having heard about and supported foreign missions since his childhood. But what he saw was a great disappointment. He became sick at heart when he observed the relationship between American missionaries and the national Christians. He saw a type of master-slave relationship, with many missionaries behaving in a high-handed manner toward the Hondurans. Our missionary, Miss Scheidt, however, never acted superior. She was a devoted, tireless worker who was putting in place many of the educational programs in the Honduran public schools.

Dr. Wierwille with Bertha Scheidt

Dr. Wierwille, immediately after his visit to the Honduran mission field, wrote, "Our missionary and some missionaries of other groups are doing almost all that is being done to alleviate suffering and poverty, and doing this in spite of much ecclesiastical and other hindrances." Unbeknownst to Dr. Wierwille at the time, this exposure to mission work whetted his interest to accept the invitation to visit India where he would teach and observe foreign missions four years later.

Bertha and the children in front of her school

Shortly after his return from Honduras, Dr. Wierwille left for Christian Workers Institute, a young Bible college in Sioux Falls, South Dakota, where he was a guest speaker at the spring graduation ceremony and banquet. He always kept himself moving to get the Word of God out, as much of it as he understood.

Receiving the Holy Spirit

One morning in June of 1951 when Dr. Wierwille went to his office in the church, he questioned his alertness because, as he entered the vestibule, he found men's shoes and army garb placed in an orderly fashion next to one of the walls. As he proceeded into the sanctuary, he found two young men asleep on pews. They were with the Royal Canadian School of Military Engineers, heading for Glace Bay, Nova Scotia. Later when the soldiers woke up, they explained to Dr. Wierwille that they had come into the city so late and they were so tired that they needed to get some sleep. When they found the church door unlocked, they walked in and used the pews for beds. Truly our church lived up to our motto: "The church with the open door and the open Bible."

By this time Dr. Wierwille had been studying in the Holy Spirit field for many years already, ever since that night in Payne, Ohio, when he asked me if I believed I had holy spirit. He continually talked to people knowledgeable about the holy spirit and went to many conferences hoping to learn about it. One day he heard about a meeting to be held in Tulsa, Oklahoma, in December 1951. He was weary of being disappointed in his search to receive into manifestation holy spirit, but he decided to try again in Tulsa. He was desperate to manifest the gift of holy spirit and to speak in tongues, perceiving how powerful this would be to himself and in his ministry.

The gathering in Tulsa was called "The Divine Healing Convention," organized by the magazine staff of *The Voice of Healing*. Dr. Wierwille flew to Tulsa on December 11 and checked in to the Hotel Tulsa, on the corner of Third and Cincinnati. He then immediately went to Convention Hall where the meetings were being held, a distance of about seven blocks.

Before the next morning's meeting began, Dr. Wierwille met a man to whom he expressed his urgent desire to receive holy spirit. After the opening session concluded, Dr. Wierwille met with a group of ministers who had heard of his desperate desire to receive holy spirit. The experience that followed was very disconcerting to Dr. Wierwille, who was so wary of being misled. A public announcement was made later that evening about a young minister's having received holy spirit that day, which was not true. What had happened was that the ministers trying to help Dr. Wierwille told him to speak in another language. So Dr. Wierwille quoted from Genesis in Hebrew. Then they asked him to speak in yet another language, so he quoted from John 1 in Greek. These were both known passages to Dr. Wierwille as he quoted them. The ministers hadn't taught him the accuracy of the Word of speaking in an *unknown* tongue, that it must be an unknown language to him, the speaker.

Demoralized, Dr. Wierwille wanted to go home. But because of severe weather conditions that were moving in very quickly through the plains—with freezing rain, sleet, and snow in Chicago, and air traffic delayed for hours due to low visibility; icing conditions in Indianapolis and St. Louis, and with sleet forecast in Tulsa by Thursday—the only thing Dr. Wierwille could do was to stay at the convention and be on standby for a flight when air traffic could begin moving again.

Dr. Wierwille had memorized every verse of scripture about the holy spirit—385 occurrences in all. But except for the exercise in memorizing, all he had were questions. Of course, God was working the timing out to answer the desires of Dr. Wierwille's heart by way of a man from California named J. E. Stiles. When Rev. Stiles first heard about the Tulsa convention, he hadn't planned on going. But then God revealed to him that there would be a man at the convention to whom he could minister holy spirit. So he obeyed God, and he and his wife went to the Divine Healing Convention.

Rev. and Mrs. J. E. Stiles

On Thursday, December 13, when Dr. Wierwille was sitting at a restaurant counter, eating breakfast and telling his reason for coming to the convention to a person sitting next to him, a woman two seats away overheard him. This woman immediately spoke to Dr. Wierwille, "I think God sent a man here to meet your need by the name of J. E. Stiles."

Dr. Wierwille related to us what happened next:

That's how this machinery started, and I said, "Well, where can I meet him?" Then she evidently set it up because she contacted me and said, "J. E. Stiles will be at such and such an entrance in the convention hall. He'll be there at 9:00," and I said in my mind, "I'll bet he won't be there at 9:00 because I just haven't seen very many people that honest," and I told God if he wasn't there at 9:00 I wouldn't have anything to do with him. I went to the agreed place at the appointed time, and there was J. E. Stiles waiting for me. He said he'd go any place to help me, but he said he'd first like to hear Oral Roberts speak. Would I like to hear Oral? Of course, that was one of the reasons I was there.

Oral preached a very stirring message, "It Is Later Than You Think." The diary of the convention read, "No one went away unmoved after this orator convinced his listeners."

We went to lunch after that meeting, and he took his wife along. I said in my mind, "No deal on this. I'm not going to have any woman around if I'm gonna act crazy and lie on the floor and whoop and holler." But I was so hungry for God and the things of God, if that would have been required, I would have acted like this if necessary, but not in front of a woman. Because I was born and raised where everything was done decently and in order and with my intellectual accomplishments, I couldn't see making a fool of myself lying on the floor and throwing songbooks or something else; so I said to myself, "No deal."

After lunch was finished he said to his wife, "Now I'm going to be with Dr. Wierwille. I'll see you whenever I'm finished. If it's tomorrow morning, don't pay any attention. I'll see you, but I just want to be alone with him." That, of course, helped me immensely. Then we went to my hotel room, and I have no recollection of how long we were there. There was one verse of scripture that he would use to settle all my arguments:
"If ye then, being evil, know how to give good gifts unto your children: how much more shall your heavenly Father give the Holy Spirit to them that ask him?" [Luke 11:13]. God wouldn't give a lousy gift. It took him maybe an hour or two to finally get me over all my fear, and that's when I spoke in tongues.

Rev. Stiles was able to answer all of Dr. Wierwille's perplexing questions and to help him receive into manifestation holy spirit by speaking in tongues. Dr. Wierwille always claimed that that night in December of 1951 in Tulsa, Oklahoma, was the greatest night of his life.

In the convention diary was written that "liberality in giving was greatly experienced." Dr. Wierwille was there when the needs of Jack Coe's Children's Home were presented, so he threw his last twenty dollars into the offering. When he returned home, he received a letter with forty dollars in it. God was backing up His Word.

The convention diary also stated, "The convention closed happily with one of the greatest services of the convention. A gratifying climax to such a meeting was the testimony of an Evangelical and Reformed pastor of Ohio who had come for the express purpose of receiving holy spirit. He electrified his listeners as he related how he had looked for this experience in colleges and universities, in churches and classrooms, from Chicago's Skid Row to the mission fields, and had asked numbers of men to lay hands on him that he might receive, but not until now had he found what he sought so long."

"THANK GOD FOR PENTECOST!" This was Dr. Wierwille's answer to a long-awaited heart's desire. "I had searched for so long and finally someone showed me from the Word why and how I should speak in tongues."

A short while, possibly a month, after he returned home to Van Wert from the Tulsa convention, he led three of the Youth Caravan members into speaking in tongues, the first two of whom were Mal and Jan George, and then Doris Mohr, one of our broadcast soloists.

Rev. and Mrs. Stiles were with us for the holidays that year, and again in 1952. We rejoiced together for our deliverance from ignorance.

Dr. Wierwille said, "The Holy Spirit field is the field God raised me up for." Thus, that exciting night in Tulsa was a singularly important milestone in the ministry of what later would be known as The Way International.

Regularly after that, we held weekly meetings in homes of our church members, some of whom we discovered were already speaking in tongues and others who were interested in doing so. Now, after Dr. Wierwille had received, he was able to help others who were interested, just as Rufus Moseley had told him he would. He knew from God's Word what God's will is for His children concerning the receiving and manifesting of holy spirit. If we were going to get His Word over the world, it was essential that those of us who had this goal operate boldly and with knowledge the manifestations of holy spirit.

Starr Daily

In January 1952 we invited a guest speaker to our church by the name of Starr Daily. We had recently formed a group called "The Spiritual 40 Club," and Starr was the first of several to whom this group extended an invitation.

The Spiritual 40 Club was made up of people interested in inviting speakers whom Dr. Wierwille believed had a message that was vital and from whom we could learn more about God and His Word. Instead of Dr. Wierwille's going alone to distant places to hear these dynamic people, he thought it would be a greater blessing to have these speakers come to us and share with all of us who were members of the Spiritual 40 Club. Dr. Wierwille asked Mal and Jan George to organize the group. Each person who wished to join "the club" paid ten dollars each time we found a speaker; this entitled the club member and spouse to attend all the teaching occasions with the invited guest. We determined that forty individuals donating ten dollars each would allow us to pay the traveling expenses plus give a generous honorarium to each speaker.

Starr Daily powerfully related his personal experience of showing how the force of love can release men and women from physical and spiritual bondage to victorious living. He had published his personal story in a book called *Love Can Open Prison Doors*. When he was with us in Van Wert, he entitled his topic of teaching "From Crime to Christ."

Jan 18, 1952

Hear Starr Daily

IN MASS MEETING AT
FIRST METHODIST CHURCH
Sunday, Jan. 20--7:30 P. M.

--SUBJECT--
"From Crime To Christ"
(Mr. Daily's Life Story)

Due to the overflow crowds, this change of location for the Sunday night meeting is being made, so that more people of this community may hear this great man.

The FRIDAY, SATURDAY, and final MONDAY MEETINGS, at 3 P. M. and 7:30 P. M., will continue to be held in the - - -

EVANGELICAL AND REFORMED CHURCH
Corner Main and Harrison Streets—Van Wert

At an Advanced Class, Dr. Wierwille said of Starr Daily, "I have seen people given brain cells through the power of God when they've been eaten out with drugs. One of the greatest examples of having one's brain restored was my friend Starr Daily, who was at one time America's 'public enemy number one' and then had become one of America's greatest church laymen, helping people in our nation reclaim the lives of prison inmates."

Coming under the influence of a master criminal in his youth, Starr by the young age of twelve had become a major juvenile delinquent and was committed to prison as an habitual criminal, where he spent the next thirteen of his first twenty-five years. His behavior while in prison was pathologically antisocial; he was consumed with hatred toward mankind. But, there in prison, Starr had a dramatic religious experience, after which he struggled with his criminal mind to become peaceful through self-discipline and spiritual rebuilding. "After someone told me about my friend Jesus Christ, the power of Christ's redeeming love literally opened the prison doors of steel," Starr later remarked.

When Starr finally got out of prison, he probably didn't have 10 percent of his brain cells left, according to the best estimates of the doctors there. Yet by God's healing grace and by his efforts to work with his mind, he became a very brilliant man. The magazine *Christian Herald* wrote that "in *Love Can Open Prison Doors* Starr shocked a sleeping Christendom into a new realization of the tremendous spiritual power lying latent in Jesus's way of life if we only practice it."

Starr believed, "The hardest thing in the world is to maintain ill health. You've got to live constantly in the sick thought if you have to defeat nature's recreative power." God made our bodies to heal themselves. This was a new, exciting observation to us.

At this occasion when Starr was our guest, Dr. Wierwille made arrangements to have Starr share his inspiring story with the entire Van Wert community at the large Methodist church in the city, as the minister cordially welcomed Starr to his pulpit. It turned out to be a packed sanctuary and a very moving experience for our town.

Of the days when these knowledgeable speakers were guests of our church and our home, our daughter Mary recalls, "We always had someone 'special' at the dinner table." Our daughter Karen remembers, "When men came to our home who were invited to speak in the church, I recall our visiting around the dinner table. It was such an interesting time just to hear people talk back and forth. We learned so much from these people whose names have become household words, such as Rufus Moseley, Starr Daily, Glenn Clark, and others. They taught us various principles because we were eager to learn and because God gave them to us. It seems to me that we took what they taught us and ran with it. What a way to grow up! I think that is still an exciting part of our heritage. God always has ways of teaching us more—through other believers, through books, and directly from reading His Word. The prospect of learning and applying is always thrilling."

Karen was right. We had been so blessed in our family to meet so many kindred hearts to enlarge our vision for our lives.

Tenth Anniversary

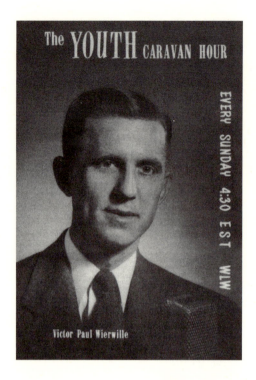

A Youth Caravan publication

> Ten years ago Dr. Victor Paul Wierwille organized this radio and public appearance group with the specific purpose of bringing to people, young and old, the best variety in the field of anthems, hymns, and gospel songs both vocal and instrumental. Every member of the cast and staff is expected to be a Christian, not only by confession, but in daily living. When youth all over the nation are being impressed by many divergent viewpoints, this work is an answer to the basic need of youth. Christianity "hits the spot" and changes situations as well as lives. This youth work is a definite counteractive to all sin and evil in the communities where the Youth Caravan appears.
>
> The cast and staff is composed of young people who desire to be "athletes of the Spirit", working together like a basketball or football team. All do their part to the best of their ability. Most of the vocal and instrumental talent has been developed under the guidance of Dr. Wierwille and the Minister of Music. It is interdenominational, cooperative, and interracial in activity. There are no written rules or regulations, only Christian love, and adherence to the principle, "Christ first, others second, and myself last."

During that tenth anniversary year of our broadcast ministry, Dr. Wierwille planned a weekend camp at a campground at Grand Lake St. Marys, Ohio, from July 24 to 27, 1952. This July camp, the harvesting of seeds planted two years earlier, was another great learning experience for us and the other people in attendance to put more of God's Word into action. One of our speakers was Tom Lasher, a chemist who had been involved in a terrible explosion at work and had not been expected to live. A believer prayed for his healing, holding on to his toes since most of the rest of his body had been burned. Tom totally recovered. This healing showed us the value of physical touch. It was the love of the believer in that touch that activated believing in the person in need.

Another speaker, Jeff Rogers of the Race Relations Department of the Evangelical and Reformed denomination, also taught at this first camp on "Thou shalt love thy neighbor as thyself," the second and great commandment as stated in Matthew 22:37-40.

Dr. Stuart Hydanus, a professor of astronomy and archaeology whom Dr. Wierwille had met at Pikes Peak Seminary, was another one of the guest speakers for the weekend camp. Dr. Hydanus's specialty was proving the detailed accuracy of the Bible through astronomy and archaeology.

Dr. Wierwille always said, "We don't have to prove it, only believe it." Yet as we learned what could be demonstrated in these fields, we saw that genuine science only serves to corroborate the accuracy of the Word.

Dr. Wierwille again was reaching out for our people to learn more about God and His Word. All of these speakers added depth and dimension to our understanding and, therefore, to our abundant walk in life. At the end of this camp Dr. Wierwille led Uncle Harry into speaking in tongues.

During that tenth-year celebration, we also held our first ever twenty-four hours of prayer at the church on February 24. Dr. Wierwille was inspired to do this. Any person who wanted to could sign up to pray for one hour, between 6:00 one evening and 6:00 the following evening.

In June at the annual Board of Directors' meeting, Dr. Wierwille reported on the past year's activities and extension of The Chimes Hour Youth Caravan, which included enlarging our mailing list to seven hundred and achieving the one-thousand-recordings mark of The Chimes Hour Youth Caravan. We had also bought a small inventory of bookstore items and a printing machine. We rented a business location just two blocks from our church that was suitable for both the bookstore and the printing equipment, and we called them "The Van Wert Gospel Gift Shop and Multigraph Printing and Publishing Co.," which opened for business on March 1, 1952. We were now able to print our own church bulletins, and

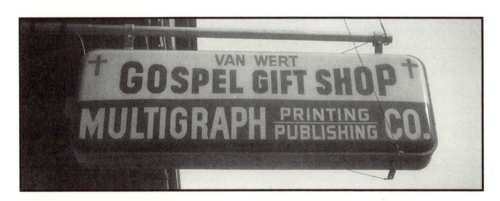

Coramae Peters working in the Gospel Gift Shop

Malvin George operating the new printing equipment

we immediately published the *Album of Verse #1*. Dr. Wierwille always loved poems which had uplifting messages, and the *Album of Verse #1* was a publication that was very popular from the moment it was printed. In March 1952 the first issue of *The Way Magazine* was released in a fourfold, 5¼" x 7½" format.

For broadcasting we purchased in 1952 a Lear wire recorder and a Gates remote amplifier. The fine wire from the recorder had a tendency to tangle easily, and it was a sight to behold when Rhoda and Dr. Wierwille would occasionally be out on the sidewalk in front of the church trying to untangle it.

At this time we also added two part-time staff members to The Chimes Hour: Ernie Atkinson, as promotional staff and choir director; and John Camp, as our radio agent for lining up more stations to enlarge our geographic range.

For the last two weeks of August in 1952, we took a group of twenty young people from the Youth Caravan and the church to a Camp Farthest Out at Lake Winnipesaukee, New Hampshire. Dr. Glenn Clark and Dr. Frank Laubach were the outstanding speakers there. This experience of being taught by these spiritual leaders in the camp setting was another time of refreshing for all of us. It was a time of putting prayer into practice and expecting results. And a time of wonderful relaxation and fun.

The tenth anniversary year then culminated in a day of great celebration on October 5. Rev. Tennyson Guyer, a friend of Dr. Wierwille's from the Van Wert area, was our guest speaker. Rev. Guyer commended the Youth Caravan on their giving. He said, "People have forgotten the joy of sharing someone else's burden; they're too busy trying to go through a revolving door on somebody else's push. . . . You can give without loving, but you can't love without giving." There were 160 people in attendance for the worship service and the fellowship dinner following. Year by year we were learning and practicing more of the Christian life-style that worked.

Mary's Healing

Our Christmas holiday preparations in 1952 were under way. Once more we were decorating the church, and I was putting in many hours helping there. At that time Dr. Wierwille and I noticed that our eight-year-old daughter, Mary, was developing a lump under her chin. Within a week another lump had begun developing under her jawbone. Mary's change in appearance was quite obvious, and people decorating at the church began asking me, "Have you taken her to a doctor?" I had to admit, "No, I haven't." These well-meaning women persisted in asking me about taking her to the doctor to the point that I could no longer answer them patiently. I knew I couldn't stay in harmony with the other helpers, so I thought I'd better do something about this. I called our dentist and made a same-day appointment.

The dentist saw Mary and with great concern said her problem was not anything in his area of expertise and that I'd better take her to see our physician right away. I had no intention of going to the physician. I didn't want her scarred from surgery, let alone the fact that anything serious could not be cured through the medical know-how of that time. But by going to the dentist, I then had a response when the ladies asked me about taking her to the doctor. I could say, "Yes, I've taken Mary to the doctor," even though the doctor was a dentist, not a physician.

B. G. Leonard

There was no way of explaining how Dr. Wierwille and I felt about this situation with our daughter because we didn't even know ourselves. We were prayerfully deciding what to do when we agreed that we would ask B. G. Leonard to minister to her. Dr. Wierwille had met him at the convention in Tulsa in December of 1951 and received publications from him following that. But the quality of printing of Leonard's publications was always so very poor that Dr. Wierwille threw his materials away without reading them; the print simply wasn't readable.

At the same time that Mary and I were returning home from our appointment with the dentist, my husband was burning his office wastepaper, and one of the pamphlets from B. G. Leonard was on the top of the pile after he turned over the wastepaper basket. He pulled the pamphlet out of the fire to keep the address. So we referred to that address, got the phone number, and called B.G. Leonard in Calgary, Alberta, Canada, to ask him to minister healing to Mary. After praying with B.G. over the phone that day, we just thanked the Father for healing her.

At the time we called him, B.G. Leonard was in the middle of teaching a three-week class called "The Gifts of the Spirit," so he couldn't come to see us; but he added on the phone that if we needed any more help we should call Lee Vayle, a student of his living in Florida, who would personally come to help us. B.G., as we lovingly came to call him, assured us that Mary would be all right. We knew that he could only have known that by revelation, so Dr. Wierwille and I relaxed and were greatly comforted. In a matter of a few days, Mary's one lump went away, and in another week the other one disappeared also.

Since B.G. mentioned it, Dr. Wierwille thought Lee Vayle from West Palm Beach, Florida, should come to Van Wert and teach us more about the manifestations of holy spirit. So in the excited afterglow of Mary's healing, we invited people to join us who were interested in this field to also learn from him when he came in the middle of January 1953. Some, but not all, of our congregation were interested.

When Lee Vayle came, he reassured us about Mary's healing and taught us more about the manifestations of holy spirit. We gathered in our living room with those interested, and Lee ministered holy spirit to anyone who had not yet received it into manifestation, which included Rhoda Becker. Lee Vayle instructed us from his knowledge of holy spirit, mainly about the inspiration manifestations of speaking in tongues, interpretation of tongues, and prophecy.

A special meeting of the Board of Directors was called for December 14, 1952. Here the President, Dr. Wierwille, introduced for discussion the possibilities of The Chimes Hour Youth Caravan's broadcasting over radio station WLW in Cincinnati. He said there would be a potential listening audience of three-and-a-half million people, and the cost of radio time was $350 a half hour. The only catch was we had to raise $4,550 before the contract could be signed. After a lengthy discussion a motion was made and carried that definite steps should be taken to contract for the 4:30–5:00 Sunday afternoon spot. It was decided that we already had the necessary radio equipment but that we'd probably have to hire more secretaries in the office.

As a means of getting acquainted with radio friends and helping to finance the broadcast, Dr. Wierwille made arrangements to personally make public appearances once or twice a week. As for the members of the board, they had to put their shoulders to the wheel and day after day lift that broadcast to God in prayer. On Sunday, January 4, 1953, in less than a month after the issue had been discussed, the initial program was aired on WLW, Cincinnati, the Youth Caravan reaching another goal in Christian outreach.

After thirteen weeks of broadcasting on WLW, Cincinnati, the Nielsen ratings taken in April 1953 showed that seventy thousand homes were tuned in to our broadcast on Sundays. But since adequate funds were not coming in to cover the expenses and since we were thinking of changing our direction of outreach, the Board of Directors decided to cancel the broadcast and renew our contract with WLW at some future date if and when it seemed appropriate.

B. G. Leonard

Ever since the Divine Healing Convention in Tulsa in December 1951, and since Rev. B.G. Leonard prayed with us for Mary's healing over the phone in December 1952, Dr. Wierwille's hunger for more knowledge about God's healing power was piqued. In late winter, February 1953, Dr. Wierwille felt the need to spend time with B.G. Leonard. He related, "I called B.G. Leonard on the telephone. He told me he loved me, but that I couldn't come up to see him because he was in the middle of teaching a class. I took the next plane to Calgary, Alberta, Canada, anyway." During the flight there, the plane flew into a tremendous thunderstorm. When Dr. Wierwille noticed that the stewardesses' faces were looking ashen and he could sense the terror of the people on the airplane, he told them not to fear because God wanted him in Calgary and that their arrival with him was certain.

B. G. Leonard with his new students. Dr. Wierwille is in the light suit.

B.G. Leonard called his work in Calgary "The Christian Training Centre." Dr. Wierwille described his first impressions there: "I walked in and B.G. was in the middle of announcements. They must have lasted an hour and a half. Then he took his violin and played hymns for a while. When he finally started preaching, he taught his heart out for another hour and a half. Then everyone left and I sat there. He said, 'I thought I told you that you couldn't come.' And I said, 'Yeah, but I didn't hear you.'"

B.G. Leonard had been a member of the Royal Canadian Mounted Police, a cowboy, a rodeo rider, and an aide in an insane asylum. He had been a Roman Catholic, then a Nazarene, a Pentecostal, and now an independent. He was put on his own in life at age eleven. B.G. had been born again through the ministry of the Nazarenes, and after that, he saw God's Word fulfilled in his own experiences. B.G. clearly had a real hunger for the truth of the Word.

In June of 1953, four months after Dr. Wierwille's initial trip, our family traveled with two other carloads of our friends to Calgary to take B.G. Leonard's class which he called "The Gifts of the Spirit." At his Christian Training Centre, a large upstairs room over a pawnshop, our son Don and I were students in this class from June 28 to July 15. Dr. Wierwille was with us, but of course, he was not a new student, though he wanted to sit through the class again because what B.G. Leonard was teaching was so thrilling and powerful about the "gifts" of holy spirit and about spiritual healing.

B. G. Leonard's class in June/July 1953. Nine of us from Van Wert were new students. Don is on the far left of the third row, and I am on the far right of the second row.

B.G. built people's believing by his tremendous, God-given ability as a teacher. On top of that, he was truly a one-man show. He was so full of life that it was exciting just to be around him. The deliverance that people received was right in the middle of the action of his ministering. We were given a giant step in knowledge by Brother Leonard, as we sometimes referred to him. He explained the manifestations of the spirit to us, particularly focusing on word of knowledge, word of wisdom, discerning of spirits, faith, miracles, and healing, demonstrating by scriptural accounts such as: Numbers 22 with Balaam and the talking donkey; II Kings 5 with Naaman and Elisha; and many other accounts from the Old and New Testaments. At the end of his class "The Gifts of the Spirit," Brother Leonard ordained several of the students, including Don.

The younger children with our group, including our Karen and Mary, who were too young to qualify to be in B.G.'s class, came to the open meetings in the evenings. Our whole family of five learned to minister healing at that time. We learned that when we ask from God, we receive from God. It was B.G.'s daughter, Connie, who led our Mary into receiving holy spirit.

Slightly over a year later, August 1 to 8, 1954, Brother Leonard and his family came to Van Wert to teach us more fully what he knew about the manifestations of faith (believing), miracles, and healing, also known as the impartation manifestations. Whatever Brother Leonard taught us, we took in with much enthusiasm and made it our own.

Dr. Wierwille said of him: "B.G. had quite an impact on my life. He's a man who loved me, and that is what really helped me. He respected my knowledge of the Word and things I had done in preparation.... B.G. really was the key person who believed in me and gave me the encouragement to move ahead in the Holy Spirit field."

Dr. Wierwille spoke of learning about revelation: "Most of what I learned [experientially] about revelation, I learned the hard way. And it was mostly a miracle. Many of my early experiences were phenomena. Before B.G. Leonard, I had nobody to teach me as I'm teaching you and going to teach you. But God was teaching me that He was God and revelation was available. I cannot tell you how thankful I am to God for His love, mercy, and grace. After God taught me a great deal about how revelation is given, as I had studied His Word, B.G. showed me in the Word how it worked."

Dr. Wierwille related the following experiences to show how God taught him about revelation before learning the scriptural accounts B.G. Leonard showed him.

"In Chicago on the sidewalk outside Marshall Fields, I would ask God if a certain person were a believer. If God showed me a picture of a black heart, I knew the person was unsaved. To check this 'spiritual' picture, I would ask the person if he loved God. The person would invariably deny any such love. Or if God showed me a white heart, I would get a loving 'Oh yes, I'm a Christian' response when I questioned the person."

Relating an incident closer to home, Dr. Wierwille shared: "At the Van Wert County Fair I would stand by the racetrack and ask God which horse would win, and He would show me." Dr. Wierwille warned, however: "DON'T TRY THIS STUFF. This is not the way revelation normally works." But this is how God showed Dr. Wierwille so that he could better teach us.

Again at Van Wert, Dr. Wierwille observed: "A fortune-teller at the Van Wert County Fair had set up her tent for business in an area near our Christian bookstore sales booth. She said that she was not able to 'get her connection' with us around, so she soon moved out of our vicinity."

Ever since we owned the Van Wert Gospel Gift Shop, we would close the store in town during fair week and set up a booth at the fairgrounds. That's how Dr. Wierwille was so close to the racetrack during the horse races and also near to the fortune-teller, until she voluntarily moved her business.

Albert Cliffe

Albert Cliffe was a biochemist from Canada who had seen miracles by believing God's promises. He had even successfully practiced his believing on herds of cattle. In the introduction to his book *Let Go and Let God,* Al wrote, "By means of faith in a living Christ, a resurrected Christ, you can gain such security that nothing can ever defeat you, no sickness can ever overwhelm you, and by the practice of this faith you can learn to gain victory over life and death." Al taught us that death only overtakes a person when he gets tired and quits believing to live.

Al described himself as "a cold Episcopalian" in his early years. All of this changed, however, when he was healed by God's power of an incurable disease. The miracle occurred one day as he lay sick in bed. The radio had been turned on when, at the half hour, the program changed and the evangelist Rev. Charles E. Fuller came on. No one was around to change the station, and Al wasn't able to get out of bed to change it himself or he would have. So although he cursed the situation he was in, he was a captive audience. As he listened to Rev. Fuller, he became interested in the message, gradually realizing that it was directed specifically at him. Then a phenomenon occurred. He said it was Pentecost in his room as he heard "like a rushing mighty wind." He was born again and healed from his incurable disease that day while hearing Charles Fuller speak God's Word on the radio.

Al was the invited guest of the Spiritual 40 Club from January 4 to 8, 1953. He was the only one of our Spiritual 40 Club guests, as I recall it, who didn't stay with us in our home. All the rest stayed in Don's bedroom in the upstairs of the parsonage. But Al thought his cigarette smoking would have offended us, which, of course, it wouldn't have.

During his four-day visit with us, we held prayer clinics every afternoon. His topic was "The Miracle of Believing." His evening teachings were titled "Lessons in Living."

Al's favorite figurative statement in teaching was "get your foot off the hose," meaning, remove all doubt and fear from your mind so the positive answers can come into manifestation. Let the prayer hose be open so that the answers can flow through freely.

Al Cliffe taught Dr. Wierwille a great principle when our family came up against the local school board on the question of inoculating our children, which we didn't want to do but that the school officials said was mandatory. Al told us to prioritize our time, to let the fight against inoculation go by the boards so that Dr. Wierwille could spend his time and energy holding forth the accuracy of the Word. This was timely, good advice which we have applied in many situations since then.

Dr. Wierwille stated that, "all those wonderful men... they were fantastic.... Somehow by God's mercy and grace, we just kept going on with the Word. That's what has made this ministry possible."

Bishop K. C. Pillai

In the summer of 1953 Dr. Wierwille's brother Harry went to Tennessee to visit a Christian children's camp called the "Tennessee Mountain Mission," which he was financially supporting. While there, Harry decided one evening to attend a nearby Baptist church in Chattanooga, where an Anglican bishop from India was scheduled to speak. This speaker was Bishop K. C. Pillai. After hearing Bishop Pillai that evening, Harry called Dr. Wierwille and enthusiastically told him of the teaching and asked Dr. Wierwille if he should bring him to Van Wert since "the Bishop," as we called him, had a couple of days open before his next engagement. Doctor responded, "If he's that good, you better bring him here!" Hastily we scheduled a few meetings, and Dr. Wierwille set aside personal time to spend with the Bishop.

It is no secret that Dr. Wierwille was always in search of a greater knowledge and understanding of God's Word. He felt there was so much more to know than he knew. One reason he had inadequate knowledge of the Bible was that he had in his formal education studied theological and other writings instead of having focused on the Bible itself. So he was forever continuing his quest to see God's Word, rightly divided.

After these few summer days in 1953 with Bishop Pillai's giving us our introduction to Eastern culture found in the Bible, we immediately made arrangements to have him return for another visit a couple of months later. Dr. Wierwille described that second, extended visit by saying, "Bishop and I sat together for six weeks and went from Genesis 1:1 to Revelation 22:21, reading every verse in the Word. And each time we saw an orientalism, Bishop Pillai would explain its meaning to me, giving the Word a whole new dimension—made it

Bishop Pillai's business card

live even greater. I'll always be grateful for that man. There was much in the Bible I couldn't understand and didn't know. I had no idea about Eastern culture. But the Bishop did; and when he explained Eastern culture to me, it became simple. An interesting thing about our relationship was that the Bishop taught me Eastern customs and I taught him renewed mind, of which he became the greatest exponent." Later the Bishop said, "I came over ten thousand miles from India to the United States just to hear the truth from Dr. Wierwille."

For years the Van Wert County Fair was one of the finest and largest county fairs in the state of Ohio. Annually, the fair began on Labor Day Monday. Since there was no entrance fee on the Sunday before opening, thousands of people milled around the fairgrounds and looked things over, as everything was pretty well set up by late Sunday afternoon. Except for

The Chimes Hour performing in front of the grandstand at the Van Wert County Fair

looking around, the people had nothing to do. In 1952 some of our young people gathered around the Van Wert Gospel Gift Shop, our fair exhibit, helping to set up and just fellowshipping that Sunday evening. Dr. Wierwille began thinking out loud that our youth should just spontaneously go over and sing at the gazebo nearby. As they did so, people came and spent some time, enjoying the songs that were sung. This experience incubated in his mind so that the next year Dr. Wierwille obtained permission from the fair board to have our radio group perform on stage in front of the grandstand. The Chimes Hour extended to the community an open invitation to the Sunday evening musical program at the grandstand. The Youth Caravan performed on the main stage at the racetrack, and a good-sized crowd came to listen. For this performance we invited Homer Rodeheaver to join our concert. With his gospel singing and trumpet playing, he thrilled the awed crowd. The next year we again performed. Our special invited guest was R.G. Le Tourneau, a lively and highly successful Christian businessman. These were both men I spoke of previously whom we had met at Winona Lake Conferences in Warsaw, Indiana. Of course, Dr. Wierwille always added a short, dynamic, inspirational teaching. We looked forward to these productions at the Van Wert County Fair, where our young people could perform with God's Word sounding out. For two years we did this. At that point, the local Van Wert ministerial association took over the program.

Dr. Wierwille closed out all broadcasts with the young people in June 1953 since our young people were getting married and/or leaving the community. Also, now that the Power for Abundant Living class was beginning to jell in Dr. Wierwille's heart, our outreach would be taking a new direction. Dr. Wierwille did continue broadcasting in the form of fifteen-minute meditations to keep contact with our listening audience. These broadcasts were over stations WIMA, Lima; WONW, Defiance; and WRFD, Worthington, every day except Saturdays. These were all gradually and individually concluded by July 1, 1955.

Though Dr. Wierwille followed much of the church doctrine, he always went beyond, inculcating more of the rightly divided Word in teaching and practice as he learned it. The radio program was a little too evangelistic for some of our church's consistory and others, but there were also some people interested in adding new members to the church, which Dr. Wierwille had done. At this time the church had 124 active members.

Power for Abundant Living

*I*n October 1953, Dr. Wierwille taught the first Power for Abundant Living class, which was held in the basement of St. Peter's Church. The first two classes were called "Receiving the Holy Spirit Today." The name was then changed to the broader title that fit better with the entire scope of what the class covers. Also, "Power for Abundant Living" would have a greater and broader appeal to people, especially to those not from religious backgrounds.

The first Power for Abundant Living class

Twenty-seven students sitting on wooden slat chairs listened to Dr. Wierwille teach from a small podium for over three hours each night.

In a letter of September 30, 1953, Dr. Wierwille wrote, "Starting October 18 to November 1, I will for the first time teach a course which will lead everyone taking it into this mighty ministry of deliverance."

There were no charts, no books, no syllabus; just the Bible and a chalkboard. Dr. Wierwille wanted to build that class in a carefully documented scriptural way with a greater understanding of our accumulated learning of the past years. He noted, "I made up my mind that I was going to tie the whole thing together from Genesis to Revelation." Many of us around Dr. Wierwille had been taught some of the workings of God's Word, but Dr. Wierwille had his unique inspiration on how to deliver this knowledge from the Scriptures in a systematic framework through a two-week-long class. Dr. Wierwille recorded this first class, and Rhoda then transcribed it.

A syllabus for the class was formed, based on the inspired teaching of the first class. This syllabus was used for each class taught thereafter, enlarged and revised according to new light gained.

Dr. Wierwille observed, "At that time, the Foundational Class and the Advanced Class were together—the whole thing in two weeks. The basic principles from the Word are the same. The class has filled out. But I knew the greatness of our age—the age of holy spirit—and that every truth must fit in the framework of the manifestations. I just had to teach it to somebody."

The content of the Foundational and Advanced Class changed very little over the years. In June 1957 the class was divided into two parts with the first "Advanced Class" held July 1 to 12 in Van Wert. One reason Dr. Wierwille separated the Advanced Class material from the Foundational Class was that people had heard they could become "faith healers" if they took the original class. Also, many people didn't have the Biblical background necessary to understand the heart of the Advanced Class. Dr. Wierwille was looking for people who were truly interested in learning about the integrity of God's Word and getting a foundation in the Word, and were not just interested in a "show of power" by "faith healing."

The people who had been part of B.G. Leonard's class on "The Gifts of the Spirit" were considered graduates and not included in the rosters of Dr. Wierwille's classes.

Dr. Wierwille had met a couple by the names of Ermal and Dorothy Owens a year earlier when they had invited him to be a guest speaker at their church in Lynn Grove, Indiana, for a week of inspirational meetings. At that time Ermal and Dorothy had a deep interest in learning more of God's Word and were regulars at our meetings. After taking the first class, they were continuously faithful in The Way Ministry. Ermal later became the first Vice President of The Way Ministry. Dorothy became our Root organist and

Ermal and Dorothy Owens

helped with Advanced Classes, Way Family Camps, and training The Way Corps in Christian etiquette and the Christian Song Service even to the time of this writing.

While Ermal and Dorothy Owens sat on the front row of the class, another student, an osteopathic physician by the name of Dr. E.E. Higgins, moved her chair to the side and back of the rest of the class. She was a strong-willed, keenly intelligent woman who had been all over the world in the previous twenty years studying religions but finding no answers to her perplexing spiritual questions. Twenty years of a frustrating quest had turned her into a skeptic. She doubted that she'd find any answers this time either in Power for Abundant Living. So she sat with her arms crossed as though she were defying Dr. Wierwille, not opening her Bible, keeping her distance from everyone. Dr. Wierwille didn't demand that she conform as she sat there, her attitude seemingly being, "you probably don't have anything to teach me."

Dr. E. E. Higgins

However, as the class progressed, her demeanor began to change. By the time the two-week class was over, she apologized for having been so rude at the beginning. But since she had been disappointed so often, she had become hardened in her search and behaved accordingly. As Power for Abundant Living answered so many of her vexing questions, she appeared as a person with a great burden lifted from her mind and emotions. After this class, Dr. Higgins frequently called Dr. Wierwille as late as two-thirty in the morning to see if he was still in his office. Her question always was: "What have you learned from God's Word today?" And Dr. Wierwille would freely share with Dr. Higgins, blessing both her to receive and him to put his thoughts into words.

E. W. Bullinger

Dr. Higgins was the person who introduced Dr. Wierwille to the great and influential works of an Englishman named E.W. Bullinger (1837–1913). She gave Dr. Wierwille his first Companion Bible, containing the notes and appendix information of E.W. Bullinger, and a copy of *How to Enjoy the Bible,* also written by Dr. Bullinger. Besides making Dr. Wierwille aware of Bullinger's invaluable research, Dr. Higgins's personal contribution to Dr. Wierwille was her knowledge of the awesome wonders of the human body, corroborating Psalms 139:14, which says, ". . . for I am [my body is] fearfully *and* wonderfully made. . . ."

After reading these books by Dr. Bullinger, Dr. Wierwille wanted to consume his *Journal of Biblical Literature, Figures of Speech Used in the Bible,* and his other writings. Dr. Wierwille obtained the book *The Witness of the Stars* which aroused his curiosity concerning the star that led the wise men to the house of the young child Jesus. He read all the research he could find at that time. We learned of an astronomer in Delphos, Ohio, just east of Van Wert, so Dr. Wierwille made an appointment for us to meet him. His name was Peltier, who also had a comet named after him. When Dr. Wierwille, after a while of getting acquainted, asked him about the star that led the wise men, he laughed. He said that one couldn't expect to base anything scientific on the Bible. It was almost thirty years later when Dr. Wierwille found his answer to "the star of Bethlehem."

At the January 10, 1954, Board of Directors' meeting a question came up concerning whether people should be permitted to use Dr. Wierwille's materials when teaching classes of their own. We did not reach a decision at this board meeting. Someone had suggested that Dr. Wierwille's teachings should be put on audiotapes and rented out, and that Power for Abundant Living should be made into a correspondence course up to and including the teaching on the first three "gifts."

On the same day of the board meeting, Dr. Wierwille began teaching his second PFAL class.

Bishop Pillai was in that second class. The Bishop had been raised in southern India as a Hindu who, as a teenager, most miraculously heard about Christ and was born again. Now he was very thrilled by the knowledge he was gaining in the Power for Abundant Living class as the teaching progressed.

During the course of the class, the Bishop expressed his desire to have Dr. Wierwille make a tour of India to teach his Indian people the same great truths that he himself was learning here in the United States. Bishop told Dr. Wierwille that the Eastern people would believe God's Word and, therefore, Dr. Wierwille would see the power of God move in a way he had not yet experienced. The Bishop told us, "India is not closed to the gospel, as you may have heard, but open to all Christians who have a contribution to make and share with the Indian people which will enable them to help themselves to stand on their own merits and to develop their own leaders in the native church of India." This was very important to Dr. Wierwille because of the unbelief he had encountered here in the American churches. Bishop Pillai was so eager for his countrymen to have the opportunity to hear the rightly divided Word of God. He felt strongly that his people would have the greatest respect for our message if our entire family went so that they could see our family ministering together.

The Bishop had talked privately with Dr. Wierwille during the class that January 1954 about the possibility of this teaching tour to India. When the news reached me, Dr. Wierwille had already settled it in his heart that we as a family would accept Bishop Pillai's invitation. Dr. Wierwille was convinced that since God wanted us to go, we would be able to make the arrangements to go—to have our financial needs met to take the trip and to have our responsibilities for our congregation and broadcasts properly delegated. For my part, I readily knew that it was the right thing for us to do. We had believed that it was God's will for us to go to India and we just acted and proceeded with that goal in mind. In early February we received Bishop Pillai's formal invitation.

A *Special* letter to our pastor...
Dr. Victor Paul Wierwille

Indian Episcopal Church
— SYRO-CHALDEAN RITE —

Jurisdictional Head:
His Excellency
The Most Rev. K. Chengalvaroya Pillai, D. D.
Archbishop and Metropolitan of India

6 Fisher Street
Greenwich, New York

February 3, 1954

The Reverend Victor Paul Wierwille, Th.D.
St. Peter's Evangelical and Reformed Church
Van Wert, Ohio

My Dear Dr. Wierwille:

    I would like to place it on record that your teaching on the Fullness of the Holy Spirit and the Gifts of the Spirit has been most original, enlightening and thoroughly scriptural. I greatly profited while I sat at your feet in the class for a fortnight, absorbing almost every word coming out of your lips. What you teach is just the Word of God, and I did not realize it until you opened my eyes to it. Why did I not know it before? I can answer that question myself. It was because I did not in total accept just what the Word of God said, but only what others said about it. I realize for the first time that this has been the reason why the Christian Church is a paralyzed institution without much power.

    Martin Luther said, "The Spirit and the Gifts are ours" because he believed in them and demonstrated them. Now, the Church acts as if the Spirit and the Gifts are not ours for today so she is tremendously handicaped and defeated. Ocassional so called revivals and rededications and surrenders which include hymn-singing and hand raising will never take the place of the Spirit and the Gifts.

    Your teaching on the "renewal of the mind" is dynamic. That is just what the believers all over the world need. I am indebted to you for this enlightenment as well. I have travelled much and seen much and heard the best of the preachers and teachers of the Word, but never as unique, original, and as scriptural as yours. India and the East will readily take to your teaching and message. This is just what we need. We have heard enough about the other kind, "having a form of godliness but denying the power thereof" and now we want to hear the truth which alone will set us free.

    I am wondering if you would care to accept an invitation to India and the East in the Fall of 1955 to quicken us from the awful spiritual decay in the Church of God throughout the world? I know that you have the key to its solution. Furthermore, because I am benefited, the Indian Church and people also will be benefited through my teaching and leadership. You have therefore done much for us and we are eternally indebted to you and can never repay our debt of gratitude to you in this

- 2 -

life, but would love to show to you our appreciation as best we can as a small token of what we have received from you.

    As an Archbishop and Metropolitan of India in the Indian Eastern Orthodox Church, and by the Canonical Authority derived by Apostolic Succession from the See of St. Peter in Antioch, Syria, and by virtue of the powers vested in me by the Constitution of our Church, established under the government of India, Act XXI of 1860, and with the concurrence of the Holy Synod of our Church I have the power to confer the honorary degree of Doctor of Literatures, (D. Litt.) on any minister in good standing and in recognition of his meritorious services rendered for the Church of God. It has been the inherent privilege of the Ancient Eastern Church to confer such honorary degrees upon Clergy with sound learning and unimpeachable character for very special work done by them. It is an ecclesiastical degree. I shall be glad to recommend your name to the Holy Synod for this honorary degree to be conferred on you in recognition of your unique services to the Church of God, if you will accept the honor?

    For your information I would state that I am currently the National Director of the Department of Interdenominational Relations on an exchange basis from India under the American Orthodox Catholic Patriarchate in the U.S.A. I may also be reached at the Chancery of our Patriarch at 162 E. 128th Street, New York City, New York, and shall be pleased to hear from you or to see you there.

    May God continue to bless you in the great work you are doing.
With kindest regards,

I am,
Yours Gratefully,

+ K. Chingalvaroya Pillai

Bishop Pillai's formal invitation asking Dr. Wierwille to visit and teach in India

HE is RISEN as HE SAID!

Seeds of The Way Corps

*I*n April 1954 at another special Board of Directors' meeting, Dr. Wierwille told the board about his idea to start a seminary in Van Wert. The name he had in mind was "The East-West Seminary."

After more thought, by the July 25, 1954, Board of Directors' meeting, the concept of a seminary was incorporated in the ministry of The Chimes Hour Youth Caravan under the working name of "The Way Bible Center." Our outreach ministry was in the process of changing dramatically, so a name change was appropriate. A new facility was discussed in which St. Peter's Church and The Chimes Hour Youth Caravan could be housed under one roof. The board of The Chimes Hour Youth Caravan told the church consistory that they would work hand in hand with them in establishing The Way Bible Center.

Dr. Wierwille reported at the October 31, 1954, meeting that the consistory, the governing body of St. Peter's Church, had discussed locating The Way Bible Center headquarters and training center on two properties next to the church. The ministry would need to buy the Hines property to the west of the church and the Eikenbary property to the east. Mrs. Owens suggested that the Youth Caravan Board of Directors should add their support to the church's in financing a new building. This center would then be in use seven days a week.

We needed to gather so much information before we would be ready to launch into such a new undertaking. Dr. Wierwille stated that the new church/seminary should be planned to meet our needs for the next twenty-five years.

Dr. Wierwille's father and stepmother, Ernst and Emma Wierwille, were in the third PFAL class that Dr. Wierwille taught, June 13–27, 1954. One of several interesting qualities of Dad Wierwille was his burning desire to help sick people receive healing through the power of God. Dad Wierwille would take sick people, if they desired, to a farmer near Kettlersville, Ohio, who would pray for them. I recall that Dad Wierwille's question after taking the class was, "What good does it do to speak in tongues if you can't understand it?" Dr. Wierwille answered, "It edifies the spirit within us; speaking in tongues is not fruitful to the mind." That answer satisfied his father.

The following dates of when our family members took PFAL show our families' support and involvement with the early PFAL classes.

Dr. Wierwille's family:
  Uncle Harry (brother) January 1954
  Martin and Lydia Kuck (sister and brother-in-law) January 1954
  Reuben and Mary (brother and first wife) April 1954
  Ernst and Emma (father and second wife) June 1954
  Annely (niece) 1956
  Bob Ed (nephew) 1960
  Sevilla Henkener (sister) July 1961

My family, the Kipps:
  Rev. Adrian Kipp (brother) October 1953
  Deloris Fischbach (sister) October 1953
  Richard Fischbach (brother-in-law) January 1954
  Jean Fischbach (niece) 1954
  Lloyd and Evelyn Ulrey (sister and brother-in-law) 1954

Our children:
  Don 1953 (with B.G. Leonard)
  Karen 1954
  Mary 1955
  John Paul (J.P.) 1965
  Sara 1965

During the spring, after having taught the Receiving the Holy Spirit class for a second time, Dr. Wierwille was very inspired to put the receiving the holy spirit part of the class in writing. He very carefully planned to do this under controlled circumstances, namely to live in a solitary environment and to eat a grape diet. He believed that if he were undisturbed for one week, Monday through Friday, eating solely a diet of grapes, he would have a clear mind to write this book. So he moved into the Marsh Hotel on Main Street in Van Wert in a room without a telephone and where only a couple of us knew his whereabouts, insuring his privacy. The product of this five-day seclusion was the first edition of *Receiving the Holy Spirit Today*.

In June 1954 while another class was being taught, we prepared to publish this first edition. The printing was done on our Multilith machine. We manually pasted the colorful yellow-on-green cover over the cardboard, and then we pasted the printed pages between the covers of the book. This was the extent of our publishing technology at that time.

Preparation to Go Abroad

Dr. Wierwille planned at this point to teach seven more PFAL classes before leaving for the India tour. He had also inquired at WIMA, Lima, about fifteen-minute daily broadcasts for a trial period of thirteen weeks. Dr. Wierwille felt that short programs would be a great way to effectively reach many people with the gospel of deliverance. This was an experiment he tested before leaving to go abroad.

By June of 1954, the time of serious preparation for our India tour was at hand. We had around fourteen months to make arrangements and get organized to be gone for eight months in 1955–1956. The consistory of the church made it clear that Dr. Wierwille's salary would continue at its current level while he was abroad and that Dr. Wierwille should find a replacement pastor for that period of time.

Bishop Pillai left the United States for India on December 3, 1954, to make contacts and set the groundwork for our visit. He would not, however, be in India during our itinerary there, so he made arrangements for Dr. J. S. Williams from Bombay to be our host. What an outstanding arrangement that would prove to be!

When first determining how to finance our trip, we considered the resources we had coming in, such as our salary (minus what we would pay a replacement minister), and other monetary gifts people might give us. Of the amount we estimated we would need from September 1955 to April 1956, brother Harry suggested that $2,000 would be taken care of by the church and $8,000 by the radio program. This was agreeable to all parties concerned. Since we calculated that $10,000 would not be enough money to cover the expenses for a family of five while traveling abroad for eight months, we decided to supplement our revenue by selling our car and our household furniture.

I was responsible for getting the clothing for all five of us organized for both hot and cold weather and for acquiring the luggage we would need for traveling. The three children along with their schoolteachers were to gather the books they would need to study, as they would be missing almost an entire year of school. In 1955 the school officials felt that our children would learn more by a year of travel than they would learn by staying at home in the local school, so they had no qualms about the children's missing all but the last month of the school year.

It took a great deal of planning to have our mail and clothing sent to specific destinations in various cities so that these items would arrive as we would be traveling through those locations. Tour itinerary, tickets, personal appointments, and many other things needed to be carefully thought through and worked out. Ermal and Dorothy Owens were a great blessing in helping us with these and many other matters.

Ermal became treasurer for our tour finances, and Rhoda was given the power of attorney for Dr. Wierwille, for St. Peter's Church, and for The Chimes Hour Youth Caravan. During this time of preparation, Dr. Wierwille still kept up a strong outreach program, teaching the third and fourth Power for Abundant Living classes in Van Wert, as well as classes in Chicago, Illinois, and Lima, Ohio.

By July 25, 1954, we had made reservations for our family to leave for India the week of September 21, 1955. We made a deposit of $350 for each ship ticket from New York to Southampton, England, with full payment due four weeks in advance of sailing. We still needed $8,000 for the tour, of which $1,730 was on hand at this time in June. Believers had promised to give us $3,276 in August.

In July 1954 our youngest child, Mary, was ten years old, and Dr. Wierwille and I thought that we would probably have no more children, even though at one time our intention had been to have five. In December 1954, having begun to make arrangements to leave the country for an extended period of time, I was absolutely stunned to discover that I was pregnant. This would have been very welcome news at any other time, but at this juncture, having an infant took some very special arrangements. I knew I couldn't get anxious for anything in spite of my circumstances. God would take care of me and our baby. So in February of 1955 I asked my sister and brother-in-law, Dee and Dick Fischbach, with their twelve-year-old daughter, Jean, to take care of what would be a very young baby while I would be abroad for eight months. They were delighted that I asked. I had confidence that they would take care of the baby as well as I.

In January 1955 Dr. Wierwille had *My Tithing Account Book* published by our publishing company, "The House of Faith." This was a wonderful little booklet to keep records of one's tithes and offerings, having space for an entire year, month by month. It also had outlines and illustrations on practical methods for persons in various occupations and also Biblical references about tithing.

JANUARY	Shows Source of Income, Wages, Profits TITHE ACCOUNT	How Much Is My Tithe! CR.	
	SAMPLE PAGE		
Dec. 30	1/10 of salary	4	00
Jan. 6	1/10 of salary	4	00
Jan. 13	1/10 of salary	4	00
Jan. 20	1/10 of salary	4	00
Jan. 27	1/10 of salary	4	00
	Total	20	00

You will notice that the "Dr." on the page to the right is equal to "Cr." on this page, meaning that your whole tithe has been given from your "LORD'S BOX."

This sample page illustrates the recording proceedure of an individual getting a straight salary plus increases of profits from his investments, bonds paying interest, etc.

A farmer, manufacturer or business man may estimate his tithe on last years net income and regularly set aside at the end of each week, or a period of time, the necessary amount for tithing through his Church. At the end of the year, after the legitimate operating expenses have been deducted and there is a net surplus, then the necessary amount making up the tithe may be given at that time or used to start off the new year of tithing. Tithers are not pharisaical in their efforts, but loving and cheerful. The tithe is an honest debt and you have not given anything unto the Lord until you have paid your tithe.

JANUARY	TITHE ACCOUNT	Where, When And For What DR.	
	SAMPLE PAGE		
Jan. 1	Sunday School		50
	Church	2	00
	Sunday Night	1	00
Jan. 4	Women's Guild		50
Jan. 8	Sunday School		50
	Church	2	00
	Sunday Night	1	00
Jan. 10	Churchmen's Brotherhood		50
Jan. 15	Sunday School		50
	Church	2	00
	Sunday Night	1	00
Jan. 20	Artho Class		50
Jan. 22	Sunday School		50
	Church	2	00
	Sunday Night	1	00
Jan. 27	Youth Fellowship Club		25
Jan. 29	Sunday School		50
	Church	3	00
	Sunday Night		75
	Total	20	00

Your tithe is distributed among all the activities of your church.

The Answer
booklet's title page

> # THE ANSWER
>
> ## THE FIRST EPISTLE OF JOHN
>
> *The Senses Coordinated with the Heart.*

The booklet *The Answer,* studies in I John, was published at this time also, funded by Mr. and Mrs. Ermal Owens.

By this time, the "Board of Trustees" had evolved, consisting of V. P. Wierwille as President, Ermal L. Owens as Vice President, and H. E. Wierwille as Secretary-Treasurer. However, the "Board of Trustees" was not legally acknowledged until June 1956.

On June 12, 1955, the Board of Trustees submitted a resolution to the Board of Directors to amend and revise the constitution of The Way. Our original charter of incorporation had been filed October 30, 1947, No. 204759, with the Ohio secretary of state.

RESOLUTION OF AMENDMENT OF ARTICLES OF INCORPORATION TO CHANGE NAME OF CORPORATION AND TO AMEND ITS PURPOSE CLAUSE.

RESOLVED, that the Articles of Incorporation of the "The Chimes Hour Youth Caravan, Incorporated" be and hereby are amended as follows:

By striking out in its entirety the First Article, which reads as follows:

"<u>FIRST</u>. The name of said corporation shall be The Chimes Hour Youth Caravan, Incorporated"

and by inserting in lieu thereof, a new First Article as follows:

"<u>FIRST</u>. The name of said corporation shall be The Way, Inc."

By adding to the Third Article, which reads as follows:

"<u>THIRD</u>. The purpose or purposes for which said corporation is formed are: For the furtherance of the gospel of Jesus Christ by radio, or by personal appearance.

the following to-wit:

television, the printed page and all things incident thereto; the receiving, holding and distributing of gifts, bequests, and funds arising from all sources, owning and maintaining suitable real estate and buildings and doing any and all things incident to any thereof; the ability to license and to ordain ministers of the Gospel and to send forth such qualified men and women to foreign fields, and to support, receive and establish real estate and properties incident thereto according to the particular state, county or land; to establish, maintain and conduct camps, institutions of learning for the purpose of efficient instruction in the Gospel of Jesus Christ, promoting biblical education in all departments of learning and knowledge and especially in those branches pertinent thereto and acquiring and holding for said purposes, money, real estate and other property necessary or proper to carry out such said objectives and doing all things necessary to the accomplishment of aforesaid purposes.

RESOLVED FURTHER, that the Certificate of Amendment of the Articles of Incorporation herewith submitted be, and the same is hereby, in all respects, approved, authorized and adopted, subject to such changes therein as counsel for the corporation may deem necessary or advisable.

RESOLVED FURTHER, that the President or a Vice-president and the Secretary of the Corporation be, and they hereby are, authorized and directed to execute and file in the office of the Secretary of State of the State of Ohio said Certificate of Amendment and to execute, deliver and file any other certificate or instrument which they may deem necessary or appropriate to render effective or otherwise fully carry out the intent and purpose of this resolution.

The new name, "The Way, Incorporated," was also deemed necessary to be attached to the class Power for Abundant Living and to our various publications. The name "The Chimes Hour Youth Caravan" was no longer used.

It seemed that Dr. Wierwille constantly stretched every fiber of his being to get the Word out to people. I think about how Martin Luther translated the Bible from Latin into German, the language of the people, so that the lay person could read it for himself and not be misled by abusive clerics. What a step to freedom that must have been, freedom from the slavery of the ecclesiastical domination. Now Dr. Wierwille was explaining God's Word in its accuracy and integrity, always interested that God's people would benefit from understanding it, first of all, in order to be able to act on the Word and then to receive in their lives what God had already given. By people's acting and receiving, God was glorified as others could see His benefits in the lives of believers.

Dr. Wierwille covered our absence from Van Wert by writing a monthly newsletter, including information of our departure from Van Wert on September 11 until our sailing date from New York Harbor on September 21. This letter went to all the mailing list of the former radio audience and to other Way believers.

Included among the schedule of dates were our specific locations so that people could write to us and catch us as we moved about. Also by having our schedule, our friends could follow our movement and pray for us all along the way.

Our official passport picture: Dr. Wierwille, Don, age 14, Karen, 12, Mary, 10, and myself. Dr. Wierwille, on the advice of Bishop Pillai, frequently wore a clerical collar while we were abroad to designate himself as a minister, a respected position.

September 1955

Newsletter

To My Beloved Friends in Christ:

Greetings to you in the name of our Lord and Savior, Jesus Christ. His love is beyond comprehension and His mercy is upon all. His favor is upon all believers of His Word and my prayer for all of you who have so lovingly stood by me with your prayers and gifts of love is that you may grow up in renewed mind love before Him in all things.

Carrying this ministry of deliverance, which is the Jesus WAY, the light of the Holy Spirit and the "gifts" of the Spirit, you will be with us wherever we are, and you will always be in our prayers and hearts.

This will not be an easy missionary tour, but we have a big God and we believe for big results. We know that His Word will not return void.

Sunday, September 11, is our final service in Van Wert, and if you can be present for the 10:30 A.M. worship hour you would make us very happy. Dr. Ernest Fledderjohann will fill the pulpit after September 11 and during my absence on this Missionary Teaching and Training Tour.

We will leave for New York City on the 13th, having some appointments there as well as in Washington, D.C., before we sail on Wednesday, September 21.

I have just visited The Way Branches in both Columbus, Ohio, and Chicago, Illinois. The believers there are enthusiastic about the things of God. As we all work and stand together as ONE in Christ, His name will be magnified and glorified in every land where we will go. Month after month I will keep you informed through this News Letter regarding the progress of our Missionary Teaching and Training Tour.

Our workers here at home will do all they can with your cooperation to keep the things of God going here in the United States. Rhoda Becker will be in our office every day. Your letters and gifts sent to The Way, Van Wert, Ohio, will be used according to your specification, will and desire.

On Saturday afternoon at 2:30 P.M., September 17, some of our workers will sell at public auction at 109 S. Harrison in Van Wert, Ohio some of our household furniture. My 1953 Nash Ambassador Country Club Automobile will be sold by Smith Auto Sales in Van Wert after we leave also.

In this news letter I am also giving you our full schedule as well as the places where you may write to me directly if you so desire. All Van Wert mail will be sent to me by Miss Becker. God bless you as we all stand in Christ, shoulder to shoulder throughout the next six months and more.

Sincerely,
In His Service,
Victor Paul Wierwille

ITINERARY FOR
DR. AND MRS. VICTOR PAUL WIERWILLE
AND FAMILY

1955

Sept. 21st—Wednesday—Sail from New York in Queen Mary to Southampton, tourist class.
Sept. 26th—Monday—Arrive in Southampton, England, in the afternoon.
Sept. 27th—Tuesday

TO } IN ENGLAND
Oct. 24th—Monday

Oct. 25th—Tuesday—Sail from Tilbury Docks, England, to Bombay, India by ship Arcadia. Tourist class.
Nov. 8th—Tuesday—Arrive in Bombay, India.
Nov. 9th—Wednesday

TO } IN INDIA
1956
Feb. 10th—Friday

Feb. 11th—Saturday—Sail from Bombay, India to Port Said, Egypt.
Feb. 18th—Saturday—Arrive in Port Said, Egypt.
Feb. 19th—Sunday

TO } IN EGYPT
Feb. 24th—Friday

Feb. 25th—Saturday—Leave Alexandria, Egypt for Beirut, Lebanon.
Feb. 26th—Sunday—Arrive in Beirut, Lebanon.
Feb. 27th—Monday

TO } LEBANON, SYRIA, HASHEMITE KINGDOM OF JORDAN, PALESTINE.

Mar. 28th—Wednesday
Mar. 29th—Thursday—Leave Tel Aviv for Haifa and sail to Naples, Italy.
April 1st on—ITALY, AUSTRIA, SWITZERLAND, FRANCE, GERMANY.

IF YOU DESIRE TO SEND MAIL DIRECTLY TO ME
SEND IT AIRMAIL TO
Dr. Victor Paul Wierwille

Sept. 13–20	% Dr. R. S. Modak, 4 East 28th St., New York City, N.Y.
Sept. 21–Oct. 24	% Bonnington Hotel, S. Hampton Row, London WC1, England.
Oct. 25–Feb. 5	% Tajmahal Hotel, Bombay, India.
Feb. 6–18	% General Delivery, Cairo, Egypt.
Feb. 19–29	% Rev. Edward Myer, P.O. Box 1973, Beirut, Lebanon.
Mar. 1–21	% Rev. M. G. Griebenou, C.M.A. American Colony Church, Jerusalem, Israel.
Mar. 22–Apr. 10	% Dr. Karl Barth, Basel, Switzerland.
Apr. 11–	% Bonnington Hotel, S. Hampton Row, London WC1, England.

Sunday, September 11, 1955

Our Sunday morning fellowship was geared to a formal farewell service for our family with the interim pastor and his wife, Dr. and Mrs. Fledderjohann, joining us to help make the transition. Dr. Fledderjohann, a retired pastor from our home church in New Knoxville, had substituted for Dr. Wierwille on Sunday morning services a few times before, so he needed no introduction. Dr. Wierwille said to his people, "I told you, there is no better pastor than Dr. Fledderjohann."

The morning worship service was followed by a dinner in the fellowship room of the church. Beautiful nautical decorations set the mood with *Bon Voyage* in silver letters across the front of the stage. Everyone gave us such a loving send-off. They seemed to feel a part of the mission we expected to accomplish. There was great expectation.

Monday, September 12

The next day after our last Sunday church services I spent getting ready for our household furniture sale and doing last-minute washing and ironing. That evening Ermal and Dorothy Owens came from Lynn Grove, Indiana, to help pack. Ermal helped Dr. Wierwille, as he was an expert packer. Others also came to help in any way or just be around; among them, of course, was Rhoda Becker.

The auction of our household goods to help pay for our trip abroad

Leaving baby J.P. at the Fischbachs

On Tuesday, after many people stopped by to wish us "bon voyage," we left Van Wert in brother Reuben's car to have a noon meal with my sister and brother-in-law, the Fischbachs, in St. Marys. It was a short and sweet time, and then we bade the baby, John Paul, and his new family good-bye. It took a real mind-set for us to leave John Paul behind; however, we never turned to look back. We choked back the tears without breathing for a while and then we moved on with goal-orientation, on our way to New York.

After visiting in several places along the way (my brother Adrian and his family in Uniontown, Ohio; Rhoda's parents in Lancaster, Pennsylvania; and the Princeton Theological campus), we arrived in New York.

We had to reconfirm our ship's travel tickets and make various arrangements with American Express. (American Express offices became regular stopping places as we traveled about. They collected our mail and helped us greatly with traveling information.) On Sunday Dr. Wierwille had accepted an invitation to preach at an African Orthodox church. The order of the service seemed like a lot of ritual to him; however, the patriarch told Dr. Wierwille how very excellent his preaching was.

On Monday and Tuesday Dr. Wierwille took care of more arrangements, including meeting with organizations that we would be representing abroad. Also, we were tutored on how the Indian people think and act so as to have a better understanding of how to deal with them and how to minister to them, acclimating to their culture.

The last night in New York before setting sail we held a wonderful "prayer retreat," as we called it, from 11:00 P.M. to 1:30 A.M., for a successful tour.

You are cordially invited to a
FAREWELL DINNER
in honor of
Victor Paul Wierwille, Th.D.

American Representative of
PEOPLES AMERICA-INDIA RELATIONS SOCIETY

on the eve of his departure for a visit to
INDIA

in the Dining Room of the Hotel Seville
22 East 29th Street, New York City

September 20th, 1955, 6:30 P.M.

Ramkrishna Shahu Modak
President, All-India Federation of
National Churches

Subscription $2.25
R.S.V.P.
4 East 28th Street
New York City
LE 2-4768

Saying good-bye after touring the Queen Mary. *(l. to r.): Myself, Lydia, Reuben, Mary, Harry, Victor, Don, and Dad Wierwille*

Wednesday was our sailing day on the HMS *Queen Mary*. Dr. Wierwille's family again showed their support when Dad Wierwille, sister Lydia, and brothers Harry and Reuben came to see us off.

We began this new experience on ship on Wednesday, the twenty-first of September. The children, Don, Karen, and Mary, enjoyed the pace as much as Dr. Wierwille and I. They each had their assignments: Don was taking all the 3-D slide pictures, while Karen took all the black-and-white photographs. Mary was our little "half-fare" and smiled a lot. Dr. Williams, our tour host in India, later called her our "advance publicity agent" because she managed to get everyone's attention with her smile. After leaving the dock with all the exciting festivities, we calmly sailed past the Statue of Liberty. Our journey had begun. Although the ship rolled a little at times, the next few days on board were relaxing and interesting, an exhilarating new adventure. On the morning of September 27, a Tuesday, we made a short stop at Cherbourg, France; and the same afternoon we docked in Southampton, England, our destination.

October 1955

Newsletter

Thus far we have had a most enjoyable and profitable trip, even though it has just begun. Our trip at sea has been most blessed and we have had a number of opportunities to witness to the greatness of our God and His wonderful salvation. We have met people from all sections of the world and what joy it is to know that Jesus still reigns supreme.

On Tuesday night before we set sail on Wednesday, Dr. R. S. Modak, President of the American Committee of the All India Federation of National Churches, and his good wife gave us a farewell dinner at Hotel Seville in New York. Some 40 prominent men and women of leadership and distinction of various races and nationalities were in attendance. Dr. A. Rouner, pastor of the Cadman Memorial Congregational Christian Church, Brooklyn, was the toastmaster for the occasion. My father and sister and two brothers, who traveled to New York to see us off, were also the honored guests at the banquet.

Telephone calls, telegrams, special delivery letters, etc., reached us from our friends on Tuesday evening and Wednesday morning before we set sail. We appreciated every thing that was done for us and is still being done by all of our wonderful friends who so lovingly believe in our ministry to which God has called us. I know that your prayers have been with us and will be with us all the way.

Just before we set sail a dozen most beautiful American Beauty red roses were delivered to our cabin from some of our Van Wert people. Such thoughtfulness almost overwhelmed us and tears of joy came to our eyes. We thank God for our wonderful helpers and friends and pray His best for all people everywhere. A wonderful group of people were present aboard ship just before we sailed, including the Modak family, Bishop K. C. Pillai, Mr. Richardson, a prominent New York attorney whom we had met the night before at the Banquet, and of course my own wonderful family, including my father, my sister Lydia and my two brothers, Harry and Reuben.

We sailed at high noon, and the Manhattan coastline of New York was an impressive sight, but nothing thrilled my heart like the Statue of Liberty in the New York harbor which we passed on our way to the Ocean. Standing so tall and stately with hand uplifted with the golden sunbeams playing so brilliantly upon her it seemed to say, 'God bless you on your way.' I am sure that when we again see the Statue of Liberty it will be even more welcome for then we shall be coming home and that means reunion with our many friends. That day we are awaiting.

Our mission in England will be well on its way by the time you receive this news letter, so in our next letter I am sure we shall be able to share with you many wonderful things that have happened.

I want you to stand with us on the words from Colossians 4:2-4: Continue in prayer, and watch in the same (prayer) with thanksgiving; Withal (always) praying also for us, that God would open unto us a door of utterance (preaching), to speak the mystery of Christ....So that I may make it manifest as I ought to speak.

God bless you and mercifully magnify His grace upon you all.

Sincerely in His Service,
Victor Paul Wierwille

England

During our stay in England, from Tuesday, September 27, until Tuesday, October 25, we had many goals set for ourselves. Of course, while in London, we walked or rode the Underground to see the historic sites: Buckingham Palace, the Tower of London (Don called it the "Slaughter House"), the American Embassy, St. Paul's Cathedral, the British Museum, the National Portrait Gallery, Westminster Abbey, and the Houses of Parliament, among others. These places all made history so real for our youngsters. It was most interesting to see the Stone of Scone, under the coronation chair in Westminster Abbey. This stone is thought by some to be the stone Jacob used for a pillow as recorded in Genesis 28:18.

Among the many treasures to be seen in the British Museum were the Rosetta stone, which is the inscribed rock that gave the world the key to decoding the written language of ancient Egypt, and the Codex Sinaiticus, an early manuscript of the Bible.

Dr. Wierwille visited the Lamp Press, where he spoke with a Dr. E. C. Carpenter, a man who had personally known Dr. E. W. Bullinger. Dr. Wierwille intentionally sought from him any information about Bullinger and his research that Dr. Carpenter might know because of his association with the man. Dr. Wierwille kept in contact with Dr. Carpenter by correspondence later in following up on his interest in E. W. Bullinger and his many works.

During this visit in England, Mary and Karen spent time visiting with other children whose parents were involved in our meetings. The rest of their time was filled with studying, learning to knit, letter writing, or helping with laundry. They frequently mentioned how they wished they could "hold J.P. up under his arms."

Mary and Don feeding the pigeons in Trafalgar Square

Don assisted his dad, as well as wrote letters and studied. I tutored the children in spelling, and we all set our sights on pulling Don through history, English, geometry, and Latin, his sophomore classes. In London his favorite place was Trafalgar Square with the pigeons. While Dr. Wierwille and I carried out our agenda, we also tried to do things of interest for the three children.

While in London Dr. Wierwille was able to get much studying done, plus make arrangements to meet the contacts that Bishop Pillai had eagerly made for us as "a door of utterance." Again, the Bishop had it so on his heart for all of his many friends in England, as well as in India, to hear God's Word rightly divided.

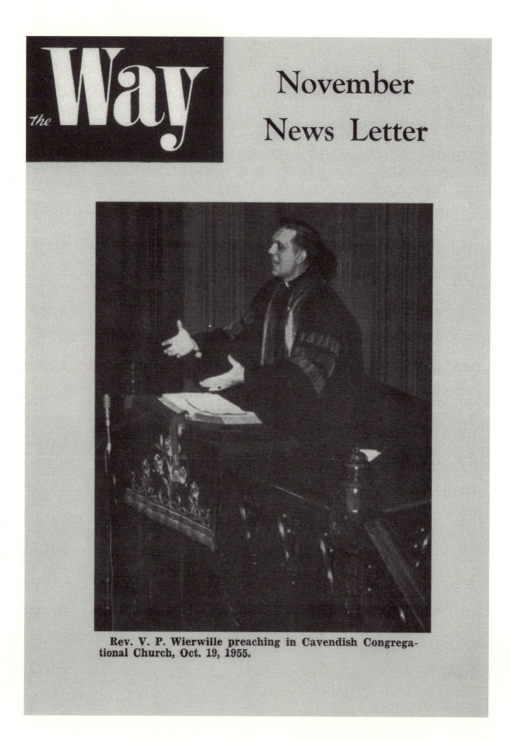

Rev. V. P. Wierwille preaching in Cavendish Congregational Church, Oct. 19, 1955.

The following is an excerpt from the November 1955 *Way Newsletter,* written from London, October 25, just before sailing for India.

> To Our Many Friends and Helpers:
>
> The sharing of our light on the Gospel with people in England was a great success. The people at first were skeptical, not knowing us; but after the first hearing, they knew that God had called us to declare great and wonderful truths of the Gospel and the crowds increased and love was manifested. People were saved, healed, and filled with the power from on high. God's blessing was upon us and He opened every door for our ministry of deliverance.
>
> We ministered at Macclesfield, Manchester, and Sunningdale, England. They asked us to stop on our return from India, if at all possible; but if not, they pressed us to return from America to England with this wonderful Gospel of deliverance as soon as possible. Macclesfield was especially hungry. Many wonderful friends were there including the Reverends Sains and Baker, and Mr. and Mrs. Ronald Hooley who first stood with us boldly and who opened the original doors to England.
>
> A Branch of The Way, Inc., was forthwith established in England with headquarters at Macclesfield and Mr. Hooley as the overseer. Praise God!
>
> At Sunningdale, which is only 15 miles outside of London, we gathered with a group of scholars for a two-day spiritual retreat. Dr. E. C. Carpenter, an outstanding English Doctor of Osteopathy and President of the Lamp Press, acted as chairman and the retreat was held at beautiful Shrubs Hill Grange. Most scholars are hungry but skeptical, yet this group's doubts were quickly quelled for the Word of God is the will of God.
>
> In His Service,
> Victor Paul Wierwille

Dr. Wierwille and Don ministering in Cavendish Chapel, Manchester

Dr. Wierwille witnessed and taught that wonderful Word of God in churches and home fellowships, many times going from afternoon teatime until midnight with packed audiences.

Because of the excitement generated in England, we were pressed to return to England on our way home from India. The Bishop had taught us how in his country, India, they didn't say "good-bye"; their parting words were "we go and come." So we could gear our thoughts to that since we had had such a gratifying visit in England. We would go and then come back.

Labeling luggage for the next leg of our journey was now the order of the day. Stopping at "The Wimpie" in downtown London for American food of hamburgers, Coca-Cola, coffee, and milk shakes had become a real treat by now, although our family did well on English food. Our newly made friends had always endeavored to bless us with their favorite recipes.

On Tuesday, October 25, we sailed from the Tilbury docks on the British ship *Arcadia*. It was another adventure by sea: a smooth trip through the Bay of Biscay, past the Rock of Gibraltar, and into the Mediterranean Sea on smooth-as-glass waters on a gorgeously bright moonlit night with the fish causing a glitter as they jumped alongside of the ship. We didn't know it would be like that, but God must have wanted to bless all of us so specially.

Several days later our ship dropped anchor at Port Said in Egypt, where the British flag came down on the ship and the Egyptian flag took its place while we sailed through the Suez Canal. The English ship's crew went in "hiding" as the brusque Egyptian crew came on to steer the *Arcadia* through the canal. Everyone stayed out of their way. In the Bitter Lakes we waited while the Egyptian ships went around us to travel ahead of us the rest of the way through the narrow canal, which accommodated only one-way traffic.

I had gotten the book *Moses* by Sholem Asch out of the ship's library, and I was so thrilled to read about the Exodus just as we sailed through the Bitter Lakes and that area. The water temperature in the ship's saltwater swimming pool recorded ninety-two degrees—not too refreshing.

Our children slept on cots on deck at night and swam much of the day in short intervals. They had met teenage friends who were en route to their homes in Australia and were having a great time with them.

Aden was a port where the ship refueled. It was our first exposure to an oriental marketplace as we went ashore there for an hour and a half.

On a Sunday afternoon Dr. Wierwille taught on deck about "The More Abundant Life." Quite a few people listened to his teaching; among them was an interested Evangelical and Reformed missionary who we weren't aware was on board. Afterward we had a wonderful visit with her.

By Monday our excitement for landing at the port of Bombay the next morning knew no bounds.

V.P. and I sunning ourselves on the Arcadia

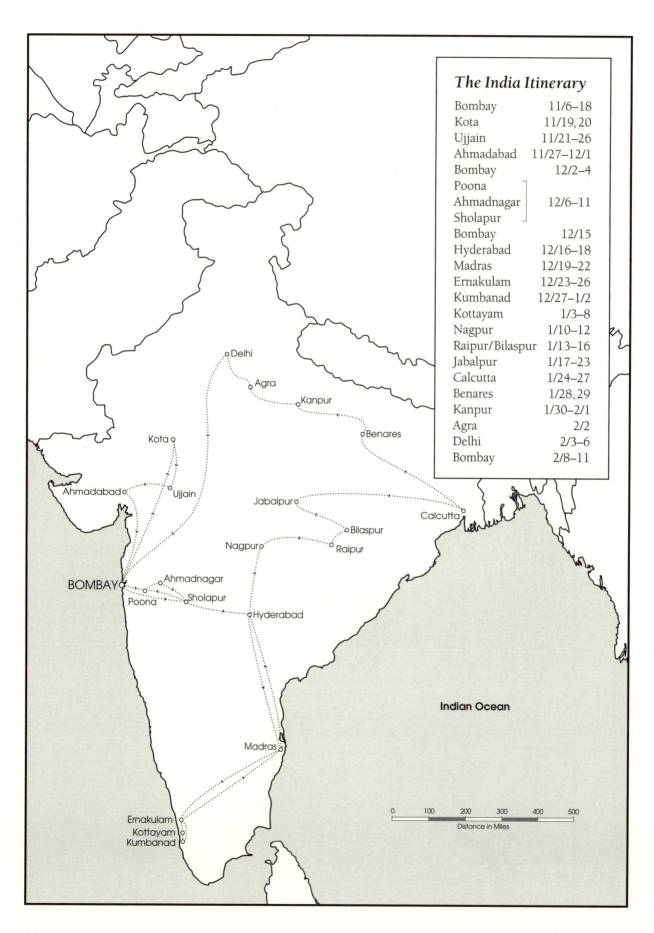

Welcome to India

I remember checking the clock at 3:30 on the morning of November 8, 1955, a Tuesday. None of us five could sleep that night because of the excitement of finally reaching India. When the boat's engines shut down in the Bombay harbor at 5:45, we had our luggage packed and were ready to disembark long before the ship docked. The five of us watched the tugboats tow our ship into port, stirring up mud in the bay.

By the time the host for our India tour, Dr. J. S. Williams, had come to our cabin to greet us, we had already left the ship to go through customs. So we met him in customs. Dr. Williams introduced us there to his wife, Dorothy, and his daughter, Joan, both of whom garlanded each of us, our first of many experiences of this gracious custom.

Mrs. Williams placing a welcome garland on Dr. Wierwille

Bishop Pillai had made arrangements with Dr. Williams to be our host in India. There couldn't have been a better person for this assignment. It was definitely God's providence that we should be making our missionary teaching tour at a time when Dr. Williams could be our host.

During the years prior to India's independence in 1948, many of the Indian revolutionaries were imprisoned for trying to oust the British. During those times, Dr. Williams contributed to the independence movement by

Dr. Williams, at the time we visited India, was the president of the All-India Federation of National Churches, the pastor of the St. Paul's Hindustani Church in Byculla, Bombay, and, to add to our personal enrichment, a devotee of Indian history. We would be able to learn so much from him.

personally carrying communications to and from these patriots. He was trusted to take correspondence and messages to those who would later become the highest political leaders in the Indian government, men such as Prime Minister Jawaharlal Nehru, Vice President Dr. Radha Krishna, and Mohandas Karamchand Gandhi, the father of India. Because of Dr. Williams's contacts and credibility, it was possible for Dr. Wierwille to meet personally, if he so desired, with the current president and any of the cabinet members in India's government and many governors of provinces. Also, being a very knowledgeable scholar of Indian history, Dr. Williams could relate so much to us about the history of the places where we traveled. Learning about India gave us great pleasure and an understanding of the nation and its people.

Part of the welcoming party with our family at the Bombay docks

126

After disembarking from the *Arcadia* and going through customs, we immediately felt the warmth of the Indian welcome. Dr. Williams was leading our way outside the customhouse while a Boy Scout band was playing. We looked around to see who the Scout band was playing for when we were informed that they were part of our welcoming party. The people seemed to form two lines facing each other so that we could walk between, thus to honor and to welcome "a religious leader." Our little Mary said she felt like Princess Margaret, as we all felt very honored. We met briefly and privately with a few people, and then we were taken to the lovely Taj Mahal Hotel nearby to settle in.

Dr. Wierwille teaching at St. Paul's Church in Bombay

Beginning the next morning, November 9, and continuing for the next ten days, Dr. Wierwille taught every morning for one hour at Dr. Williams's St. Paul's Church. These teachings were open to all. People of several religions came to listen because they were eager to hear about the Bible and its teachings. Their experience was somewhat like Acts 17:21, Dr. Wierwille mentioned, "For all the Athenians and strangers which were there spent their time in nothing else, but either to tell, or to hear some new thing."

The next evening after our arrival we were given a very cordial "at home" at Dr. Williams's church, where about 150 people gathered to

The mayor of Bombay presiding at our welcoming banquet

Mr. James John (left) and Dr. J. S. Williams (second from right) were the pillars of our India visit.

officially welcome us. Among the people there were Mr. James John (Dr. Wierwille's honorary secretary for our tour), Dr. E. Nevalkishore (a retired officer of the Pakistani government), Dr. S. Soman of the Haffkine Institute (where cholera serum was first developed), His Honor the Mayor Papula, and other friends who lovingly promoted our tour.

After Dr. Williams introduced our family, everyone there was eagerly waiting to hear from Dr. Wierwille. After giving his greetings, Dr. Wierwille explained the goal of our tour, telling that we were interested in the people of India spiritually, economically, and culturally and wanted to share mutually with them on a people-to-people level.

Dr. Wierwille said that ours was the first mission to be invited to India by the indigenous church of India, rather than by foreign mission churches. Other non-Indian businessmen, politicians, and missionaries had come to India without invitations, "but our tour here is not sponsored by any foreign mission," he explained. The mayor then made a few remarks, extending to us the cordial welcome of the citizens of Bombay.

In the context of the times, this aspect of our visit seemed particularly important. India had just been freed from English colonial rule in 1948. So in 1955 the Indians were still highly sensitive to foreign institutions on their soil. Colonialism in any form, including mission churches, was suspect by many of the nationals.

The morning after the "at home," we were busy with telephone calls from the Indian press wanting to interview Dr. Wierwille. These were arranged. Dr. Wierwille explained again that the object of our tour was to make closer contacts with the people. He said, "What is most needed in the world today is love and fellowship." This was to be a three-month spiritual goodwill mission. Speaking engagements kept him moving. After the usual morning teaching at Dr. Williams's church, he and Dr. Williams went to a Hindu home to informally meet with fifty people. They had questions about Christian beliefs, and then they provided Indian-type entertainment.

Each afternoon for the next several days we went to see points of interest in the Bombay area. We went to the milk colony, where both buffaloes and cows were milked. This was a lovely setting in the green countryside. We visited the Duke of Windsor Museum and saw all kinds of historical arts, industry, and natural things pertaining to various sections of India. We found the local YMCA quite interesting, a nice place with a good moral program.

Although the American consul in Bombay always seemed too busy to greet us, I did go to register at the American Consulate.

During this time in Bombay, Dr. Wierwille was asked to speak to the Society of the Servants of God. This group had been formed the year before (1954) to help people lead a "god-guided" way of life, to introduce a new system of economics based on spiritual values of life, and to spread the

The Free Press Journal

MBAY, THURSDAY, NOVEMB

Closer Contacts With People

BOMBAY, Wednesday: Dr. Victor Paul Wierville, International Representative of the American Committee for the All-India Federation of National Churches, who is on a four-month tour of India, told pressmen here this morning that the object of his tour is to make closer contacts with the people.

Dr. Wierville, whose tour is sponsored by the All-India Federation of National Churches, added that he was here primarily on a people's level to receive what "I feel the people of India have to share with us in the West."

He said people the world over wanted to share the richness of India's inner spiritual light and truth.

Later in the evening speaking, at an "at home" given in his honour by the Indian National Church of St. Pauls'. Dr. Wierville stated that what was most needed in the world today was love and fellowship, adding that he had seen definite evidence of this in his short stay in Bombay.

Shri N. C. Pupala, Mayor of Bombay, presided.

The Bombay Free Press *clipping, November 10, 1955*

teachings and the message of the six prophets: Christ, Zoroaster, Krishna, Buddha, Ram, and Muhammad. At the meeting, Dr. Wierwille spoke on "The More Abundant Life in Jesus Christ." On Saturday, November 12, Dr. Wierwille addressed a group of Hindus at the Ram Krishna Ashram, again teaching about Christ. They were a delightful, receptive group.

That afternoon we went to the Haffkine Institute, where we received the first of two typhoid shots which we would need later in order to visit the Bible Lands. Dr. Soman, who was a part of our welcoming party previously, showed us around the institute. One item of special interest was watching the technicians extract venom from a snake. The cholera serum was perfected here by a Russian, Dr. Haffkine. This work was contemporaneous with that of Louis Pasteur and Robert Koch.

During our stay in India, Dr. Wierwille was sometimes introduced by Dr. Williams as a representative of "PAIRS," the acronym for the Promotion of America-India Relations Society in an industrial, economic, and cultural exchange, and also as the guest of the All-India Federation of National Churches. Dr. Williams was the head of the Federation of National Churches, and therefore at various times during our tour Dr. Wierwille was invited to speak in their local churches.

Dr. Wierwille had been asked to speak about community life in America at a Hindu New Year celebration on November 14 in a mixed community of Hindus, Moslems, and Christians. He complimented them profusely for the wonderful cooperation they showed in their community. While we walked through the housing settlement to see how the Hindus celebrated their Festival of Lights, another name for the celebration, our family was asked by one of the Hindu families to come into their home and pray for the healing of a young lady, a medical student. She had been bedridden for over a year, though no one was able to diagnose her problem. Our family with Dr. Williams and others went in to pray and minister to her, as she was meek to God's Word. Later, when we returned to America, we had a letter stating that this girl was resuming her medical studies, completely recovered.

The trains in India have compartments where there are berths flush with the walls that can be lowered for travelers to lie down and sleep at night. During the day more people are permitted to be in a compartment than can be accommodated for nighttime sleeping. As often as possible we traveled at night in order to conserve on hotel bills.

Our first experience of train travel came soon after arrival. On Friday evening, November 18, we boarded a train in Bombay to go to Kota. The next morning as the train made stops en route, more people came into our compartment. We made friends with them and, of course, always looked for the opportunity to witness and share about God's Word. That noon we arrived at Kota and were met and garlanded by the native minister. In the evening a meeting was held in a church with four local missionaries present. Dr. Wierwille taught about 150 people, a hungry audience for God's Word, on Galatians 5:22 and 23, the fruit of the spirit. The next evening we had an open-air meeting, and the one hundred people present sat on the grass. A few people returned to our hotel with us for special prayer.

An overflow crowd as Dr. Wierwille taught in a private home

A tonga, pony and cart, was one common means of our transportation.

One historic place we saw in Kota that was new and somewhat shocking to us were the suttee memorials. These memorials were erected in a garden setting for the wives of notable Indian leaders. The tradition was that after their husbands had died and while their husbands' bodies were being cremated, the wives would throw themselves on the burning funeral pyres. According to their culture, the wives were showing their devotion to their husbands since there was nothing more for the wives to live for once their husbands were deceased. This practice was banned in 1835.

On November 21, 22, and 23 in the city of Ujjain, Dr. Wierwille addressed a three-day annual convention of the Terapanthi Jains, known as the Anuverat Movement. Dr. Wierwille was the first Christian ever to be invited to address this body. The Jains are a sect of Hindus and their leader was Acharaya Shri Tulsi, who spent much time in private telling us about the whole movement and asking questions of us. Dr. Wierwille remarked, "I can say that the Acharaya is doing much for the building up of the moral and ethical structure of the Indian peoples."

The Acharaya. The Jains kill absolutely nothing, as they believe that the spirit of God is in every living creature. They even cover their noses and mouths with masks to prevent themselves from accidentally breathing in a bug.

Krishna Murti

Approximately four thousand people listened as Dr. Wierwille spoke on "The Abundant Life in Jesus Christ." It was our first time to be hosted by the Jains, whom we found very congenial. Our four days with them was an unusual blessing, both giving and receiving, as we saw the different culture and were exposed to their logic.

Our lodging in Ujjain was a room in a long line of bedrooms, each with an entrance from the outside. Next door to our room was India's foremost Hindu philosopher at that time, Krishna Murti, who was also a speaker at this Jain convention. He said after he had talked with Dr. Wierwille, "This is not of man's doing that we should meet here, for only God could arrange this." Their discussion about Jesus Christ and our witness was clear and bright, and we thanked God for all that was done and the seed of God's Word that we planted.

Our designated host at the Jain convention was a family by the name of Sethi who owned a cotton mill and were quite wealthy. Here we ate vegetarian food served Indian fashion, their usual hot spices omitted. Don played badminton with the sons. We went sight-seeing and saw the famous large temple of Shiva. People were ringing bells as they entered their various shrines to awaken the god or goddess before saying their prayers.

132

The next day Dr. Wierwille was again one of the speakers at this huge Jain convention. He taught from Matthew on the good Samaritan.

During our second evening we were in the town square area for the reception of the Jains, where we witnessed men and women being initiated into full-time religious service for their lifetime as sadhus or sadhuis as Jains, somewhat similar to becoming priests and nuns in the Roman Catholic church. As we were seated there in the town square for this occasion, a bridegroom passed, dressed in a red and silver garment riding on a white horse, followed by his groomsman, also on horseback, and a company following carrying lanterns high and beating drums on the way to the bride's home. What a thrill to see the custom in Matthew 25:1-6 reenacted before our eyes.

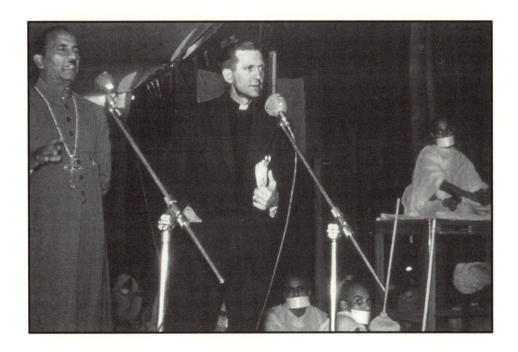

Dr. Wierwille addressing the Jains with Dr. Williams interpreting and the Acharaya listening

On Saturday, November 26, we boarded the train in Ujjain and traveled to Ahmadabad. I remember that when Dr. Wierwille offered me a piece of gum, I said, "It might take up a little gravel in my mouth." The air was dry and dusty as we moved about.

Since we had to change trains in Baroda at 2:00 A.M., all five of us played a game of Rook to stay awake. Baroda had the most beautiful train station I had ever seen, with a lovely park and beautiful flower beds and palm trees.

We arrived in Ahmadabad at 6:00 A.M. to a heartfelt welcome by a reception committee of seven. We retired until noon, after which we got organized. A small group began to gather at 4:00 P.M. at our residence, the Ritz Hotel.

That evening, at 7:45, our first service in Ahmadabad began at the church. With about six hundred people present, Dr. Wierwille taught on "Fear versus Faith." The next morning, from 8:30 to 11:00, Dr. Wierwille taught on Luke 5:1-8, Peter's response to Jesus after catching the draught of fish. Several hundred people sat inside and another fifty stood outside, all seemingly wanting to absorb every word. That evening he preached from John 9 about the man who was blind from birth. There were at least a thousand Christian people present.

We continued meeting on Monday, Tuesday, Wednesday, and Thursday, from November 28 to December 1, with between six hundred and twelve hundred people gathered as Dr. Wierwille taught for the various evening teachings. Hindus and Moslems also came, and all heard the Word of God. I felt sure many would turn to the true God. During the day people would come to our lodging to be taught God's Word and to be prayed for.

Dr. Wierwille teaching in the garden of a hotel

We hardly had an hour of our waking time alone. Among the topics Dr. Wierwille taught were "Paul's Thorn in the Flesh," "Abraham and Believing," and "The Three Men in the Fiery Furnace." One time a Hindu came to see Dr. Wierwille about what to do to become a Christian, and he immediately believed. People just kept coming; we hardly had time to eat.

On the evening of December 1, we left the Ahmadabad meeting at 9:15 and went directly to the train to return to Bombay. At this time

Dr. Williams and Mr. John, our secretary, were able to map out definite plans for our next two weeks. Doors of utterance were swinging open as our visit to India proceeded.

Dr. Williams had been able to arrange an appointment with the chief minister of Bombay state, who offered him five minutes. However, the chief minister talked with Dr. Wierwille thirty-five minutes and then asked him to come back again.

On December 5, a Monday, Dr. Wierwille, accompanied by Dr. Williams, went to Poona to speak on Indian-American relations to the students at the Poona University. The next day in sight-seeing, they visited the Indian Military Academy, the "West Point" of India, which was at that time a new facility.

On the Sunday prior to this, the Indian pastor of the largest church in Poona, trained in America and married to an American woman, publicly and vehemently expressed his opposition to Dr. Wierwille's presence in Poona, exhorting the people not to attend Dr. Wierwille's teachings. Immediately after making this statement in the pulpit, this pastor fell down and died on the spot. On Monday Dr. Wierwille attended his memorial service. There was "no small stir" about this.

Dr. Wierwille returned to Bombay on Monday, December 12, from making his tour engagements in Poona, Ahmadnagar, and Sholapur. The children and I were not invited because it was thought to be too strenuous a trip. At this time we were receiving testimonials of many physical healings which had occurred because of our ministering in Kota and Ahmadabad.

During the next two days Dr. Wierwille wrote individual letters and made arrangements for a rental car and a driver's license which he would need later in Europe. He was advised to get an Indian driver's license, making it simpler to get an international license when we got to Italy. There was always so much to consider, to plan ahead for, and to learn.

Many friends we had made already in India came to visit us at our hotel in Bombay, though we were having no scheduled meetings. We were invited to a Jain's home for tea, where Mary, Karen, and I "visited" with the women, though because of the language barrier we could not communicate verbally. They showed us some beautiful jewelry, as that was the family business. Among other gems, we were shown a large ruby perfectly cut so it looked like jello as it was turned. They said its market value was around $400,000. The family had a canary-colored (bluish green) perfectly round pearl, which was priceless, and other gray-black pearls and white pearls. They gave each of us five a tiger stone while we had a three-course tea with them.

The timing of an event that evening, December 15, was clearly worked out by God; it had not been planned. Our packing had been finished and our luggage moved, as we would be traveling by train later that evening, when at 7:15 the phone rang in our hotel room and Don answered it. The person on the line asked for Dr. Wierwille. We soon realized it was a long-distance call, as Dr. Wierwille heard London answer and then New York. In a little while he heard Ermal Owens's voice. We were all so happy that tears came to our eyes. All of us took turns saying hello to both Ermal and Dorothy, but not much more. It was such a joy just to hear their voices; and how happy we were not to have missed their call. A telephone call from the other side of the globe was a very rare treat in 1955.

We then left to board the train at 9:30 P.M. for Hyderabad. Some Jain friends, Mrs. Williams, and some Boy Scouts and Air Force men were at the Bombay railroad station to see us off.

We were on the train all that night and the following day until 6:30 in the evening. Dr. Wierwille and Dr. Williams quickly went to the service which had been scheduled for 6:00 P.M. Obviously they were late for the meeting, but on this occasion we simply took advantage of the Indian culture, which habitually ran behind schedule.

The next morning all of us went to see the ruins of Fort Golconda, which was built by the Moslems 450 years before. A most interesting

Can you find me in the rickshaw?

thing was how they raised the water for the palaces to a higher level by waterwheels, like fans, since the palaces were built on different rock levels. On the way back to our lodging in Hyderabad, we stopped along the way to watch a young man make pots on a potter's wheel, just as in Biblical times. One spin of the wheel and he could form a whole pot.

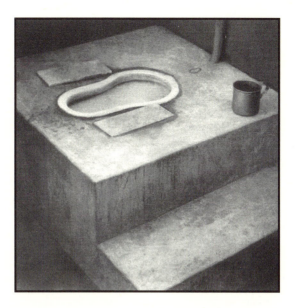

A common Indian privy with toilet cup

The next day being Sunday, December 18, Dr. Wierwille had been invited to preach at the Indian National Church in Hyderabad, a fully self-supporting Pentecostal fellowship. The minister mentioned to Dr. Williams that the church did not approve of wearing lipstick and jewelry. So when Dr. Williams told me of this concern, I immediately blotted off my lipstick and removed my jewelry. When we arrived, there were six people gathered. After handclapping and singing accompanied by a type of organ called a harmonium and drums, the people asked Dr. Wierwille and me to sing. So we quickly decided on "There's a Lovely City." By the time Dr. Wierwille was beginning to teach, one hundred people had gathered and a wonderful mood prevailed throughout the two-hour service. Dr. Wierwille spoke on "The Birth of Jesus."

That afternoon Dr. Wierwille, Dr. Williams, and our host Mr. Samuel, along with others, gathered in a room at the hotel while the girls and I met with Mrs. Samuel and her three daughters. We ministered holy spirit to the eldest daughter in our one-hour appointment, which stretched into four hours. We then excused ourselves from tea and got ready to meet the train to go to Madras.

A dozen men escorted us to the train station. As usual, at every station where the train stopped we were inundated with beggars. Even when the trains began moving, the young boys would edge their way on the outside of the train cars from window to window. One boy even brought his shoeshine kit as an excuse to come into our compartment. If a beggar should find a train compartment door unlocked and the occupants gone, the beggar would throw all the belongings out and then jump off the moving train to retrace the train tracks and collect the stolen goods.

During this train trip to Madras, we saw so many wonderful, interesting sights, such as drawing water from wells for irrigation, banana groves, and many rice fields. We were coming into the wet part of a mostly dry country, so the rich vegetation was impressive.

A form of Indian irrigation

Winnowing grain in the fertile south of India

At the Madras station we were met by Bishop Pillai's son and daughter (our first time to meet), some church members, and several pastors. All of these people went with us to our Ambassador Hotel, where we could visit only briefly with the Bishop's family.

Thomas, one of the twelve apostles, is said to be the first Christian to witness in southern India after Christ's ascension. So the next day we went to see the memorial church dedicated to him which was built over the spot where it is believed Thomas was martyred.

Dr. Wierwille was then taken to the palace of the governor of the Madras province, where he and Dr. Williams spent some time visiting with officials on issues concerning the independent Indian church and the United States-India relations. The allocated five minutes for the appointment with the governor extended into an hour. The governor acknowledged that only the missionaries were actively working among the lepers and harijan, the underprivileged. He expressed his dismay that these harijan, who were so attached to the missionaries, suddenly became better individuals but that they gave up their native allegiances and customs in the process.

That evening there was a reception for us at St. Margaret's Cathedral, where Dr. Wierwille had a short teaching. Immediately afterward we were taken to the orphanage behind the church, where Dr. Wierwille spoke and presented each of the children with little plastic scripture cards and ten rupees for a holiday gift.

As we later met with the pastors of the cathedral, Dr. Wierwille impressed on them that they must remain indigenous, independent of the control of foreign missions. At the time of our visit to India the Indian National Church for the whole of India consisted of thirty fellowships.

The next day was Wednesday, December 21. Since St. Peter's Church in Van Wert had sponsored the building of one of the indigenous churches for the Christians in this nearby area of Madras, we had wanted to see it and take pictures for our Van Wert congregation. Our hosts, however, discouraged our making the trip because it was extremely muddy from recent rains. But Dr. Wierwille insisted on going; so the men left alone. They were able to drive ten miles on paved road. Since the path from there looked fairly dry, they determined to drive as far as possible through the ruts, finally walking the remainder of the trip, about one mile.

News of their coming had reached the congregation, so according to Indian custom, many of the villagers had walked the mile to greet them and show their respect. (The same courtesy was observed on their

The Van Wert Memorial Church

Rev. and Mrs. Peters, the pastor and his wife, in front of the parsonage

Dr. Wierwille and Dr. Williams again visiting with Krishna Murti

departure.) The church building and parsonage were built like all the homes in the area, as mud huts with thatched roofs. After Dr. Wierwille and Don were garlanded, Dr. Wierwille spoke briefly to them words of loving encouragement. His English was translated into Tamil, which was also Bishop Pillai's native language.

Once back in Madras Dr. Wierwille had another delightful visit with the philosopher Krishna Murti, who remained very interested in the Bible as Dr. Wierwille discussed it with him.

The next afternoon, December 22, we left Madras, our destination being further south in Ernakulam. On this train the men and the ladies had separate compartments. An Indian lady with me told of the wonderful broadcasts she enjoyed from America. She did not believe in celebrating Christmas because the Hindus there in southern India celebrated their goddess Isis's birthday at that time. By custom a Hindu family would gather at the father's house where they would lay out all the family wealth for the goddess, who supposedly enters sometime during the night to observe. If she is pleased, the family will enjoy a prosperous new year. The family will stay up all night to watch their money and jewels, shooting firecrackers to stay awake and to keep the thieves away.

The Indian lady told me that she had not seen signs, miracles, and wonders in the Church and concluded that power must have died with the apostles; so the woman was very interested when I told her in a short time about the holy spirit and the "gifts."

For those riding the train at night, no breakfast was served, so we carried bananas and oranges with us for sustenance.

We arrived at our destination, Ernakulam, at noon on Friday, December 23. A local woman minister, Anna Mamman, a Mr. Kurian, and Pastor George were at the depot to welcome us. We had an awful time getting a taxi. They had no meters there, so we had to bargain for a price of five rupees. That was robbery! On top of that, the taxi driver was drunk, and we had to believe God to get us safely to our hotel—at least the driver drove slowly.

Mr. Kurian, thinking that all Americans were loaded with money, did nothing to help us conserve. He was our host for a few days while Dr. Williams returned to Bombay to attend to his other responsibilities. We felt very much left on our own, not a good feeling in a foreign country with a language we could neither speak nor understand. The train had been late, and our host had changed our hotel reservations from the lovely Malabar to the Terminus Hotel because the former was filled. What a letdown. However the rates were more reasonable.

After we had waited a couple of hours to get in a room at the Terminus, we were so hot, disoriented, tired, and dirty that none of us were able to go to the meeting that night, as we were supposed to leave a half hour after arrival. Instead we took a "water taxi" to the Malabar Hotel to get our mail. There were many wonderful holiday cards with notes waiting for us, including pictures of baby John Paul. This definitely picked up our morale. That evening we spent writing letters.

Our meetings in Ernakulam were held on a small island, so we traveled by water bus, stopping at various places to take on and leave off other passengers. Here we drank only coconut water, as purified water was unavailable. Someone would split the coconuts and we would drink directly from them. It was a beautiful four-mile trip with shorelines of the islands all lined with coconut palms and many stretched fishnets drying in the sun.

In the mornings the fishermen would let down their nets as the fish would come near the shore to feed. The kingfishers were immediately on hand to steal some fish if the fishermen were not quick enough in dealing with their catch.

The children and I went after our mail and did a little Christmas shopping at the Malabar Hotel. It was a beautiful place with a lovely lawn and water on two sides. There were many German people spending the holidays there. How wonderful! We received more pictures of John Paul just in time for Christmas, among other cards, notes, and letters. We had our gift opening on December 24 before retiring, as we had purchased some small gifts for each other. The local celebration was noted mainly with firecrackers.

A 1955 holiday photo of the Fischbachs and J.P.

On Sunday, December 25, we arose early and left by boat at 7:45 for the island where Sunday school and church services were held, arriving there at 9:45. Dr. Wierwille spoke to all about the mustard seed and the great power which we have in Jesus Christ. Karen and Mary sang "For God So Loved the World," and Don took pictures after the service. We returned to our hotel for lunch. At 4:30 Dr. Wierwille and Mr. Kurian began the return trip to the island for an evening service. I wrote a letter and went to the Malabar Hotel afterward to sit and relax while the children took a swim. At 8:00 p.m. we returned for dinner, eating the same thing we'd been eating two times a day since arriving—chicken stew. Dr. Wierwille returned at 10:00 p.m., having preached a powerful message on "The Three Men in the Fiery Furnace." This teaching was always such an inspiration to Moslems, Hindus, and Christians alike, wherever Dr. Wierwille taught it.

Although Dr. Wierwille had specifically told Mr. Kurian not to make any engagements for him the next morning, Mr. Kurian invited some people

Tropical Ernakulam

to a 9:00 meeting anyhow. Dr. Wierwille simply could not see them. He had personal letters to write and other public occasions coming up for which he needed time to prepare, so Mr. Kurian had to handle the situation himself.

That evening we had a meeting at a children's home which two American women, missionaries under the Independent Pentecostal Association, were in charge of. The children, about twenty-five of them, sat on mats in the middle of the floor; and there were about two dozen adults present, among them a young Jacobite priest. The adults sat on benches around the walls, many of them having been at the island meetings. Dr. Wierwille talked to the children about the clock and keeping time. The lesson of the clock is its faithfulness. After they had been dismissed, he talked to the adults on the lesson of the hinds' feet and on the three ways the Bible interprets itself. After teaching those basic principles, he read Acts 2:1-4, where the twelve apostles "began to speak with other tongues, as the Spirit gave them utterance." Then Dr. Wierwille asked them, "Who did the speaking?" Ninety percent of them answered that the Holy Spirit spoke, so Dr. Wierwille taught them further.

From the island meetings we sometimes walked in semidarkness back to the boat dock. Some of the adults following behind us said that they would become Christians if we'd give them some rice to eat. They knew that this was one way people had previously "bought" converts.

The mission there was quite young and had only a few converts; so of the three hundred to four hundred people at the meetings, most of them were Roman Catholics and Hindus. We had three days of meetings on the islands of Ernakulam and always had a wonderful response with people asking, "Why are the meetings stopped so soon?"

On Tuesday, December 27, we traveled by bus to the village of Kumbanad for a Pentecostal convention. The countryside was beautiful and the land was fertile, rice being the main crop. There were fewer beggars because the people were more prosperous. Arriving there early, we had time for a good night's sleep on beds made of heavy rope stretched on wooden frames. The next evening, December 30, Dr. Wierwille and Mr. Joseph, a Christian from the Pentecostal camp, went to Kottayam, about twenty-five miles away (three hours of travel). The two men stayed there for three days of meetings with about four hundred people attending. It was physically demanding for Dr. Wierwille to continue through these days of teaching because the heat was oppressive. At the final meeting in Kottayam he spoke on Luke 5:1-8, teaching that we must act to see the promises of God fulfilled.

During the days when Dr. Wierwille was teaching at the meetings in Kottayam, a large tent consisting of two-by-four braces and uprights fifteen feet apart was being erected for the Pentecostal convention in Kumbanad the next week. The roof was constructed of woven palm leaves for protection from the sun and heat. All the buildings were whitewashed and looked nice. By attaching handles to empty coconut shells, the carpenters made dippers for the serving of curry and rice. For the convention I took off my earrings and did not wear any makeup, as the people would have found them a stumbling block from hearing God's Word.

On Tuesday, January 3, at 8:00 A.M. the Pentecostal tent meetings began. Dr. Wierwille opened the meetings and taught on how the Bible interprets itself. Again at 2:00 that afternoon he taught on the original Pentecost of Acts 2. That evening another American minister taught on "We Are Sons of God."

Services the next morning began with a prayer meeting. Actually the praying had begun the night before, with people "tarrying for the holy spirit." All the speakers the days following were teaching the crowds to break the custom of "tarrying." The teachers explained that the custom must be broken, that the holy spirit did not have to be "tarried for" because it was freely available to any believer when he or she wanted to receive.

On one occasion Dr. Wierwille taught on man as a threefold being in the original creation and twofold after the fall. The congregation was thrilled with that new knowledge. Although the largest crowd numbered two thousand, over the course of the meetings, ten thousand to fifteen thousand people cumulatively attended. Meetings were held morning, afternoon, and evening. And the tarrying for holy spirit continued. Every night the tarrying meetings became louder, with intermittent singing for a few minutes followed by the furious beating of drums and people's moaning and screaming very loudly "in the spirit." There were plenty of "spirits" present to cause all this confusion.

On Saturday, January 7, our final day there, Dr. Wierwille preached on the topic, "You Get What You Believe For." After he concluded, fifty-eight people stood to receive salvation according to Romans 10:9 and 10. Our entire family had ministered healing on several occasions.

On Sunday, January 8, we left Kumbanad at 3:30 A.M. by taxi to go to Kottayam and then by bus to Ernakulam, waiting five hours in 100-degree temperature for a train to Madras. We were so tired, but we believed big. (I'm glad we didn't faint in adversity, as we are told of in Proverbs 24:10.) In Madras we changed to the Grand Trunk Express to Nagpur. Once on the train we could lie down and sleep. We arrived on Tuesday, January 10, at 9:15 A.M. There at Nagpur, the capital of Madhya Pradesh state, we were gratefully rejoined by Dr. Williams, who was among twenty-five Indians greeting us so warmly and garlanding us so graciously. At 6:30 that evening we had our first appointed meeting at the Union Church (Presbyterian independent), with about 125 people filling the church. The people were moved by the power of God, although at first they had come wondering about us, since the local missionaries had spoken against us.

Dr. Wierwille and Dr. Williams met with the chief minister of Madhya Pradesh, Patta Bhai Sitaramaya, a seventy-three-year-old. After being invited into the waiting room and being under scrutiny of the CID (Indian security), they were invited to meet the governor in his library. During the time before Indian independence, he had been imprisoned in the Ahmadnagar prison. He was the former historian of India, writing two volumes of the history of the Indian Congress while imprisoned. He asked Dr. Wierwille in what capacity his visit to India was and why he didn't bring his family to visit him. He said that in the Indian tradition, children are expected. He added that the children are the ones who should observe things. This really impressed us.

The governor then related how foreign missions had done commendable work in building hospitals, schools, asylums, orphanages, leper homes, homes for "fallen women," and such; but he said that the black mark against Christian missions was, first, that charity was not given impartially (for example, Christian lepers were charged three rupees for a shot of medicine while non-Christians were charged fifteen rupees); and second, he didn't think this kind of favoritism was conducive to good nationalism.

The governor then told the difference between something "private," something "confidential," and something "secret," according to William Gladstone. Something private you tell your wife; something confidential you tell your friend; and something secret you keep to yourself. The governor then took them through six rooms of his home, showing them many samples of Madhya Pradesh cottage industries. He gave Dr. Williams and Dr. Wierwille an hour and a half of his time.

The next day we had tea with Dr. Nyogi, the chairman of the Missionary Enquiry Committee. The topic of conversation, as usual, centered around the Indian National Church—whether the Christian churches of India should be controlled by Indians or by foreigners, by nationals or by foreign missionaries.

Dr. Nyogi had been educated at a Christian school and was quite knowledgeable about the Bible. Yet he had many questions about its apparent contradictions. He was so excited when Dr. Wierwille was able to answer these for him and was so hungry to know more. He constrained us to spend more time with him.

For our educational pleasure, Dr. Nyogi was able to give us a brief overview of Christianity in India, one of his areas of expertise. We left him to go to a preaching engagement at a packed church. After Dr. Wierwille's teachings from Daniel, he invited people to come forward to be ministered to for healing.

At 10:30 the next morning, January 12, after another 8:00 Bible study, we went to our appointment with a Mr. Bhatty of the National Council of Churches. Soon after we were seated, Dr. Seybold, Mr. Essebarger, and Mr. Singh, who was a worker with the National Council of Churches, along with a lawyer whose name was also Singh, joined our meeting uninvited. They had come in from Raipur. Our appointment had been arranged with Mr. Bhatty, but the others showed up also. We had two issues we wanted to address with Mr. Bhatty: first, a negative statement Mr. Bhatty had made about Bishop Pillai to the World Council of Churches, and second, the reason for his issuing a personal statement maligning our visit here. The meeting resolved nothing.

At 11:30 we were back for another Bible study at the Union Church. At 4:00 we met with a smaller group at a home and went on to tea at another home. At the beginning of the evening service Rev. Sontakey, the minister, read a formal vote of thanks to us from the reception and program committees for our visit, which we appreciated very much. After the evening teaching then, Dr. Wierwille singled out some physically and mentally afflicted people so that our family could minister healing to them. There were about three hundred people in the building all crowding around the pulpit, with about one hundred standing outside trying to listen. Our family ministered to some and then stopped to shake hands. Too many began pressing in to be ministered to, but all of us felt led to call it an evening. It had been a very busy schedule in Nagpur with Bible studies every morning and services every evening from 6:30 to 8:30.

On Friday, January 13, we said good-bye to our new friends in Nagpur and went by train to Raipur. There we stayed in various homes as we spent several days visiting the United Church of Christ Mission, which at that time was our denomination.

The next day, January 14, they showed us the boys' high school and the girls' middle school. The girls demonstrated their cooking and grinding for us. We saw the Gass Memorial, like a YMCA. Rev. Bauer, who was in charge of the leper compound, showed us those homes outside of Raipur. He also showed us through the hospital wards, accompanied by a nurse who explained different phases of the work: the treatment of the disease, tendon transplant, skin grafts, rehabilitation, and exercise. There were no X-ray machines, and their sterilizing "autoclave" was a pressure cooker. The electricity there was only turned on from 6:00 A.M. to 10:00 P.M., so at the other hours they had to use oil lamps.

Sunday, January 15, I woke up at 4:30 in the morning with dysentery, which turned out to be only temporary. Don had just had a siege of it two days before.

On Monday, January 16, we were on our way by Jeep to meet the train at Bilaspur. This was a very dusty trip over dry, dirt paths. We went through a forest, following a trail through the plains—a shortcut. We encountered large families of baboons sitting in the middle of the road, causing us to stop till they decided to move out of the way. Our train then left at 8:30 A.M. and made a quick stop at Raipur. Then on to Gondia, where we had quite a few hours' wait. As we got off the train some people we hadn't met or weren't expecting came to see us. They had heard of our meetings in Nagpur previously and knew of our train connections in Gondia, so they quickly and tentatively arranged a meeting for us. We unpacked and washed a few clothes in the railroad station. It was so hot that our clothes dried almost as quickly as we could bathe and shampoo our hair right in the depot. The church leader in Gondia, Mr. Daniels, had arranged to invite us for lunch and dinner in the evening and also for a service in his church at 6:00 P.M. A few dozen people assembled, and we had a quality meeting. After dinner we boarded a train on the final leg of our journey to Jabalpur.

We arrived in Jabalpur on January 17 at 9:15 A.M. and were met by a lovely delegation. After taking a few pictures, we were driven to our hotel, which was quite a dreary place with hardly any windows. No nice veranda either. The girls did a big washing detail, while Dr. Wierwille and I wrote some letters and cards. Some men came in to discuss various things about our program, which took the better part of the day. Mostly Dr. Williams dealt with them.

At 6:15 that evening we left for the first meeting at St. Luke's Anglican Church. They had decorated the walkway from the street to the church with small banners on either side and a sign, "Welcome," overhead. The welcome program consisted of garlanding and an Indian dance in front of the church entrance by four girls. Next the municipal street sweepers, who were Christians, did a highly disciplined drill routine. Then we proceeded into the church, which was being lighted by lamps that needed to be pumped several times during the service. After proper introductions were made, some ladies sang a welcome song composed by one of them, Mrs. Singh. They gave us copies of the translation in English so that we could better appreciate it. Dr. Williams spoke first on the independent Indian National Church. Then Dr. Wierwille spoke on "Fear versus Faith," and the people's interest was greatly stirred. While we were waiting for our car to take us back to our hotel later, two bulls almost got into a fight on the street in front of us.

All morning Wednesday I spent writing letters and updating my diary. I had gotten behind in the past five days. At 10:30 A.M. Dr. Williams and Dr. Wierwille went to the Bible study at Mr. Benjamin's home with about three dozen people present. At noon they went to the Leonard Theological Seminary, an interdenominational theological school just across the street from our hotel, to have an interview with Mr. Harper, the president, who was an American and a graduate of the Chicago Divinity School.

At 5:00 P.M. we left for a service at the municipal sweepers' place of worship. It was a building closed in on three sides with a roof, all of galvanized sheeting. They did another drill for us, accompanied by singing and drums. Some of the wives and children also came, all very poor. They were wonderful people and excellent entertainers who loved God.

On Thursday, January 19, Dr. Wierwille, Dr. Williams, and I returned to the Leonard Theological Seminary, this time to tour the campus. The new chapel was of special interest, as the Evangelical and Reformed Church had paid for it. There were about one hundred students, of which eighteen were married. The chapel was modernistic in design, having a cross in front of it that was almost as tall as the building and silhouetted by lights at night.

At 10:30 A.M. we returned to the Benjamin home for the usual Bible study, and Dr. Wierwille taught on "The Bible Interprets Itself." After lunch everyone left us, and Dr. Wierwille worked on *The Way Newsletter* and then rested. When 3:30 came around, the men returned, and at 4:00 P.M. there was a news conference. Mary and I had done some laundry and shampooing that morning.

At 6:00 P.M., Dr. Wierwille, Dr. Williams, and I went by rickshaws to the evening service, which was held in the open air. The crowd was restless. In the middle of Dr. Wierwille's sermon, a stone fell just a yard from him; but nothing more came of it. The chairman of our visit to Jabalpur said he had requested police protection during the meeting.

After the service, the local pastor asked us in for coffee and some Indian sweets. While we were waiting for the coffee to get ready, someone came to the pastor's home requesting us to minister to the wife of Wellington Lazarus, who lived next door. So we went next door, followed by an entourage. The house was lighted by a lantern. As we began to minister, we immediately knew by discerning of spirits that devil spirits were in control of this woman's body. Her mother-in-law was bedridden on the bed behind us; and as Dr. Wierwille began naming the name of Jesus, the spirits in the mother-in-law began to object. She became violent, so the two sons tried to control her to keep her on her bed. When Dr. Wierwille commanded the spirits in her to leave, she became quiet. The revelation to us was that so long as the daughter-in-law lived with the mother-in-law, she could not be healed. The young woman had nothing to live for, as the old lady was so domineering; the daughter-in-law had very little vitality left in her.

After we had done all we could under the circumstances, we did not return to the pastor's home to have coffee, but immediately went to our living quarters. Others asked us to come to minister to their sick, but we were very tired. Mr. Singh escorted us home on his bicycle, with Dr. Williams in one rickshaw and Dr. Wierwille and I in another. Very romantic. A convertible too!

Mr. Singh had dinner with us. Our children, who had stayed home, had eaten earlier and were sleeping when we returned. The fire was still burning in the fireplace, so we added a few more pieces of wood and sat there talking until midnight. Dr. Williams was just amazed at the way the devil spirits acted as we ministered to the sick. Mr. Singh told us of his deep desire to be in full-time Christian service.

The next morning Dr. Wierwille's first meeting was at 9:30 with a group of Jains; then the usual 10:30 Bible study. A Mrs. Hamilton and Mrs. Singh came home with the men after the meeting and remained quite a while, so we didn't have lunch until 2:30. Mrs. Hamilton told us of the healing of a hernia which her three-and-a-half-year-old son had received instantly during the meeting. She had come from Nagpur to Jabalpur to tell us and to learn more about God's powerful Word. After lunch we had a quiet time until 4:30, when several men came to talk. At 6:00 we left for the evening meeting, a new place in the open air. Since the car didn't arrive to take us, Dr. Wierwille and I went in one rickshaw and the children in another—a distance of three or four miles. We had a good meeting with a crowd of three hundred. We were observing, however, that when we moved from place to place each night, it was impossible to build the believing and expectation of a mostly new audience at each teaching. We had coffee and sweets with the local pastor, after which we returned home again by rickshaw. Mr. and Mrs. Singh and Mrs. Hamilton had dinner with us, and later we all sat around the glowing fireplace to talk more of the Word. Soon it was midnight.

There was a temple near our lodging which was unique in that each idol in it had had some part of it amputated.

The children studied and I tried to catch up on our correspondence and scrapbook on Saturday morning, January 21. At 2:00 P.M. a Jain friend sent his car and driver to take us sight-seeing. That day we again had an outdoor meeting scheduled for the late afternoon. Quite a few passersby stopped along the way to listen to Dr. Wierwille's teaching.

Don typing a letter to a friend back home

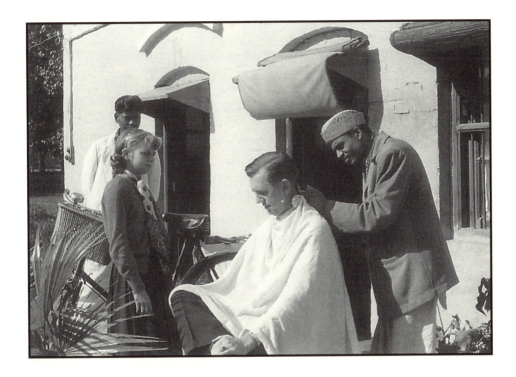

Dr. Wierwille getting a haircut with Mary inspecting

Dr. Wierwille went to bed that night at 8:30, as he was very tired. Mr. and Mrs. Singh, a Mr. Johnson, and several others stayed, and I talked with them of the things of God until 10:30.

Sunday morning began a most exciting day. Our host in Jabalpur, Mr. Benjamin, had asked and received permission to use the St. Luke's Church for the 10:00 A.M. and the 4:00 P.M. services. Until we arrived on January 17, St. Luke's Church had been closed, not in use for services anymore. By 10:00 A.M. the church was filled with people, and Dr. Wierwille preached on "The Power in the Name of Jesus." After the service many pictures were taken. I was quickly and privately informed that Dr. Wierwille, Dr. Williams, and I were to return immediately to the Lazarus home by rickshaw to minister again there. As we arrived, Pascal and Wellington Lazarus and Mr. S. D. Singh were the only others present besides old Mrs. Pascal Lazarus and the daughter-in-law, Mrs. Wellington Lazarus, whom we had gone to see a few evenings before. We entered the home and, for the sake of privacy, closed all the windows and doors. Immediately the devil spirits in the old woman began to act up. She became very restless, and words blurted out of her mouth in Hindi. Dr. Wierwille snapped his fingers for Dr. Williams to quickly interpret. "The 'guru' [master] has come to send us out, but we will not go. We've been here for a long time, and we're going to stay."

151

Dr. Wierwille and I commanded these devil spirits to come out in the name of Jesus Christ. The woman then became violent. Again her two sons could hardly keep her on the bed. Dr. Wierwille spoke to the devil spirits in English, "How many years have you been here?" They answered in Hindi, "Thirty years." Dr. Williams continued to interpret. Dr. Wierwille commanded, "You are going out NOW!" They replied, "We will not go!" And then the devil spirits said, "We are burning!" So Dr. Wierwille commanded the "fiery" spirits to leave in the name of Jesus Christ, and they left. Then the other devil spirits said, "We are going now," which was a lie; they were trying to deceive us. Next I commanded the "animal" spirit to leave. Then came some mumbling and the spirit said, "Janwar" (animal), so Dr. Wierwille commanded the second "animal" spirit to leave. Next, Dr. Wierwille commanded the "spirit of the tombs" to go. Then we commanded the "possessive" spirit, and he also commanded the "infanticidal" spirit to go. (The latter he commanded without saying it out loud because he didn't want the others to know. This woman had attended to her daughter-in-law each time she had given birth. The only living child was delivered when the grandmother wasn't present!) After casting out all these devil spirits one by one, the old woman was finally in her right mind. She was an entirely different person.

Now she was able to relate that her own angry brother was responsible for introducing the devil spirits into the family in an effort to destroy the family. He had hired fifty witch doctors to put these evil spirits on the family. She said that if it had not been for the sun, moon, and stars to protect her twenty-four hours a day, she would have been destroyed long ago. Then I said, "You'd better forget the sun, moon, and stars and look to Jesus only." With this knowledge she was completely delivered.

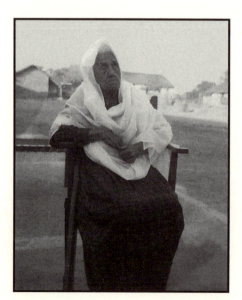

Mrs. Pascal Lazarus

Mrs. Lazarus told us how she saw a cat and a hog, followed by a man, leave her as the spirits appeared to her. She knew that God had been with her, otherwise the evil spirits would have killed her; they had killed her husband long ago. Before becoming oppressed by the Devil, Mrs. Lazarus had worked for thirty years with a mission doing Christian work. She praised and prayed and quoted Psalm 113.

*Praise ye the Lord. Praise, O ye servants of the Lord, praise the
name of the Lord.
Blessed be the name of the Lord from this time forth and for
evermore.
From the rising of the sun unto the going down of the same the
Lord's name is to be praised.
The Lord is high above all nations, and his glory above the
heavens.
Who is like unto the Lord our God, who dwelleth on high,
Who humbleth himself to behold the things that are in heaven,
and in the earth!
He raiseth up the poor out of the dust, and lifteth the needy out of
the dunghill;
That he may set him with princes, even with the princes of his
people.
He maketh the barren woman to keep house, and to be a joyful
mother of children. Praise ye the Lord.*

Dr. Wierwille asked if she believed that the devil spirits would never control her again. She replied fervently, "Yes, definitely." So Dr. Wierwille told her that she must declare to others that she had been delivered so that others would also be delivered. Dr. Wierwille then ministered healing and strength to her body in the name of Jesus Christ. She thanked us profusely, and she thanked God for having brought us to Jabalpur to deliver her.

Next, we turned to Mrs. Wellington Lazarus, the daughter-in-law. She had been ill for a year—just helpless, crippled up with great pain. Dr. Wierwille talked to her about a desire to be well and also about God's ability to heal her. She said that if her husband would take her to the hospital at Poona, where she had already been, she would be healed. Dr. Wierwille responded, "Now you have just seen your mother-in-law healed; do you believe that God can heal you right now in the same way?" She answered, "Yes." She also related how at the Poona hospital she had kept looking at a picture of the "bleeding heart" of Jesus hanging on the wall and how she had been spared this long because of it. Dr. Wierwille proceeded to minister healing, first commanding the pain to leave, which it did. Next he commanded the rheumatic spirit to leave, and then he prayed for her; he asked me to finish the ministering. She continued speaking of the "bleeding heart," so I ministered to her and commanded the spirit of the "bleeding heart" to leave and for her blood to become normal. Then I told her that she must never again look to the bleeding heart, but to Jesus Christ only. We blessed the house and proceeded back to the hotel by rickshaw at 2:00 P.M. for lunch.

At 4:00 P.M. we returned to the church, where Dr. Wierwille taught on "The Blessings of God" from Ephesians 5. Later when we were back home in Van Wert we received word by letter that this church building in Jabalpur had been fumigated after our meetings to rid it of any vestiges of our presence.

After the service we were invited to tea at one home. Then, we blessed another home and finally returned to our hotel at 7:00 P.M. Many came to visit us until we finally excused ourselves to have dinner at 8:00 P.M. After dinner we joined them again and talked about God's Word until midnight.

On Monday, January 23, Dr. Williams and Dr. Wierwille went to keep a speaking engagement at a Jain meeting. With about five hundred men, women, and children gathered, they reported a wonderfully receptive gathering. Dr. Wierwille spoke on Jesus' law of discipline. Dr. Williams also spoke in Hindi to the crowd for fifteen minutes. I remained home to do some urgent typing, mailing, and packing. We had lunch at 12:00. At 12:45 our Jain friend took our luggage to the train station and returned to take us to meet some local Jain sadhus who had wanted to see us, especially our children. The leader stated that Dr. Wierwille spoke from the depth of his heart.

We left for the railway station early to meet the afternoon train to Calcutta. This was our first dark, overcast day in India. On our way to the depot, we passed a bagpipe-and-drum corps in beautiful red-and-white uniforms, wearing turbans. We learned they were coming to escort us to the train. By the time we reached the train, each of us had received twenty-five lovely garlands and various small tokens of affection. They sure did say it with flowers!

As we were putting our luggage into our compartment on the train, a man came running, calling for the man of God to heal his arm.
Dr. Wierwille stepped out of the compartment and asked him, "Do you believe God can heal your arm?" He answered, "I believe if you pray for me I will be healed, but I don't believe in your Jesus. I'm a Hindu."
Dr. Wierwille repeated the question and received the same answer. Then Dr. Wierwille prayed in the name of Jesus Christ, laying his hands on the man. He commanded him to lift his arm. When the man realized he could raise his arm a little, he lifted it up over his head. He was ecstatic and thanked Dr. Wierwille profusely. Dr. Wierwille told him he was healed in the name of Jesus Christ.

One of the Jain leaders asked Dr. Wierwille to have a special blessing for all of the Jains also, which he did. Dr. Wierwille quickly stepped back into our compartment as our train lurched forward. We stood in the doorway, waving as they waved their hankies until we disappeared from each other's sight.

When the train came to its first stop, a man from the next compartment came to our door, saying that his master would like to meet the man of God. So we extended an invitation to the master to come to our compartment. When we had introduced ourselves, he said, "We would like to pay our respects. It is not often we get to travel with such a man of God who blesses *all* the people." He told us he was a member of the central government on his way home to Allahabad. He gave Dr. Wierwille the key to that city.

As we stopped in Allahabad, where two "sacred" rivers flowed together, the Ganges and the Yamuna, many people got off the train because that was the destination of their pilgrimage. Mary offered a beggar who came to our door a piece of candy, but he refused it, wanting only money. We continued on the train to Calcutta.

It became very cold about three o'clock in the morning so we doubled up in our narrow berths to keep warm. At the next stop around ten o'clock in the morning we ate breakfast, and we arrived at the Howrah Station, Calcutta, by noon, Tuesday, January 24. A crowd of Jains met us. Also many Pentecostals introduced themselves who asked if we might arrange a meeting with them, which Dr. Wierwille consented to. They had heard by the grapevine from Nagpur about our coming to Calcutta. We then had a meeting in the center of town at a wonderful Pentecostal revival center. This was followed by a second meeting at another YMCA. They asked for more, but our schedule already was full of other speaking engagements.

In Calcutta we stayed in the home of Jains, the Sarana family. Our children went with the men, Dr. Wierwille and Dr. Williams, to visit the National Library, formerly the

Our Calcutta host, Mr. Sarana, with Dr. Wierwille

home of the English viceroy of India before independence in 1948. After visiting the Victoria Memorial, a noteworthy museum which the occupying English had built, they then went to visit the governor of Bengal, an eighty-year-old Baptist who was very favorably disposed toward both the National Council of Churches and the All-India Federation of National Churches. Next, after seeing a Jain temple, they went to the Pentecostal church where Dr. Wierwille had accepted their recent invitation to teach. It seated three hundred, but only one hundred were present. Dr. Wierwille spoke for an hour and a half, inspiring everyone—including Dr. Williams and our children, who were still bubbling when they arrived home.

On Wednesday we visited places of interest, with our chief concerns being to obtain tickets for the remainder of our trip in India and to have a camera and shoes repaired. Later Dr. Wierwille spoke on the disciplined life at a public meeting with the Jain group.

The next morning, Thursday, January 26, Dr. Wierwille spoke at a Jain school celebration on the Indian Republic Day, their Independence Day. They played the drums as we were shown to our seats. After a drill by the physical education class, there was a flag-raising ceremony. Dr. Wierwille and Dr. Williams both gave short talks to the students of the school.

We stopped to see a great banyan tree which covered a couple of acres, on our way to lunch with the Sethis.

In the afternoon our host, Mr. Sarana, an attorney, showed us around his large and lavish house: on the ground floor were offices, the second floor was temporarily unoccupied, the third floor was for his family, the fourth floor was his

A Republic Day program at a Jain school

Mary and I marveling at an immense banyan tree

brother's floor, and the fifth floor his cousin's. After our tour, our host invited us to dinner. We left the Western-style living room, where we had been entertained by a musician playing a harmonium, to go to an area where individual trays had been arranged in a U-shaped configuration on the floor. We sat against the walls on lovely carpet runners with pillows behind our backs. The men were seated on the wall opposite from Karen, Mary, and me. Dr. Wierwille, Dr. Williams, and Don, as guests of honor, were seated on a tapestry-covered mattress at the head of the room. Our host ate with us. A few times previously when we ate in Hindu homes, the host served us our food but did not sit down and eat with us.

The inner court of the Sarana home

During our sight-seeing tour the next day we saw a jute mill where burlap was being made. Next we were taken to see the Kali temple, where they had just sacrificed four goats to their idol. The sadhus were reading their Vedas and selling items to be offered to the idol. The idol was adorned with a girdle of human skulls. Outside this Jain temple was a dead tree where infertile women were tying ribbons on the branches and praying that they might have a child.

The fertility tree

An elephant ride at the Calcutta zoo

A cremation grounds on the Ganges River in Benares

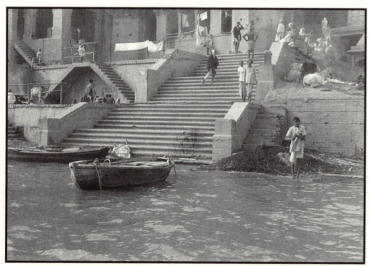

In the afternoon we went to the Calcutta zoo, and all of us took an elephant ride. We were riding high, the entire family at once. We went to get our income-tax exemption, which only took fifteen minutes since our host there had a friend in the office who expedited the matter. From there we went to a market and bought a few things, picked up photos we just had developed, and returned home to do our packing.

We bade good-bye to the Sarana ladies as we left to meet the train. We were again beautifully garlanded. A Jain friend came to talk to Dr. Wierwille concerning the Christian teaching about "soul." At 7:30 our train left as we traveled northwest to Benares.

On Saturday, January 28, we arrived at Benares at noon. As we traveled north, we could feel the temperature drop. Rev. Das, a former Hindu converted to Christ, had an ashram there where he taught the Bible. He was to be our host.

When we were being taken to our Benares hotel, to my amazement our taxi stopped in the middle of the congested marketplace. "Oh no, not here," I thought. But yes, this was the location of our hotel. We went up a stairway and found a fairly pleasant environment, though the fumes floating up from the street below were putrid.

After moving into our quarters, we walked to the Ganges for a riverboat ride. There was a Hindu crematorium on the banks in the open air with a corpse draped in red (meaning a woman) on a stretcher drying in the sun. The dead person on the wooden pallet had already been dipped in the river for the ceremonial washing away of sins. After drying, the covered body would be placed on a pyre and cremated. There were three pyres already burning. As we rowed down the river, we passed a dead, bloated body floating along. There would be crocodiles around the bend of the river to eat it as soon as it floated far enough downstream.

Rev. Das invited only the men for tea that afternoon, since he had a very small home. He apologized; but since he couldn't entertain all of us, we women went shopping in the markets. At 5:00 P.M. we went to a meeting at which Dr. Wierwille taught a group of Christians who worshiped with Rev. Das. Dr. Wierwille extended an invitation to him to teach to our Way people in the United States, but at seventy, Rev. Das didn't feel he could make the trip. Our family left after the teaching while Rev. Das and Dr. Williams ministered privately to the people. We visited with several men in our hotel room after dinner, where all of us wrapped up in blankets to keep warm. We spent the next day visiting with Rev. Das and a few other Christians, and writing letters and cards.

Rev. Das with us on a boat ride

On Monday, the thirtieth, at 3:45 A.M., a hotel servant woke us for a 5:00 breakfast. We thought we didn't need an hour and fifteen minutes to get ready to leave, but we couldn't get to sleep again as it was so noisy outside our room. The hotel management had brought us an electric heater at bedtime the night before, so we had it to keep us warm while dressing early in the morning. A taxi came to take us to the Benares train depot, where we arrived at 6:05. We were quite cold, as the taxi had half of its windows missing. The train came in at 6:50 and, thankfully, we were able to find a compartment without anyone in it. All of us took naps to compensate for getting up so early.

At the Ansons' school

A few people met us at the train at Kanpur and escorted us to our hotel. We came to Kanpur specifically to meet with Rev. and Mrs. Anson and to see their Christian school.

While we were having dinner in the evening, a delegation of sixteen from their school came to greet and meet us. Later we sat around the fireplace and served coffee to our guests. They were such sincere and interested people. At this informal gathering, Dr. Williams talked about the Indian National Church, and Dr. Wierwille explained our mission in coming to India and about the power we all have in us as sons of God. Most of them left at 11:30 in the cold night. Two of the men, Dr. Williams's brother-in-law and a Moslem friend, stayed to talk about hunting, to Dr. Wierwille's delight.

The next morning we visited the two schools which Mrs. Anson oversaw, and then went to a reception at the home of Mr. Tal, executive secretary of the YMCA, where a tent was pitched in his backyard for our meetings. Many of the Kanpur church leaders were present. After tea, the dining tables were removed and the chairs were rearranged for the meeting. Dr. Wierwille spoke on "Our Christian Freedom and Power" to about 150 people. Afterward a few people came to talk with us around the fireplace in our hotel, discussing the teaching Dr. Wierwille had given that afternoon.

The following day, Wednesday, February 1, we received correspondence from the Mackinon Mackenzie travel agents that our ship from Haifa to Naples would be leaving on March 6 instead of March 13.

Dates were occasionally adjusted anyway as we got a specific feel of how to pace our traveling. This change would work out for us except for mail, as per dates given in *The Way Newsletter*.

We went to an "at home" at Attorney Bose's residence. Many prominent men came for the occasion. Dr. Williams made an introductory statement, and then Dr. Wierwille again explained what prompted us to come to India. All of this was well received by both the non-Christian and Christian guests. The leader of the Congress party of Kanpur spoke in response. We then left for the tent meeting. The atmosphere was wonderful, though a bit formal. Dr. Wierwille taught on "The Three Men in the Fiery Furnace," after which he prayed for several individuals in the meeting. After we returned to our hotel, a couple of people came over, hypocrites, who were trying to cause trouble. Dr. Wierwille asked them to leave. They were the same people who had been troublesome to Rev. Anson before. We learned that the Ansons had been concerned that these people would disrupt our meeting earlier that day.

The next morning we traveled by train to Agra. At noon on Thursday, February 2, we arrived there, getting a glimpse of the beautiful Taj Mahal

The Taj Mahal

Karen and Mary pointing out a delicate carving on the Taj Mahal

Dr. Wierwille speaking to a water carrier transporting water in an animal skin

as we drove past it on the way to our hotel. As soon as possible we had lunch, and before 2:00 we were on our way to see the sights.

We went through the Agra Fort, a fort built in the 1500s and still looking very sturdy. Only one-third of it was open to visitors, while the rest was still being used by the Indian military. Built on the Yamuna River, the fort gave us a perfect view of the Taj Mahal. The next day we went back to the fort to mail many cards with the fort's postmark.

We had definitely "seen it all" once we had seen the Taj Mahal! It was impressive beyond our wildest expectations. The building is a mausoleum which a Mogul king built for his beloved wife, Mumtaz Mahal. The white marble structure was inlaid with semiprecious colored stones forming designs of different flowers and their foliage.

That evening we were invited to tea at Dr. Nazareth's home. We had met him on the ship coming to India as he was returning to his home after studying medicine in the United States. We had witnessed to him on the *Arcadia,* and he wanted us to visit and bless his home while in Agra.

On Saturday we were on the morning train headed for Delhi. Stopping at every crossroad, we finally arrived in Delhi, a distance of eighty miles, six hours later.

The children and I spent the evening by the fireplace in our hotel room, writing letters and studying. Dr. Wierwille and Dr. Williams went to the market by rickshaw to buy a suitcase. Since we were all very tired, we went to bed early, having talked over our sight-seeing schedule for the next day.

Red Fort

Actually, Dr. Wierwille didn't go to bed early; he worked until 3:30 that night, so we got a late start for sight-seeing in the morning. First we went to the Red Fort. In the part of the structure called the House of Lords was inscribed in Arabic, "If there is a heaven on earth, this is it, this is it, this is it." It was indeed beautiful.

We went from there to the mausoleum of Mahatma Gandhi at Rajghat,

where Dr. Wierwille placed a wreath of flowers. At this location Gandhi was cremated. In this tourist spot, everyone removed one's shoes out of respect. (Because I was in my stocking feet, several Indian women began looking at my hosiery, so I stopped to give them a good look. They were very impressed!)

The next morning we did more sight-seeing again. We passed the India Gate, built in 1921 by the Duke of Connaught in memory of the brave Indian soldiers who were killed in the First World War.

The Gandhi Memorial

163

The Kutub Minar

The Asoka Pillar

From here we got an overview of all the national government buildings. We went on our way to see the Kutub Minar, a tower 238 feet high and with 379 stairs to the top, dating from the thirteenth century and regarded as one of the most perfect towers of the world. The children climbed to the top; Dr. Wierwille and I didn't even try. Nearby was the iron Asoka Pillar built by Maharaja Asoka in 250 B.C. and inscribed with the teachings of Buddha. This pillar is said to be made of solid, pure iron. It is twenty-two feet high and sixteen inches in diameter, weighs eighteen tons, and never rusts—which is unexplained! Next we went to the Jantar Mantar Observatory built by Maharaja Singh II of Ambeo in 1725, designed to observe the sun's course as well as the lunar and stellar altitudes with masonry instruments. These

The Jantar Mantar Observatory

are all unique, one of a kind. What a memorable day! Bishop Pillai many times remarked that Americans are interested in how new things are, while Indians are interested in how old things are. That day we saw some impressively old achievements.

On Tuesday, February 7, the three children and I boarded a train, leaving Delhi for Bombay. Dr. Williams and Dr. Wierwille saw us off while they stayed in New Delhi, keeping appointments with the minister of education, the minister of defense, and the vice president of India. We had bought a large trunk in Delhi and were wondering if we would be permitted to take all our luggage plus this trunk on the train. But everything came along without question, in our four-berth compartment.

The minister of education

The minister of defense

The vice president of India

We arrived in Bombay Central Station at 9:00 on Wednesday morning, February 8. Dr. Wierwille, Dr. and Mrs. Williams, and others were there to meet us, Dr. Wierwille and Dr. Williams having flown back to Bombay from Delhi. We went to the Taj Mahal Hotel with all our luggage and found room #540 very lovely, with a veranda overlooking the bay. If only we had had the time to enjoy it! We were afraid to ask the price of the room because the hotel was filled and we had no choice but to take whatever was available. So many tourists! However, when we later received our bill, it was the same charge as when we had previously stayed at that hotel.

Before noon I went to our travel agent to exchange our passage order for the ship tickets. I found that I also needed a tax exemption. Immediately, I took a taxi to the government tax office and within fifteen minutes I had our exemption in hand. I returned for the tickets again with success this time. When I got back to the hotel around 2:00, Dr. Wierwille had gone to get a haircut. One could sense that our incomparable visit in wonderful India was coming to a rapid conclusion.

At 4:00, Dr. Williams and Dr. Wierwille left to keep an appointment with the governor of Bombay state. After they returned to the hotel, we discussed with Dr. Williams and Mr. John our meetings for the next two days, including our regular morning meetings at Dr. Williams's church.

The next morning, Friday, February 10, Dr. Wierwille spoke on I John at the regular Bible study. The girls and I finished our major packing, and Don went to the shipping agent to get our boarding regulations. He was told that each passenger was allowed one guest pass. Immediately after lunch Don and I went back to the travel agency to get the passes and to see about insurance for forwarding packages unaccompanied to Southampton, England. This worked out well.

That evening, February 10, a grand farewell dinner was held at a Hindu park with about fifty people invited. At this, leading men of various communities expressed their appreciation to us for our coming to India, and to all the people of America who supported us and made our mission possible. They expressed their gratitude that we had extended to them the love of Christ and the positive gospel of the Word of God with its deliverance.

Dr. Wierwille and I and each of our children spoke at this lovely

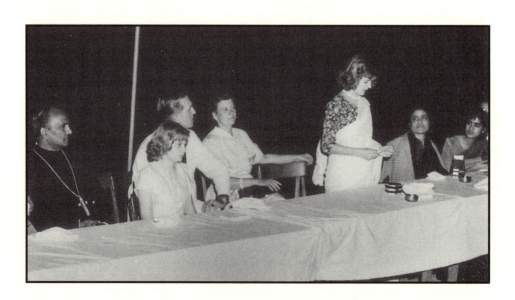

Our farewell dinner

occasion, expressing our joy and appreciation of their kindnesses to us and for the many experiences they had made available to us. Karen wore a sari and other Indian accessories for the occasion, which really pleased the people.

On Saturday, February 11, 1956, our departure day had arrived. I arose early to write a few letters, sitting out on our little balcony overhanging the street below and overlooking the bay where sailboats floated idly by.

We were invited to Dr. Soman's home for morning tea at 8:30, and he gave us the second cholera shots required for our entrance into the Bible Lands. All day long visitors called on us from such distances as Ahmadabad, Jabalpur, and Poona. Some of them brought gifts for us to take to friends in the United States, which meant we had to do a little repacking. We had invited Dr. and Mrs. Williams for lunch. We invited two other people who were visiting us also to eat with us. After all, they had treated us very kindly in their home previously and we wanted to be hospitable, so I constrained them. Groups came in all afternoon to bid farewell. Because of these visitors, we delayed our departure as long as we could and were garlanded profusely by all; the girls and I also received bouquets.

At 5:30 in the afternoon we boarded the ship *Chusan*. We found a secluded place to have prayer with the five people who had passes to come on board to say good-bye. At 9:00 P.M. we heard the ship's motors begin whirring, which meant that our guests with passes had to disembark. "Parting is such sweet sorrow," and many tears were shed as we waved and waved when the ship pulled away from the dock. The three months we spent in India left a wonderful, indelible imprint on all five of us.

Dr. Wierwille and I about to say good-bye to Dr. and Mrs. Williams

The following were governmental officials with whom Dr. Wierwille had appointments during our tour:

S. K. Patil
president of the Congress Party
of Maharashtra state

B. S. Hiray
minister of revenue and agriculture
of the central government

Mr. DeSai
chief minister of Maharashtra state

Sri Prakash
governor of Madras of Tamil Nadu state

_____
governor of Calcutta of Orissa state

Patta Bhai Sitaramaya
chief minister of Madhya Pradesh

Dr. Nyogi
chairman of the Missionary Enquiry Committee

Dr. S. Radha Krishna
vice president of India.
Discussed the Indian National Church movement.

Dr. K. N. Katju
minister of defense of the central government.
Discussed the Indian National Church movement.

Dr. N. A. Azad
minister of education of the central government.
Discussed the Indian National Church movement.

J. S. Patel
minister of industry of the central government

Krishna Murti
foremost philosopher of India.
Professor at Madras University.

_____
governor of Bombay state

_____
governor of Bengal (a Christian)

N. C. Papula
mayor of Bombay

The following are most of the topics Dr. Wierwille taught on as we traveled in India:

The Abundant Life in Jesus Christ
The Good Samaritan
The Birth of Jesus
The Marching Orders of Jesus Christ
The Original Pentecost of Acts 2
Galatians 5—Fruit of the Spirit
Fear versus Faith
Paul's Thorn in the Flesh
Abraham and Believing
The Three Men in the Fiery Furnace
The Mustard Seed—Great Power in Jesus Christ
Hinds' Feet
How the Bible Interprets Itself
Who Did the Speaking?
How Wide Is Your Boat?
We Must Act to See the Promises Fulfilled
The Power in the Name of Jesus
The Blessings of God
The Great Commission
Creation and the Threefold Being
You Get What You Believe For
Jesus' Law of Discipline
Community Life in America

During our three-month tour in India, we visited twenty-two major cities with about forty-six speaking engagements: eight with the Jains, three concerning "PAIRS," two with Hindus, and thirty-three with Christian groups.

Besides our public occasions, many people came to our lodging places to learn more about God's Word. We were able to lead many into receiving holy spirit into manifestation.

In the newsletters each month to our believers in America, Dr. Wierwille summarized the activities in which he was involved.

December 1955

Newsletter

I wish that we all might have the joy of being with you in America at this season, but God has seen fit for us to be ministering in this part of the world at this time. We praise His name, as we know you too are doing, for the many doors He has opened to us and the light on the Word which has been shed abroad in our hearts by the Holy Spirit.

Our mission in India is a wonderful answer to your prayers. You could not possibly even imagine what good has been accomplished, how many souls won for Jesus Christ nor how many were filled with the Holy Spirit. What an opportunity to see the peoples of India on the level of the people in their towns and villages. They are a great peoples with millions perhaps poor in things of this world as we would think of it, but rich in their spiritual heritage and their great spiritual hunger. They gave us a wonderful reception every place we went including the reception where there were many of India's great leaders and scholars. I have been greatly humbled in their presence, for Hindus, Moslems, Jains and many other non-Christians were always in attendance and showed us the greatest love and courtesy, some things Christians many times don't even show among themselves and especially so among the denominations. I thank God for the privilege of representing Him in this missionary tour and we also thank Him for your wholehearted support of this trip.

I will share with you just one of the opportunities we have had so that you may rejoice with us, for others are in store. At Ujjain I was invited to be one of the speakers at the yearly convention of the Jains, [the first foreigner (Christian) permitted to address this audience], an all-Hindu group numbering some three thousand at the convention. I was asked by them, the Hindus themselves, something no denominational missionary would perhaps find offered to them, to speak on The Abundant Life in Jesus Christ. Souls were saved, healed and delivered under the power of our Lord and Savior.

God bless you this Holy Season and always, and we know that you won't forget us in your prayers and financially. You will surely stand behind us with your special gifts for the need to do this work here is great and I do need your help. Don't send your gifts directly to me, but to our Van Wert office and then they will be sent to me. God bless you and may you have A Merry Christmas and a Happy New Year.

Sincerely in His Service,
V. P. Wierwille

Newsletter

January 1956

Every place we have gone to share the Word of God we have found great spiritual hunger for the true light on the Bible, not that we have the only true light and that all we have is true, but to the extent that we are built on the Word of God we could not be wrong. But, the people have been so "denominationalized" that they have much "Churchianity" and their hearts hunger for loving, true Biblical Christianity. I have been teaching to hundreds and preaching to thousands. In addition to all this we have had the privilege of meeting with many of the Governors of the different states of India, as well as the Chief Ministers and others of prominence as officials both in the Nation, State and Cities. We have been in the outlying Villages where the truest life of the Indian people can be seen and understood.

Dr. J. S. Williams, who is a wonderful man of God here in India, is my constant companion and has done so much for THE WAY ministry in India that I shall never be able to thank him enough.

At Ahmadabad 7 different Christian groups banded together, hired a special hall and we filled it night after night, even though there was organized resistance from certain other "Christian" groups. Thousands were blessed and many were led to the Lord and also delivered of many diseases including epilepsy, T.B., etc. Letters are almost daily coming to us here yet in India telling of the blessings.

Only after we write a full report will we possibly have done even a half way description of all that was accomplished in His Precious Name. At Kumbanad, where they held an annual pentecostal convention, as I mentioned before, 5,000–7,000 gathered together for eight nights to be saved, filled with the power from on high and to find Jesus Christ as their complete deliverer. Previously, they had been taught that they must tarry for the holy spirit and still, much tarrying and begging went on in the morning hours beginning about 4:00 A.M. every morning.

Mr. James John is Hon. Sec. of our tour and has spent so many hours of his time, all without pay, and has done such a wonderful work carrying out all the arrangements.

Sincerely in His Service,
V. P. Wierwille

Newsletter

February 1956

Your prayers are being answered. All over India our mission is making its spiritual inroads with the love of God which we have for all peoples.

By the time the newsletter reaches you, we will be on our way to Egypt and Palestine.

At the close of just a few days of meetings in Nagpur, the following letter was read by the leader [Rev. R. Sontakey, chairman of the reception committee in Nagpur] and then given to us. I thought that if you could read the letter yourself it would give you an idea and indicate to you the tremendous spiritual success of our mission. The following is the letter:

February 1956 Newsletter

January 12, 1956

I thank God for this joyful occasion which He has very graciously given us of witnessing and spiritual blessings which our Lord God Almighty during the past three days in an United Assembly consisting of members from all local denominations, after a long period of 20 years. Formerly, as some of us remember that members of all denominations in Nagpur used to have combined social and spiritual gatherings very often and specially at Christmas and Easter Occasions but such meetings could not take place during the last 20 years.

Thank God that He has again made a beginning of His gathering in these last days by sending His servant Dr. Wierwille and family in our midst who has presented us the pure word of God without mixing up denominational doctrines; with signs and wonders, and we pray that God may send more of His servants in the near future for the extension of His Kingdom at Nagpur in particular and India in general.

I as Chairman of the reception Committee of Dr. Wierwille party and the free United Christians of Nagpur gathered here this evening the 12th day of January, 1956, thank Dr. Williams, president of the Federation of Independent Churches, for bringing about the visit of this great Scholar and expositor of the Bible to our city. The Nagpurians have been very fortunate that they could learn so much from him in such limited time. Dr. Wierwille has not only been able to disclose to us the hidden truth in scriptures but has strengthened and built up many who were weak in their faith. This is the first time in the history of this City that Nagpur has seen last evening and also this evening when the sick which were prayed for received healing. It would not be out of place to mention the great sacrifice that Dr. Wierwille has made so that he could visit our beloved land. He has come to this land at his own expense and without any strings attached to any Mission. We are also grateful to his beloved wife Mrs. Wierwille. She too is a good scholar of the Bible and a spirit filled lady and has been of much help to us during our private Bible studies. It is her sacrifices and her love for the people of India that made her to leave behind her two months old Baby in U.S.A. and accompany her husband in his great evangelical service.

The children are also a real blessing to their parents and are full of love for the Indian people.

In the end I sing with the great poet 'God be with you till we meet again' depending on God to make our next meeting possible, Amen.

Rev. R. Sontakey, Chairman,
Reception Committee, Nagpur

Your prayers, love and support has meant so much to us in this ministry, and we pray God that you will continue with us as we complete this teaching tour. God bless you as you continue trusting Him and stepping forth on His wonderful promises.

Sincerely in His Service,
V. P. Wierwille

The following is an excerpt from a letter Dr. Williams wrote to a friend of his in England describing our visit to India.

My dear brother in Christ,

We found in Dr. Wierwille a great expositor of the Bible we have so far come across. His special ministry is the teaching of the Word of God, and he expounds the Will of God only through the Word of God. They all possess a wonderful believing Faith in Jesus Christ and signs, wonders and miracles are spontaneously wrought through them all. I had the most wonderful joy and special privilege of being in the closest contact with them in India and the great honour and pleasure of being their Chief Host.

. . . Throughout their stay in India they never complained of the dirt, dust and filth of India. Their only desire was to be helpful to the people of India and to teach them the Word of God. They bore all sorts of hardships in India, and their spiritual joy was so evident in their daily life. They had come to India for the first time and in spite of bad food they all gained in weight. They are a family of beautiful members. I am sure that their ministry among your people will be a source of abundant blessings to them. The Wierwilles I must say are the loveliest Christian people I have ever met in life; and you and your people, I am positive, will be richly blessed by their Christian Ministry.

The Wierwilles have been a source of blessings to me personally, and thank God I have now a new vision of service to my Saviour and my people.

J. S. Williams   March 1, 1956

The following is another excerpt written to us as we left India.

Dear Dr. Wierwille & Mrs. Wierwille,

. . . I think I have started a new life. It was very interesting to learn from you. . . . We need a person like you to teach us and teach us the simplicity of the Word. . . .

Mrs. Helen Hamilton   February 3, 1956

Dr. Wierwille had designated Dr. Williams as the general overseer of The Way of India, with its headquarters in Bombay, as had been voted at the convention held on February 9 and 10. Branches for each state of India were to be established as soon as possible, all under and by the independent national Christians without a foreign system of control. Mr. James John was to be secretary for The Way of India.

Excerpts from the March 1956 *Way Newsletter*

Greetings to Our Many Friends and Helpers:

Our three months spiritual goodwill mission to India is a memory, but what a joy. We shall never forget the wonderful people we met or the doors that were opened to us, nor shall we or thousands of people in India forget the victories that were wrought in the precious Name of our Lord and Savior Jesus Christ.

The three months passed rapidly, but it did allow us ample time to visit 13 states of India, 20 major cities and many other towns and villages. We lived and ate with many of the different communities that make up the life and culture of India. We were with Christians, Hindus, Moslems, Sikhs, Parsees, and Jains. We visited and studied Foreign Missions in India as well as the Indian National Christian work.

In Delhi, the seat of the Central Government, we were graciously received and invited for special interviews on February 7th by the Vice-President of India, Dr. S. Radha Krishna with whom we had tea in his residence.

Before setting sail from Bombay, India on February 11 we were again entertained in the most royal Indian way. We returned to Bombay from Delhi on February 8th to begin our packing, which after all is a task when traveling with five people, and when I could not help because of engagements.

The Governor of Bombay had invited us for an interview on the 8th, and because of the success of our goodwill mission and the information we had gathered on the Foreign Mission system, the Governor was further interested and concerned and invited us for a special tea on the 10th.

In Delhi, the Defense Minister, Dr. K. N. Katju and Naulana Abulkalam Azad, Minister of Education, both accorded us much time and discussed with us the Indian National Church situation and the continued goodwill between the people of India and America.

On February 9 and 10 we also held a convention in Bombay at which it was voted to launch a branch of The Way ministry with headquarters in Bombay and with branches for each state of India to be established as soon as possible, all under and by the independent National Christians without any foreign system of control. The Bombay headquarters will have as a general overseer, Dr. J. S. Williams and Mr. James John as secretary.

On February 11th at 2:30 P.M. we left the Taj Mahal hotel with all our belongings to board the ship *Chusan*. Many friends from various places in India and Bombay paid visits to us in our hotel on the 9th and 10th and more than fifty of them came to see us off. At 4 P.M.. we started through the Health Department, then emigration, passage and finally customs and by 5 P.M. we were on ship which, however, did not sail until 9 P.M. Yet, many of our friends waited outside in the visitors area for our sailing. The Williams family and a few others had passes and were allowed on ship with us until 8 P.M.

Yes, at 9:00 P.M. the *Chusan* loosed anchor and with our handkerchiefs waving from the ship's port side and their handkerchiefs waving from shore, until the ship moved out to sea that neither of us could see the other any longer. "Parting is such sweet sorrow" but the contributions and enriching fellowships that we mutually made will continue to bear fruit both in America and India.

Many people throughout India responded so lovingly to the positive Gospel of the Word that people were saved, healed and made whole. A young boy was healed of hernia instantly, and a miracle of the casting out of many evil spirits was wrought on an aged mother 84 years old who had been bound for 30 years. After deliverance she was free to talk about her former enslavement by the evil spirits and she blessed God and us for her deliverance.

Sincerely in His Service,
Victor Paul Wierwille

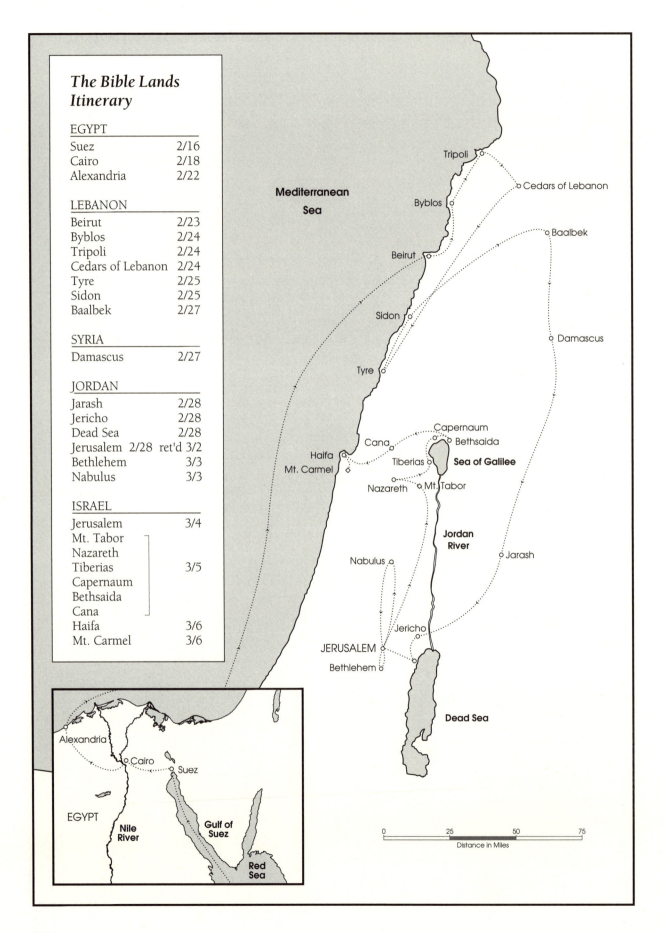

Bible Lands

After leaving India, our family's winding tour back to England was primarily intended to be an educational experience. Our journey took us back to Suez by way of the Indian Ocean and on through the Red Sea. During our week on board the *Chusan* from Bombay to Suez, Egypt, Dr. Wierwille became very interested again in the history of Moses and the Exodus. He also wrote the monthly *Way Newsletter* to send to Rhoda. And our family studied maps together, preparing for our trip in the Near East.

We disembarked at Suez on Saturday, February 18, and traveled by taxi to Cairo, a distance of about ninety miles, being stopped en route by police many times for no apparent reason. By the time we arrived in Cairo we could read "Coca-Cola" in Arabic, since we had seen it so frequently along the way. We had hired two cars in Suez to carry our family, along with another young American who helped direct our taxi, to our destination in Cairo, the Windsor Hotel. Rev. Bailey from the American Mission Church came to meet us at the hotel to welcome us and to make sure that we arrived safely. Egypt in general seemed expensive; but through Rev. Bailey, we made good connections.

Later that same day Dr. Wierwille wanted to see the traditional place where Joseph and Mary stayed with the young child Jesus when they fled into Egypt. The St. Mary's Coptic Church has a crypt under it where custom says the family stayed for a while before returning to Judea and Galilee. Also we were shown a tourist spot called the "Hanging Church," believed by some at that time to be built over a Roman tower, actually using the tower as its foundation. We hired a man with a car to take us to all these places.

The Pyramids were the first sight to see the following day, Sunday, February 19. We went into the pyramid at Giza, where the ceiling is so low one has to stoop as one walks. The king had it purposely built this way so that it would be necessary to bow as one entered the king's and queen's burial chambers. After being impressed by the age and labor involved in building such an imposing structure, we mounted camels and rode a half mile to the Sphinx. How impressive, if very weather-beaten by time, sun, and sand.

Guess who's riding a camel at the Sphinx?

 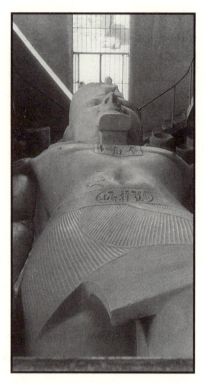 

Dr. Wierwille in Arab dress

A statue of Thutmose III

The front of the Egyptian Museum with papyrus plants behind Mary, Karen, and Don

After this a car took us south to Memphis, known as "the city of the living," the ancient capital during the dynasty of the Thutmose family. Here we saw the seventy-five-meter marble image of Thutmose III, now reclining but originally in an upright position. A sandstorm suddenly blew up while we were walking around Memphis. Our faces and arms stung from the pelting sand, and we could hardly open our eyes to see where we were going as we searched our way back to our car. After this we understood how a tower could be buried and become a foundation for a building. We also drove to Zakorah, called "the city of the dead."

Being a Sunday, we attended the Sunday evening English church service at the American Mission with Rev. Bailey preaching. On Monday morning Dr. Wierwille spent more time visiting with Rev. Bailey, who became interested in the research Dr. Wierwille shared.

The next day we took in some of ancient history's most impressive relics, some dating back as far as 3000 B.C., at the Egyptian Museum in Cairo. We had looked forward to visiting this museum ever since traveling through India. So many times when some beautiful pieces of stained glass or other works of art would be missing from historic sites in India, we would be told that it was in the Egyptian Museum in Cairo or the British Museum in London. We all had such an impressive time learning about ancient artifacts at the Egyptian Museum that we returned the next day to take in more.

Leaving Cairo on Wednesday, February 22, we took a train to Alexandria to sail later in the day to Beirut, Lebanon. While waiting at the dock, we were inundated with Egyptian merchants selling their wares. Among them was one who singled out Dr. Wierwille, pressuring him to buy a pair of house slippers. When Dr. Wierwille shook his head no, the man said, "You have only one wife to keep; I have four wives." In spite of this plea, we needed no house slippers so Dr. Wierwille bought none.

At 3:40 P.M. our ship, the *Esperia*, left the port of Alexandria in an overnight trip to Beirut. We again spent time reminiscing about how privileged we were in seeing places of such historic significance; so many names and places were familiar to us from our study of the Word.

Docking in Beirut, Lebanon, at 9:30 the next morning, Thursday, February 23, we were eagerly anticipating seeing many more places which we read about in God's Word. We had arranged to be met at the port in Beirut by a Christian tour guide and travel agent, Mr. Monsour, who would be with us as we traveled through Lebanon, Syria, and Jordan until we reached the border of Israel. At that time, 1956, people traveling through Syria and Jordan could not be Jews or Israelis. Our travel agent had to write a letter to swear that we were Christians, not Jews. In Lebanon there seemed to be more religious tolerance than in other Arab cities and countries in general.

The Myers family and Mr. Monsour greeting us at the Beirut docks

In Beirut we were guests of wonderful missionaries, Rev. and Mrs. Edward Myers. We invited them later that fall of 1956 to Spencerville, Ohio, as Uncle Harry's guests. They lived very modestly in Beirut and were really bighearted and wonderful.

As we traveled around beautiful Lebanon, we were blessed to see, as we drove by hired car, so many places of Biblical interest as well as other historical landmarks. The cedars of Lebanon were uppermost on our list. On our way to the cedars, we passed by Byblos, where archaeological digs reveal buildings and artifacts from the Amorite, Hyksos, Egyptian, Phoenician, Greco-Roman, and medieval times. The remains of buildings date back to 3200 B.C. and are considered the earliest monumental stone construction in the East.

We followed the coastal road to Tripoli, fifty miles north of Beirut. There we turned inland through the Qadisha Valley on the way to the cedars, about one hundred miles from Beirut. We were amazed by cliff-side monasteries and many snow-fed waterfalls. Most of the steep mountainsides were terraced in order to grow vegetation on them. There were no guardrails along the mountain roads, only a few low stone walls built around the hairpin curves, which took my breath away. At the very top of the mountains majestically tower the cedars of Lebanon. These are the same type of trees that David had chosen in building the Temple in Jerusalem. They are very beautiful, stately, and impressive. Snow-laden, these trees swayed tall and gracefully.

The Myers and us at the beautiful cedars of Lebanon

The next day we visited Tyre and Sidon, learning much history of the area and its previous civilizations. On Sunday, February 26, Dr. Wierwille had been asked to preach at a church in Beirut. Since there was no English interpreter for the Arabic services later, we excused ourselves from the rest of that day's meetings.

On Monday, February 27, we left Beirut, on our way with Mr. Monsour, our tour guide, and Rev. Myers, our friend. First we went to Baalbek, taking a picture of Mount Hermon in the distance. Baalbek, fifty-six miles from Beirut, was originally built as an imposing Roman religious center when the Roman Empire was at its peak. The ruins of many of the temples there are still massive and impressive after two thousand years.

We crossed the Syrian border without so much as a guard stationed there. In Damascus we visited the Omayyad Mosque, where the head of John the Baptist is supposedly buried. We went to the location of the house of Judas (Acts 9:11), now a mosque, where Paul was taken after his experience on the road to Damascus. The original street "called Straight" is somewhere buried under the present one. We continued with this Biblical account to find the home of Ananias, "a certain disciple," who ministered to Paul for his sight and for receiving holy spirit into manifestation. The house is now well below the street level, resembling a basement room. We also saw the spot where Bible scholars believe Paul was lowered down in a basket over the wall of the city of Damascus in order to escape the Judeans who had taken counsel to kill him because he preached Christ.

Dr. Wierwille on a street in the walled city of Damascus

Crossing the Jordanian border and continuing on toward the Jordanian part of Jerusalem through fertile but very stony soil, we visited the ruins of Jarash, noting

The borders of Jordan and Syria

the famous columns and excavations being done, considered among the most magnificent of ancient cities. Historians say it had become a strong Christian center by the fourth century. Its glory was completely ended by a disastrous earthquake, perhaps in 746 A.D.

Archaeologists at work in Jericho

Before entering Jericho we were excited to see the Jordan River, a natural landmark spoken of so frequently in the Bible. We entered the country of the Jordan River through beautiful hills. Here many soldiers were stationed along the way. We visited several ancient sites; some, the actual Biblical locations and others, where custom or tradition dictated. We visited Elisha's fountain and saw many women carrying water pitchers on their heads. We passed the site where Zacchaeus climbed the "sycomore tree" to see the lord pass by. Just across the road were world-renowned archaeological digs at ancient Jericho with a new dig going on, so we could observe the archaeologists at work. The size of the fruit grown in and around Jericho, especially lemons, was very large. I still remember how very impressed I was.

We headed to the Dead Sea, not far away. All five of us went wading in that amazing water, after which we had a glaze on our skin which running water couldn't rinse off. We had a song in our hearts, and we sang hymns and choruses as we entered the Jordanian side of Jerusalem.

A segment of the Jordan River

The next few days we visited sites in Jerusalem, beginning on Wednesday, February 29. We saw so many places mentioned in the Bible that we became overwhelmed: the Brook Kidron; the Mount of Olives; the Galilean hills or the Mount of Bad Council (where the plot was made against Jesus); the Mount of Ascension; a panoramic view of the city of Jerusalem, including the golden gate (walled off by the Moslems in 1543); the Dome of the Rock (the site where Abraham was said to have gone to offer Isaac); a small minaret marking the place of the last supper; the Palace of Caiaphas; the home of Mary, Martha, and Lazarus in Bethany; the place that is thought to be Calvary; the Garden Tomb; the valley of Molech (the pagans used to burn human sacrifices in the hands of his statue there); the Wailing Wall (or the western wall of the Temple); Gethsemane; and many more places.

On March 2 we again passed over the Brook Kidron on our way to Bethlehem. We stopped on the Mount of Olives to get a distant view of the Pool of Siloam. By way of the old road to Bethlehem the distance was four miles from Jerusalem. But at the time we were sight-seeing, parts of the "Bethlehem road" were in "no-man's-land," a buffer zone between Jordan and Israel. The current route to Bethlehem from Jerusalem was about twenty-five miles long as it wound up and down the mountains. On our way to Bethlehem we stopped at Rachel's grave. We visited the vicinity of Bethlehem where Jesus was born, saw a traditional shepherd's grazing field with a shepherd's cave on a Judean hillside, and viewed the field of Boaz.

A shepherd's cave near Bethlehem

Located near Bethlehem was the Christian Approach Mission, which cared for many orphaned children and was run by Mr. Handel and Mrs. Van der Linden. We had had previous knowledge of their work through their literature and had arranged to spend some time with them. While our guide, Mr. Monsour, stayed at the travel agency, we stayed at their children's orphanage a couple of days as we visited the Bethlehem area. The Christian Approach Mission was doing a wonderful Christian work with many children.

The Samaritan synagogue

The next morning was Saturday, and Dr. Wierwille spoke at the mission's morning chapel service. After this we went back through Bethlehem, through Jerusalem, and on to Nabulus, a very beautiful scenic trip with terraced hills and a green-and-brown patched valley. Here we visited first of all Jacob's well, where we drank the water. We also visited the only colony of Samaritans who date their ancestry back to Bible times. There were only about 350 of these Samaritans remaining in 1956. They did not believe in cutting their hair; some of them braided theirs while others let it hang straight. We were arriving just as the weekly Sabbath services were to begin. Our family felt especially blessed to be invited in to observe. Their ritual might possibly have been very similar to that of the synagogues in Jesus' day. There was chanting for an hour and a half—through the entire reading of the Torah, it seemed. An hour and a half of chanting in a language one doesn't understand can seem like an extremely long time. After the service was over, the head priest read for us from an ancient Hebrew scroll. The scroll was kept in a Persian case, and the three knobs projecting above the case represented the tribes of Levi, Ephraim, and Manasseh. There were eight priests in this synagogue who claimed to be descendants from the line of Levi.

We were told that this scroll was the oldest manuscript of the Torah in extant.

Our family entered the Israeli side of Jerusalem through no-man's-land.

We returned to the city of Nabulus, where a peaceful rally was celebrating the departure of a general from the English army the day before. In Jerusalem that evening they were also celebrating the same event of the English military authority's leaving. At last the country of Jordan was on its own without any English military or political persons overseeing the affairs of their country.

At this time, because of extreme tension between Israel and its neighbors, the border between Israel and Jordan was closed. The only way to enter Israel by land was to cross by foot from Jordan to Israel at the Mandelbaum Gate in Jerusalem. To explain the situation, Jerusalem was a divided city in March 1956, with part of the city in Jordan, part in Israel, and a strip of no-man's-land in between. Since Jordan would not honor passports that were stamped "Israel," obviously we had to plan our itinerary to visit Israel last on our Near Eastern excursion.

The Mandelbaum Gate was heavily patrolled with armed military guards walking back and forth. It was a very tense experience. Without any exchange of words, we walked from the Jordanian guardhouse with two boys carrying our bags halfway through this buffer zone. We turned around to wave good-bye to Mr. Monsour. Then two men came from the Israeli side and carried our bags into their customhouse where we were given a warm greeting. The customs officials called a taxi for us and we were taken to the YMCA, where we had lodging reservations. It was said to be the nicest YMCA building in the world. We very much appreciated our brief stay at the "Y" with heated rooms, hot water, and a shower. It was the first time since leaving Beirut that we had such creature comforts.

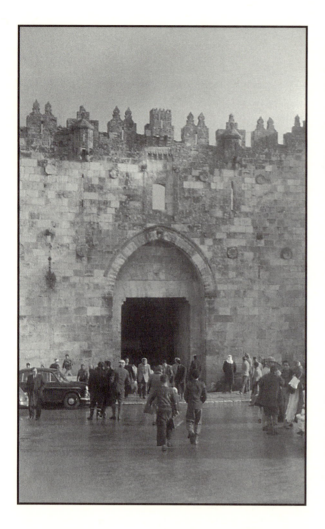 

Herod's Gate

Dr. Wierwille walking up an ancient, narrow street in Jerusalem

At 8:00 A.M. on March 5 we started our tour of sights in Israel in Mrs. Duce's station wagon, as she wanted us to use it. Mrs. Duce was an enthusiastic helper at the YMCA. A visiting evangelist, Rev. Stewart, drove the car and a Scottish Presbyterian, Rev. Scott, also came along with our family. We headed north and were blessed to see Samuel's monument (I Samuel 7:12) and Gibeah (II Samuel 6:3), where the ark of God was left and David came back for it. Then ten miles from Jerusalem we came near Samson's birthplace. We stopped to take pictures of Mount Tabor in the distance from the plain of Jezreel. Next we came to Nain, where Jesus raised the widow's son, spoken of in Luke 7. To our right was the valley of Endor, with great patches of blue lupine flowers growing wild. Suddenly, between the Galilean hills, we spied the Sea of Galilee. The fishing nets were spread in Tiberias, a winter resort.

We drove on around the seashore to Capernaum, viewing the YMCA and the ruins of Magdala (Arabic ruins three miles north of Tiberias).

Looking back, we could see the Maccabean hills and Pigeon Valley, the path which Jesus followed to Capernaum and the site of battles during the Crusades. We stopped on a hillside which sloped down into the Sea of Galilee. The terrain formed a natural amphitheater with perfect acoustics. Dr. Wierwille stood on stones in the sea and read Mark 4. It was very likely the same place where Jesus stood when he taught the account we were now reading. The rest of us stood about a fifth of a mile from the shore as Dr. Wierwille read, and we could hear him plainly. We passed through Capernaum's gateway and saw the ruins of the synagogue there. Capernaum was by that time an archaeological site, not a living city.

Dr. Wierwille standing at the edge of the Sea of Galilee reading from Mark 4

Don on a hillside overlooking Nazareth

We continued on, taking pictures of the monastery on the hillside of the Mount of Beatitudes, Bethsaida, the well at Cana, Mary's Well, and Mary and Joseph's Grotto where Jesus worked in the carpenter's shop, all in Nazareth. We came to Haifa through the plain of Sharon.

Dr. Wierwille expressed great feelings of gratitude and rejoicing in visiting the Near East and wrote, "Our hearts are thrilled to think that we have had the privilege to visit all these Bible lands and to see so many things, especially as a family. It is a joy of inexpressible words to walk the way and see the places where Jesus Christ walked and talked; to traverse the land where men of God, the prophets, apostles and disciples labored that we might know Him."

On the morning of Tuesday, March 6, we called for our mail at the Shoham Maritime Services and received many newsy letters for which we were very excited and thankful. We then took the city bus to Mount Carmel but didn't go up as far as to the site where Elijah called down fire to the altar in I Kings 18. We returned on the same bus to our hotel. After eating at a lunch stand nearby, we immediately got a cab to take us to the pier. We had no difficulty in customs and boarded the Israeli ship *Negbah* at 3:30 P.M., ready to sail to Italy.

Dr. Wierwille summed up our tour of the Bible Lands in the April *Way Newsletter.*

April 1956

Newsletter

In every land where we have traveled with the light of **The Way** ministry, which God by His grace has given us, we have endeavored to show people the greatness of the rights and privileges of every believer in Jesus Christ. We have found nothing but a most welcome reception in every land, and have been asked to return quickly or to send someone else who could teach and share more with them. Little can you realize the doors that have and are open for the Abundant Life, and the responsibility that rests upon us, as Christians, to meet these obligations. God has called us that we might meet the great challenge of the world in this day.

Our tour through the Holy Land has been a blessing to all of us. We had no meetings planned as our tour here was not geared for teaching primarily, but for us to personally orient ourselves with the Holy Land so we might be more efficient in knowledge and better qualified to teach others. However, several meetings were arranged for us and we had many wonderful personal contacts who we could witness to and we thank God always for the privilege of witnessing for Him. We believe that His sheep will hear and the goats only will not listen.

I know that to **The Way** ministry will be drawn, by the Spirit of Christ, souls who are great in love and good works; those, who like to be associated with a cause that has meaning and purpose beyond the self. When we return to the United States we will continue to work even more enthusiastically and effectively than we have ever done before, because we realize not only the greatness of **The Way** ministry but also the urgency of getting the truth out to all who will hear. I trust that you may be one to join hands with **The Way** ministry to carry on this work.

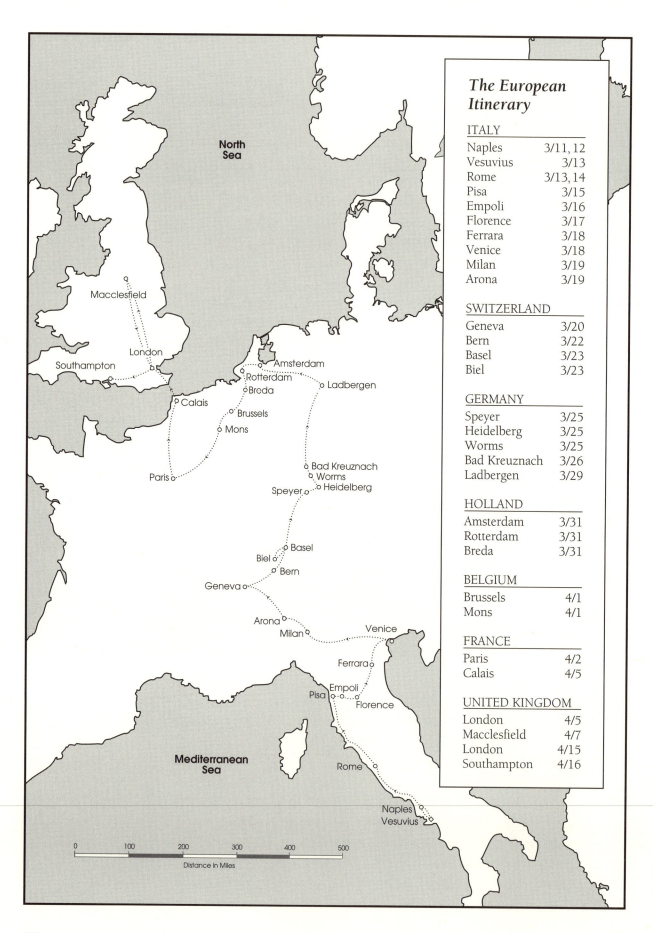

Europe

On Wednesday morning, March 7, we found ourselves anchored about a half mile from the shores of Cyprus, where some passengers got off the *Negbah* and others came on. The shore of the island seemed to be green with vegetation, but the hills farther back looked like sand dunes. By 11:00 A.M. we were sailing again and traveled west along the shores of Cyprus until late afternoon. After teatime, we had a lifeboat drill. As we got out in the open sea, the water became increasingly choppy. By the time the second seating for dinner came around at 8:00 P.M., many people did not show up in the dining room. Others left in a big hurry. I wonder why! Don and Mary didn't eat, and Karen ate only sparingly. Dr. Wierwille and I were on the verge of dizziness, but we ate heartily. So long as our minds were occupied with something else, the boat's rocking didn't bother us. We had to practice conscious relaxation.

Because we were on an Israeli boat, we discovered at breakfast the next morning that we couldn't have milk and meat at the same meal since it isn't kosher. So we drank cream with our coffee only at breakfast and teatime; at the other meals we drank our coffee black. This was our first personal experience with the rigidness of Old Testament dietary laws.

On the next day, the sea still churned. Dr. Wierwille and I both wrote letters and then worked on the organization of The Way. Dr. Wierwille was doing some thinking and writing in connection with the future expansion of The Way Ministry. The thought again presented itself that the Church as we know it today must be revitalized by holy spirit in God's people so that God can communicate with them, giving them spiritual power that is greater than the adversary's. We also gave more thought to our trip through Europe. By midafternoon Thursday, as we were passing the island of Crete, the water quieted down considerably.

Friday evening, March 9, was the beginning of the Sabbath, another learning experience on an Israeli ship. Candle lighting by the women at 5:20 for the memory of the dead began the celebration. At 5:30 the rabbi had a service in the synagogue which only men attended. At the beginning

Mary and I during a safety drill on the Negbah

of our dinner the rabbi chanted something in Hebrew and then drank a swig of wine before we began our meal.

On a rainy Sunday, March 11, we docked at Naples, Italy. An American Express representative came aboard the *Negbah* to help us get oriented for the European leg of our trip. After going through customs with us, he helped us load the luggage into his car and took us to our hotel.

Every time we arrived at a new destination listed as our mailing address, we found letters waiting for us. We looked forward to these "mail days" with great anticipation. We were thrilled again to get pictures of J.P.

After reading our mail, as treasure, we discovered the California Restaurant and enjoyed American food. We had eaten mostly native foods on our trip so far, so when we occasionally found foods familiar to Americans, we were delighted.

First thing on Monday, March 12, we went to inquire about a car rental as well as to get an international driver's license for Dr. Wierwille at a cost of twenty dollars. We also sent some excess luggage with our lightweight clothing to an address in England, as it was still winter in Europe. Dr. Wierwille decided to rent a Fiat 1100 for us to drive through Europe, from Naples to Paris. The car was just large enough for the five of us to get into; our luggage had to be put in the carrier on top.

Pompeii was our first destination for sight-seeing in the area, about seventeen miles south of Naples. Dr. Wierwille became accustomed to driving the car, while we tried to be helpful in reading the road signs written in Italian. Since it somewhat resembled Latin, I could get the gist of what was meant some of the time. (At that time there were no international road signs.)

Visiting Pompeii

In approximately 54 A.D. Pompeii, a resort city for the wealthy Romans, had been badly shaken by an earthquake, after which much of the city had been repaired. Then in 65 A.D. the nearby volcano of Mount Vesuvius erupted for three days and destroyed three cities in the lava's path. When we visited Pompeii, only two-thirds of the city had been excavated, but we saw the House of the Faun and the House of the Vettii from the classic book *The Last Days of Pompeii*.

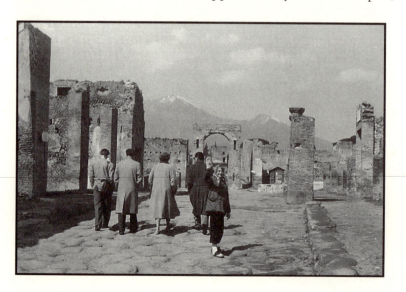

The road to Rome had a fresh layer of snow most of the way with little traffic and a few hairpin curves. The mountains seemed to surround us. Having arrived in Rome after dark, we found our hotel with some difficulty. In the morning we called the American Express office to procure a guide for the duration of our stay of one-and-a-half days there. In the afternoon we began our tour at St. Peter's Basilica. The celebration of the thirteenth anniversary of Pope Pius XII and his eightieth birthday had been held on Sunday and all the beautiful red draperies were still up. The many colors of marble were impressive; the size of the church and the works of art were outstanding. Dr. Wierwille was thinking, "Would that God's Word might have first place here."

Other points of interest in Rome were the Roman Forum, the Palace of Justice, the obelisk known as Trajan's Column, the Vatican Museums, the Sistine Chapel with the famous paintings by Michelangelo, the palace with the paintings of Raphael, Mussolini's Forum (sports center), and the Pantheon, which was saved from ruin because it was changed from a pagan temple to a church in Alexander's time. The latter had the largest dome in the world at that time, vaulting a span of forty-three meters. Of course, we had to see the Colosseum, and then we traveled down the Appian Way to the catacombs. What Dr. Wierwille wanted to see most of all in Rome at a Vatican Museum was not there at that time, the Codex Vaticanus.

The road to our next point of interest followed the shoreline of the Mediterranean Sea. Near Livorno we reached a high elevation, enjoying a scenic panorama of the shore. As we arrived at Pisa, on a rainy day, we

The ruins of ancient Rome

Inside the Roman Colosseum

marveled at its leaning tower built during the years of 1173–1372. Since tourists were at that time permitted to climb its stairway to the top, we did.

On the next cool, crisp morning, we arrived in Florence, where we went to see the bronze replica of Michelangelo's *David*, the home of Elizabeth Barrett Browning, and also the palace of the de' Medici family, who ruled not only the city of Florence, but practically all of Italy due to their influence in banking and the arts during the late Renaissance.

That afternoon we headed for Venice by way of the Futa and the Raticosa passes, the entire trip being about thirty-five miles. It was all snowy, and we passed two cars that were stuck on the inclines and one truck-car collision. The clouds were hanging low in the mountains and visibility was quite poor, but we drove slowly and had no difficulty. The next morning after having stopped at a hotel for the night, we arrived at Venice. Our car had to be parked in a garage on the outskirts of the city. Doing the tourist thing, we took a gondola, known as a water taxi, on the Grand Canal—a new experience for us; it took us to our hotel.

Since the next day was St. Joseph's holiday, everything in the Piazza San Marco was set up for rides, fun houses, and toss games. It was good for a few snapshots.

As we arrived in Milan the next morning we found the same celebration going on, so the museum was closed and we didn't get to see da Vinci's painting of *The Last Supper*. We wanted so much to see it but decided not to wait.

We drove on to Arona, a small resort town on a lake in northern Italy. We stopped at a guest house for the night—no heat and no hot water, but the scene over the lake was absolutely breathtakingly beautiful. And to think that heaven will be lovelier!

Karen on a gondola ride on the Grand Canal in Venice

Transporting our humble Fiat (the car with the carrier on top) through the Italian/Swiss Pass

A typical Swiss chalet

It was now March 20 as we headed toward Geneva, Switzerland. Domodossola, Italy, was the point where we had to put our rental car on a train flatbed. We shipped it to Brig, Switzerland, as the Simplon Pass was still closed for the winter season. To go from country to country, we had to get a permit from customs for the car. We were crossing our first European border here. It was about a forty-five-minute trip, passing through thirteen tunnels; the longest one was twelve kilometers. The train was crowded, so we stood all the way. Since our car was being transported on a train which followed the one we were riding on, we had time to purchase postage stamps and go window shopping while waiting in Brig.

The drive from Brig to Geneva was most beautiful, with snow-covered peaks all around. That night we felt indulged with the warm room and hot water in our Geneva lodging. Switzerland is so clean and pretty. Dr. Wierwille visited at the World Council of Churches' International Headquarters and spent some time seeing the work of that headquarters. After that we did some sight-seeing: the United Nation's European Headquarters, the Wilson Memorial Building, and Memorial Square, which is a park with monuments of the fathers of the Reformation. We regretted that we could not enter the John Calvin Church because it was under repair. Seeing this church and getting a feel for John Calvin and his work by going to his church had been a great desire of Dr. Wierwille's heart.

We had a beautiful drive to Bern, partly through freshly fallen snow, so gorgeous on the branches of the evergreens. As a part of our random conversations as we drove along, we discussed in what order we were going to hold J.P. when we saw him at the dock in New York. We were what could be called "planners ahead."

As we passed through cities, the fashions in the shop windows made such an impression on us. Our trip to Basel was through plains with beautiful farmlands and homes with the barns attached, all so immaculately kept.

The evening before meeting Dr. Karl Barth, Dr. Wierwille met a seminary student from Akron, Ohio, who was studying for his doctorate degree. He became quite interested in the Holy Spirit and healing fields. In Basel we were excited to meet Dr. Barth, an internationally known theologian with whom Dr. Wierwille was most eager to converse. Dr. Wierwille spoke of him as "the great European theologian." We arrived at the Barth home and found he was sick with the flu. His secretary granted only a short meeting with Dr. Wierwille, while the children and I sat in on the conversation.

Dr. Barth was very kind and also eager to hear about Dr. Wierwille's research, the difference between "manifestation" of the spirit and "gift" of the spirit. Dr. Wierwille had already taught this truth in the third PFAL class in June 1954.

Dr. Barth was planning to publish a book he was writing about the gifts of the spirit. However, when Dr. Wierwille pointed out that the Bible in I Corinthians 12 speaks of them as manifestations, Dr. Barth checked his Greek text and couldn't believe his eyes. Truly, it read "manifestation." Dr. Barth gave us names from the seminary in Basel of people of mutual interests on the Holy Spirit and healing fields. Dr. Barth also inquired about and was eager to hear of Dr. Wierwille's other interests.

The Reverend Mrs. Cox, one of the seminarians Dr. Barth had mentioned, came to talk, and we were in discussion that afternoon from 4:30 to 8:00, and later that evening from 10:00 to 3:30 A.M.

Dr. Wierwille wanted to find the location of the Ecumenical League, which we discovered was in Biel. So we backtracked a little the next day for an appointment there.

We met Dr. Erni, the secretary of the league. He spoke only French, no English or German, so he had an interpreter with him. However, he could not give us the particular information Dr. Wierwille wanted. After Mrs. Erni served tea, we were on our way back to Basel.

Our next destination was Bad Kreuznach in west-central Germany. It was not as scenic as our drive through Switzerland had been, only foothills. Much of the highway was brick road and not very smooth, and the blacktop roads suffered from freeze damage. All the Germans were out walking the day we drove to Bad Kreuznach, as it was Sunday afternoon. At Karlsruhe we drove through a part of the Black Forest made up of beautiful Kiefer evergreens with very little underbrush, and we frequently saw the sign "Deer Crossing." Since we were passing only seven miles from Speyer, we decided to visit some relatives of our church members, the

Schramms. They seemed very happy to see us; and though our children understood very little German, they enjoyed the company. We had to ferry across the river to Speyer because the bridge had been blown up during World War II and had not yet been rebuilt.

In Heidelberg we saw ruins yet from the 1940s and their very old and famous university. And in Worms we stopped at the Martin Luther Memorial to take a picture and remember that Luther was pronounced a heretic of the Roman Catholic church there by the Edict of Worms. We returned to the autobahn on our way to Bad Kreuznach, a distance of another sixty kilometers. Along the way farmers were busy preparing the ground, planting potatoes and seed, working mostly with horses, some oxen, and a few tractors.

The Luther Memorial in Worms

We arrived in Bad Kreuznach at the Maus home and were given a hearty welcome. Since our church in Van Wert had sent "CARE" packages after World War II to the German people, Mrs. Maus and I had become pen pals and thus our family had been extended an invitation to visit. She had invited an English teacher as interpreter for the evening; but since we could get along quite well understanding one another in German, we canceled with the interpreter.

The Mauses had butchered a pig in anticipation of our visit. Mrs. Maus's brother lived in the house where they were born, which had a very large social room, like a town hall used for harvest and folk dancing. This is where we spent the evening, meeting quite a few of the Maus's relatives. They were most hospitable, and we did a lot of reminiscing about the war and after. Mr. Maus before his retirement had been in the German military. (Fourteen years later Mrs. Maus and daughter, Heidi, made a return visit to us.)

We continued the next day on to Mainz. The entire drive again was beautiful, with rolling hills and beautiful woods. All along southern Germany the farmers lived together in villages. Much of the war damage was still evident in the larger cities. As we came up north from Kassel, the land was more level. We made our way to Ladbergen, Westphalia, the area where Dr. Wierwille's great-grandparents and my grandparents had emigrated from to come to the United States. It was interesting to see the familiar surnames in the churchyard cemetery, the same surnames that we have to this day in New Knoxville, "Kipp" (my maiden name) and "Wierwille," of course, among them.

The owner of the "Gasthaus" (guest house) in Ladbergen had some hunting dogs, German longhairs, which were a great point of interest to Dr. Wierwille, being an avid hunter and already a lover of German shorthaired pointers. Dr. Wierwille himself had raised German shorthairs and Labrador retrievers so that every fall of the year he could go hunting with them. His dogs were always a joy and a point of interest and relaxation to him. Ever since our sons were old enough to carry a gun, Dr. Wierwille took them hunting in the fall of the year and taught them with care.

Ladbergen with its Protestant church

As we were in Ladbergen on Good Friday, we joined the people there for the communion service at the church the night before. Though Dr. Wierwille and I had both been raised in the church in New Knoxville where we were brought up in the German-speaking services, we did not recognize the hymns they sang at this occasion. There were about six hundred members in attendance, and they were having another service the next morning. This church claimed thirty-six hundred members. We learned that the membership was so large because there was no separation between church and state. In other words, every citizen of the community was counted in the church membership, divided into two groups: Protestants and Roman Catholics.

The next morning we had a wonderful visit with the town historian. He showed us a well-worn wood-carved plaque in the hallway of the Gasthaus with the name of a former owner as being "Kipp."

Now we were ready to go on to Holland. At the Dutch border we discovered that we didn't have the proper permit to bring our car into the country. So we were required to give them the money for the value of the car, to assure the Dutch government that we wouldn't sell our car while in their country. The auto club wouldn't do anything for us except call someone who might be our benefactor and deposit the money with the government on our behalf, as we certainly didn't have that kind of money ourselves. Our benefactor arrived; and as he and the interpreter were conversing, we found we could understand and speak the same language. It was Low German. When the benefactor heard that Dr. Wierwille was a minister, he immediately urged us to let him put down the money for us; and he no longer insisted that we needed to leave Holland at this same point of entry.

Having the privilege now to enter Holland, we drove to Amsterdam. As had become our custom, we looked for the American Express location there. A man near the Holland-Germany border said he was driving that way, so he led us for miles into the city, even finding a parking place for us. We got a map of the city and then walked to the canal boat station, arriving just in time to catch a departing sight-seeing boat. It was again a unique experience, riding on streets of water in Amsterdam. And though it was a dreary day, we had a beautiful tour with a guide who could speak in four languages.

We traveled the next day through Rotterdam, Dordrecht, and on to Belgium. Though the weather was quite cold, we enjoyed the great beauty of the tulip fields and the many picturesque windmills along the way. We stopped at a Dutch Reformed church for services that Easter Sunday morning. This church had family pews, hence we were ushered to the front of the sanctuary, practically next to the minister. Dr. Wierwille and I understood some of the Dutch service, and what a thrill it was for us to be singing a verse of "Christ the Lord Is Risen Today." (This was the melody at least; Dutch words.)

Don in front of what Holland is famous for

That afternoon, we drove through Belgium and into France. The trip into Paris was beautiful, through rolling hills, hedgerows, and the forest near Verdun, where we saw the World War I Memorial. It was very difficult to communicate because we could hardly speak a single word in French. And since the hotels we stopped at didn't accept children as guests, we went to three hotels before we could register. We were so glad to find a heated room and hot water. In 1956 this was still a treat in Europe. We again enjoyed hamburgers and chili soup as we found the American Embassy restaurant. The hostess was lenient to allow us access though we weren't employed by the embassy, inviting us to come every day at the less busy hours. We took pictures of the beautiful fountains, the Tomb of the Unknown Soldier, the Arch of Triumph, the Champs-Elysées, and also the Eiffel Tower and the original Statue of Liberty. We went to a movie theater to see the newly released *Hans Christian Andersen,* starring Danny Kaye, and then did a little shopping, some "regrouping" of letters, tidied up our suitcases, washed some clothes, and wrote many letters to people back home.

On Wednesday afternoon, April 4, we went to the American Express office to turn in our car, which they noted was nice and clean, and settled our account quickly. The car fee was $330.00, and the gasoline for the trip had cost us $56.22. The total mileage we drove in Europe was 2,517 miles in twenty-two days. After we turned in our Fiat, we had to get around on the Métro, the Paris subway. The next day we left Paris, headed for London by way of the train to Calais, France, and then by ferry to Dover, England.

The following are two letters from India that were awaiting us as we arrived in England.

My dearest Dorothea,

Dr. Williams has been very happy since he has come in contact with Dr. Wierwille. He has found in him a genuine friend, which he needed most. He has been keeping good health and sleeps so soundly. He hardly worries about things which used to bother him much. It appears as if his friend Dr. V.P. has taken most of his burden off his shoulders. He would talk with pride to people about Dr. V.P.'s wisdom and his exposition of the Word of God. He talks about the Wierwilles almost every day and rejoices in their great ministry in India.

I thank you all most heartily for having helped my husband by your kind and courteous manners and by your abundant love and sympathetic understanding of his work and personality. He had always entertained a confidence that someday he would be truly understood by someone, endowed with spiritual insight. Whereas he has met with unkindness he is now happy that there are the Wierwilles who can understand him, trust him and sincerely love him. He loves the American people, you must have known by now, as much as he loves his own countrymen. He made no secret of it in Russia and so boldly and courageously gave vent to his innermost feelings, and wished the very best to USA at a public reception held in Moscow in his honour at his birthday.

Dorothy Williams   March 19, 1956
[Wife of our host in India, Dr. J. S. Williams]

The following is a letter from a Christian layman who attended all the meetings in Ahmadabad, India.

My dear Wierwille, Mrs. Wierwille, and Children.

. . . "The Bible is the revealed Word and will of God" was my base for preaching the gospel and I spoke in 5 meetings on this truth and to Christians and non-Christians individually in the suburbs and nearby villages. Dr. Raj was also with me and he also gave messages to people in the trains, motorbuses and meetings on this very truth. On our program of the nearby villages, 8–9 persons joined with us and we all were much happy to preach the gospel. I concluded my work on 3/56 and submitted a short account of my 'Individual work of Gospel preaching during the Evangelical weeks' to the Secretary who read with other reports, in the morning service of 5/3/56 in my church and on hearing of my report, some of my friends astonished and they congratulated me for good work done.

Now I feel a quite new experience in my life and wonderful courage and strength to speak without any shame or fear. As I read more and more the Word of God, with the help of the explanation and exposition given to us by you, I experience a quite new vision from the Word of God and new light in my life. I gather new courage and strength to be firm in Way upon which I want to walk now. But still however, without the perfect knowledge of the Word of God, I fear, it would be very difficult to face the world, because Satan is at his work. So I have started studying the Word of God, very carefully, no doubt, Dr. Raj is helping me, but I may confess here that from the wonderful experience I got from your fellowship during your short stay in my City and the messages I heard, a new appetite for the Word of God and thirst for the Water of life has opened for the first time in my life. I longed to be more and more in close with you even at Bombay, with the deep desire of my heart that I may be imparted with the blessing of the <u>Saint of God.</u> Those morning meetings and your fellowship during your stay in India, are sweet memories of my life and in my loneliness, when I remember those days, I feel great joy and peace in my heart, and when I read the Word of God, I feel that My Master is near me.

Now though I am poor, I feel rich in Jesus, though I am weak, I feel strong in Christ, though I am empty in all things of life, I feel that I am abounds in all in Jesus Christ who is my Lord of all. . .

At Bombay at the time of our departure, each one of us wanted to express our last desire, but departure at the last moment was so sudden that we could not do it, and we also were somewhat disappointed and had sorrow of departing for a while. But now I take privilege here to express that last desire "LET THE DOUBLE PORTION OF THY SPIRIT BE UPON ME." This is what I wanted from you at the last moment, because I believe that you have been bestowed with the power from High and I look upon you to pray for me to get the double portion of the power from High, to strengthen me to work in this region of Gujarat and this great nation of Bharat.

Yours in his fellowship,
Harry Henry   March 27, 1956

Now back in England, Dr. Wierwille and the rest of us made another itinerary to Macclesfield, as planned. Karen and Mary stayed with Miss Luce again, while Dr. Wierwille, Don, and I were guests in the home of Ronald Hooley. I couldn't stay up at night past 11:30, however; I was too tired. Mr. and Mrs. Hooley and others stayed up with Dr. Wierwille until 1:00 or later.

During this itinerary of another nine days, Dr. Wierwille taught on these subjects: speaking in tongues; faith (believing); two seeds; the unforgivable sin; God's giving good gifts; Luke 11:11-13; Acts 1, 2, and 9 on receiving holy spirit; the renewed mind; the threefold man; and I Corinthians 12, 13, and 14. There were around forty to fifty people in these meetings. Our children were either baby-sitting in one of the homes during these gatherings or attending "Crusaders" meetings at the Gowars' home (a youth group from their church) or just visiting with the Gowar children.

Ronald Hooley with Dr. Wierwille in Macclesfield

Dr. Wierwille and Mr. Hooley, on Mr. Hooley's day off, discussed extensively the organization of The Way. The last evening of our stay all who wanted to receive into manifestation holy spirit were invited after the meeting to come to the Hooley home. We retired at 2:00 A.M. Dr. Wierwille was very blessed about how the message of the Word had been so eagerly received.

The following excerpts are from a letter written by our interim pastor at St. Peter's Church in Van Wert. To hear his good report was a great blessing to us.

Dear Dr. Wierwille and Family,

Mrs. F. joins me in many thanks for your kind letters and now for the lovely Easter Greeting. We are all glad that you are having such a profitable time, but most of all that you will soon return to good old U.S. and Van Wert. You have certainly trained these good people to be co-operative and in the true Christian Spirit.

Sunday evening (Easter) the Choir rendered an Easter Cantata. I've never heard one better. They had worked very hard and the rendition certainly indicated it.

Your members are very faithful and attentive as long as I preach the Word and they serve as an inspiration.

I just feel that it is useless to go into details as to the work here because Rhoda told me that she writes to you regularly and keeps you thoroughly informed. Rhoda has been most faithful and a great help all along the line. She is a truly consecrated laborer in His vineyard.

Your consistory have also been very faithful as well as all the S.S. [Sunday School] and other workers.

Katie [his wife] and I hope that you will have a safe return home and this is also our prayer. With this I must close, for it is almost time for the evening mail to leave.

May the Lord richly bless and keep you,

E. [Ernest] Fledderjohann   April 2, 1956

On Sunday, April 15, we returned by train to London and finished up the day by labeling our suitcases for the SS *United States,* preparing to board ship the next day at Southampton.

The day of our sailing, Monday, was very happy since we were heading home. We purchased cards and stamps and wrote away on our train ride from London to the port. We immediately boarded our American ship, Dr. Wierwille having exchanged our remaining English pounds for American dollars. My sister and brother-in-law had mailed another letter and pictures that were at Southampton for us—such a joy to see how our little John Paul was growing.

Return to the U.S.A.

Sailing from Southampton on the SS *United States*, we docked at Le Havre, France, to take on a few passengers. Our mid-April trip crossing the Atlantic was not an opportune time to go out on the open deck. The average speed of this new ship was 32 knots per hour, adding to the wind factor on deck. These days were good for catching up on reading, as well as doing crossword puzzles, playing checkers, and seeing several of the latest American movies. At one point on this last stretch, our room steward informed us that ours was the only family in his care that wasn't bed-bound with seasickness.

Our family, along with everyone on the ship, cheered as we passed the Statue of Liberty in the New York Harbor. This sight signaled that we were happily home again. Soon our boat moved into dock. My sister Dee with little J.P. and my two brothers-in-law, Dick Fischbach and Lloyd Ulrey, were there to greet us. Dr. Wierwille's family had seen us off, and now my family blessed us by welcoming us back. They brought the following letter with them to the boat:

Little J.P. being reunited with his family in New York customs

Dear V.P. and All,

Greetings, Salutations, congratulations, etc. and bless you all from all of us and I can say from all the congregation at Main and Harrison. Believe me, they will all be glad to welcome you back. Rhoda especially. Boy, she is sure a queen. Dr. Fledderjohann is very good and everybody likes him very much but I don't know where or when a church was more Christian and loved one another more than our little church and of course we owe it to you and yours so naturally all will be anxious to greet you. Bless you all and God's love abound on you and your return and do hurry back.

Lloyd, Evie, etc.   April 21, 1956
[My sister and her husband]

We needed to spend a few days in New York, where Dr. Wierwille reported to people who were interested in our tour, such as the Promotion of America-India Relations Society and representatives of the All-India Federation of National Churches. We also made a personal visit to the American Express office, which had served us so well all along our way.

Anticipation now ran high for our return home to Van Wert. We made it a goal to ease our way back into little J.P.'s heart on the way.

Dr. Wierwille and I at our welcome home pound shower

Things happened in rapid order as we arrived back home. One of the very first issues to deal with was our empty home, including our empty cupboards. Uncle Harry had given us new bedroom sets: twin beds for the girls, a Western-style for Don, and a lovely walnut double for Dr. Wierwille and me. All of our immediate needs were met, and we gradually again added more furnishings. In the meantime we also used a folding table and chairs from the church basement in our kitchen. The church members gave us a "pound" kitchen shower, which means that they brought a pound or several pounds of a staple food to get our kitchen restocked.

The Wierwille family gave our family a wonderful welcome home at a get-together, April 25, to break bread at Sevilla and Walter Henkener's farm near New Knoxville. Then on May 20, Karen was among the three girls who were confirmed at our church and taken into church membership. Dr. Wierwille was faithfully carrying on denominational practice, but always extending himself beyond. On June 7 the Wierwille family gathered again with fifty-eight present to give a short report of our tour and show the slides Don had taken.

When we were in Chicago for a meeting later in June 1956, just two months after our return from our seven-month tour, Dr. Wierwille received word that his father had fallen asleep, having developed chest pains twelve hours before. (We had sent Dad Wierwille a telegram from India on his eighty-first birthday in January.) He had lived a full life, always sought answers on what he didn't understand, wonderfully supported Dr. Wierwille's interests, always loved the Lord and contributed to His work. Dad Wierwille had been a man of firm will; he was, of course, a Power for Abundant Living class graduate and always worked heartily and acted deliberately on his beliefs.

In his last will and testament, Dad Wierwille bequeathed the farm he had lived on and owned to his three sons. His will read as follows: "I Give, Devise and Bequeath to my three sons, Harry Wierwille, Rueben [sic] Wierwille and Victor Wierwille, my farm of One Hundred and Forty-seven (147) acres, more or less, situated in Van Buren Township, Shelby County, Ohio, jointly, their heirs and assigns forever, in fee simple; but with the proviso and upon the condition that they pay my grand-son, Charles Wierwille, the sum of Twenty-four Hundred ($2400.00) Dollars in cash within one year from the time of my decease, to represent and cover his share or interest in said farm premises."

After the three brothers had paid the required $2400 to their nephew, the only child of their deceased brother Otto, they each had their share of the inheritance. As life has its certain dynamics and though Reuben and his wife Mary's hearts were very much with the ministry, Reuben felt the necessity of keeping his share of the inheritance. Reuben and Mary were both graduates of the April 1954 Power for Abundant Living class. Being an avid reader, Mary carried out many assignments in research for Dr. Wierwille, and Reuben was always generous in his support, helping in various ways.

The warranty deed for what was to become The Way Headquarters

So H.E. Wierwille and Victor Wierwille paid Reuben for his share of the farm and then they freely deeded the farm as a gift to The Way, Incorporated, henceforth to be used in every way possible for the furtherance of the goals and principles of The Way, Incorporated, as set forth in its charter, amendments, and testimony of belief.

The first meeting of the Board of Directors after our return from the World Missionary Teaching and Training Tour was held on June 10, 1956. At this meeting the revised constitution and the revised bylaws of The Way were read and discussed in detail. Both were unanimously accepted as revised.

The revisions in the constitution included the auditing of the books once a year, the necessity of notifying board members of a meeting ten days in advance, and the number of members required to be present at a board meeting in order to transact business.

The Way Testimony of Belief was read, giving an outline of our learning at that time.

Dr. Wierwille was authorized upon a motion by Mr. Owens to officially appoint the Trustees for The Way, Inc. In actuality Ermal Owens and H. E. Wierwille had been carrying the responsibilities of Vice President and Secretary-Treasurer, respectively, for several years already.

Dr. Wierwille reported that the formation of a branch of The Way of Florida was under way. This then would bring the number of branches as of the summer of 1956 to a total of three in Ohio and two in Florida.

Mrs. Owens suggested that we should work toward establishing educational headquarters in various countries and teach them in their own countries and environments.

THE WAY TESTIMONY OF BELIEF

1. We believe in the Scriptures of the Old and New Testaments as verbally inspired by God and inerrant in the original writing and that they are of supreme, absolute and final authority in faith and life.

2. We believe in one God manifested as Father, Son and Holy Spirit.

3. We believe that Jesus Christ was conceived by the Holy Ghost, born of the Virgin Mary, and is true God and true man.

4. We believe that man was created in the image of God; that he sinned, and thereby brought immediate spiritual death, which is separation from God and also physical death which is the consequence of sin; and that all human beings are born with a sinful nature, and, in the case of those who reach moral accountability, are sinners in thought, word and deed.

5. We believe that Jesus Christ died for our sins according to the Scriptures, as a representative and substitute for us; and that all who believe in Him as their personal Lord and Saviour and that He was raised again from the dead are justified and made righteous on the ground of His eternal redemption.

6. We believe in the resurrection of the crucified body of our Lord, His ascension into heaven and in His present life there for us, as high priest and advocate.

7. We believe in the blessed hope of Christ's return, the personal return of our living Lord and Savior Jesus Christ.

8. We believe that all who receive by faith the Lord Jesus Christ are born again of the spirit of God, receiving eternal life and thereby children, sons of God.

9. We believe in the bodily resurrection of the just and the unjust, the everlasting blessedness of the saved, and the everlasting punishment of the lost.

10. We believe in the receiving of the fullness of the holy spirit, the power from on high, plus the corresponding nine workings of the spirit, for all born again believers.

11. We believe we are free in Christ Jesus to receive all that He accomplished for us by His substitution and promised us in His Word, according to our believing faith.

Dr. Wierwille gave a report of the World Missionary Teaching and Training Tour which took place from September 1955 to April 1956. He told how the doors to the various countries were miraculously opened to the ministry of The Way.

In July 1956 Dr. Wierwille gave a verbal report on the dilemma of foreign missions in India and tape-recorded it. This he published in the late 1956 issues of *The Way Magazine*. On the following two pages are excerpts from the November/December issue.

> Foreign missions have such little spontaneous spiritual expansion in them on a national basis. The Indian mission-Christians under the foreign system are 'spiritual hitch-hikers,' if not parasites. A spiritual starvation diet plus a foreign system of control always produces denationalized and nominal Christians. This foreign ecclesiastical mission system has led to spiritual sterility and in many cases is beginning to manifest itself in antagonism to the sponsors.
>
> More than a century of this same foreign system has so denationalized the Indians that they have been for the most part solely dependent upon foreign authority, foreign leadership and foreign money. This system has so isolated the Christians from their neighbors, the non-Christians, who are their fellow-countrymen that the common life of India has been hurt.
>
> All foreign systems tend to create the inevitable separateness which causes isolation and makes it almost impossible for the missionary to be identified with the culture of the people.
>
> Mission WORK in India has dwarfed the 'making of disciples of the Lord Jesus Christ.' The mission strategy has been and is a composite of better farming, medicine, education, chicken raising, livestock breeding, etc. etc., with the hope that SOMETIME the Christian life will become known and take root. They rationalize their actions by saying, 'We are interested in establishing goodwill and brotherhood, and not in establishing the Church and imposing our faith upon anyone.' Thus the missions gave education, rice, compounds, schools, churches, hospitals, mission houses, salaries, positions, free trips to Europe and America, denominations and most of all a foreign church administrative system of legislation and control.
>
> The very system that may give prestige to an American in America or character to an Englishman who is an Anglican in England means enslavement in India. For instance, can an Indian ever become the spiritual head of the Church of England?

CHRISTIAN WORK:
            SPIRITUAL VS. INSTITUTIONAL:

Facing this spiritual dearth, the missionaries tended to build their own colonies known as compounds where the adherents to the foreign mission system could live and thrive. Here they built houses for the missionaries, churches, schools, hospitals, leprosariums, orphanages, etc. etc., because the spiritual impetus and success was lacking, institutional work looked more tangible, solid and rewarding. The buildings were at least there and visible to the supporters and donors. If people were not becoming Christian in sufficient numbers, so what, at least a 'great work' was being done and the attitude of SOMEWHERE, SOMETIME, SOMEHOW they will become Christians permeated their thinking, attitudes and actions.

Thus having such meagre success in discipling people for Christianity, the institutional work was developed under the foreign system and the SECONDARY aims of Christianity became the PRIMARY concern of missionaries and missions systems. These multifarious activities relegated the real cause of missions into a secondary place and a casual but honest visitor to almost any mission station might inevitably come away with the idea that the Church is only a small portion of the mission, but that its MAJOR emphasis lies in mission WORK and not the Church.

As electricity flows best where there is a good point of contact, so does genuine Christianity. Indians have been MISSIONIZED, but not spiritually CHRISTIANIZED. Spiritual inabilities and defeats have caused foreign missions to steer away from the primary task of Christian missions to secondary undertakings. They sincerely and successfully in most instances defend the change-over to the more mundane things, secular, with spiritual connotations, not only to themselves, but to their home boards and the individual churches and people who sponsor them.

In September of 1956 our first foreign student arrived in Ohio. Joan Williams, Dr. and Mrs. J. S. Williams's daughter, came from Bombay to be with us and to receive her formal higher education at Defiance College in northern Ohio. Benjamin McWan also arrived from India the same month to attend a university in New York City for postgraduate study.

Classes on Power for Abundant Living had resumed already in May, a few weeks after we got back from abroad. Also, planning once more commenced immediately for The Way Biblical Seminary.

New printings of several studies were needed: *The Joy of His Fellowship, Paul's Thorn in the Flesh, Release From Your Prisons,* and *The Accuracy of the Bible.*

A new, fourth edition of *Receiving the Holy Spirit Today* was considered for publication at a cost of $1,000 to print. We also requested a reconditioned IBM Executive Typewriter, the price of which could vary between $300 and $450. This information was to be disseminated by the Board of Directors to the believers in their local areas.

Eddie and Donna Doersam of Columbus, Ohio, took the PFAL class in October 1956. This class began with "The Way Bible Campaign," where Dr. Wierwille showed some slides of the India Tour. Eddie tells of the thoughts he had of Dr. Wierwille: "He wasn't exactly what you would think of as a minister because he was talking about reaching up into Daddy's cookie jar and all this kind of stuff. I thought, 'Well, he's a little bit all right.' So we ended up taking the class, and we're here. We've been holding Bible studies, now known as Twig fellowships, in our home since sometime in 1957."

Eddie and Donna Doersam

Eddie's wife, Donna, relates, "We asked our minister if we could meet someplace in the church on Sunday night and study the Bible. He said not unless it was Methodist doctrine. So from there we started meeting in our believers' homes.

"At that time in The Way Ministry, fellowships were not meeting in the home. I think the first home fellowship began when Dr. Wierwille had received the holy spirit and led Mal and Jan George into speaking in tongues. Then Mal and Jan had one also when they were living at the Wierwille family farm, so ours was the first Way fellowship to start outside of the Wierwilles' and Jan and Mal's homes. After we went to church on Sunday mornings, we would meet in our home with another couple and a girl from the church. Then we would go around our circle of five and practice speaking in tongues. We got bold in speaking in tongues and interpretation, overcoming any fears of doing so. Then we talked to people in the church about taking the class and got the first class together, which involved mostly people from our church. And so we continued meeting in our home."

Donna continues, "The church got so cold with us that we quit going; but I continued to go to Sunday school, because we had a son that was around two years old then, and I wanted him to have some type of teaching. My sister made the suggestion that we go over to Van Wert, Ohio, so we started traveling to Van Wert every Sunday, which was a three-hour drive from Columbus. This, I think, helped us to become more stable with the ministry. You have to realize that outside of the class, there were no ministry activities to keep people involved and active so it was easy for people to get pulled back into their church. So, I believe that our weekly trips to Van Wert helped us to become more faithful and steadfast."

The Troy class and class graduates in the spring of 1958

Dr. Wierwille taught classes in Ohio in Piqua, Troy, and Xenia. Right after the class in Columbus that Eddie and Donna Doersam were in, Dr. Wierwille taught one in November in Troy, Ohio. Donna shares, "I drove back and forth every night for two weeks, except Saturday night, which was 'bath night,' Dr. Wierwille always said. So I had another class right away. Eddie didn't because he worked at night. Then the next year, Dr. Wierwille taught a class in Troy in May of 1957, and we drove back and forth to that one. But anyway, what kept us faithful is that we kept contact with the ministry that taught us the Word. Of course, more activities did develop as they moved to the farm, not so much in the Columbus area, but in New Knoxville where there was summer school available."

George Jess

George Jess, a barber in Piqua, Ohio, took the class in October 1956. Lawrence Dale, a mail carrier from Troy, Ohio, along with another recent graduate of the class, went to the pastors of churches in the Troy/Piqua area so each of them could get names of five people who would be interested in more in-depth Bible study. One of the pastors gave George Jess's name to Lawrence. George commented, "I was a real worker in the church, and my pastor wasn't afraid of losing me. He gave Lawrence my name for my benefit. He knew I had applied to Moody Bible Institute to go there to study. It was one of the best schools I knew of at the time for real fundamental evangelistic work.

"I stayed in the denomination after I took the PFAL class because at that time Dr. Wierwille encouraged people to take the Word back to their churches and be the best workers they ever saw. There must have been twenty-five graduates of the class at the church after I took it.

"I didn't start going up to Van Wert for Sunday night fellowship until 1960, when the Wierwilles were on Washington Street. Previously I had been tithing to the church. But after I took the PFAL class, I stopped giving to the church and supported the teaching ministry of The Way because its message filled the greatest need of the world. The deacon of my church couldn't understand it at all, as his life was the denomination. But the pastor, he understood it very well."

At this time my brother-in-law and sister, Dick and Dee Fischbach, and their daughter, Jean, lived in Punta Gorda, Florida, the location of the southeastern United States branch of The Way. This was where Ermal and Dorothy Owens had started witnessing in nearby Fort Myers and where the first class in Florida took place. Soon the Fischbachs moved to Arcadia, which became the center of The Way fellowship meetings for the next four and a half years, in the Fischbach home. Dr. Wierwille then taught four PFAL classes in Arcadia. That Arcadia group was one big happy family in the Word.

George M. Lamsa

When we met Dr. George M. Lamsa, he had already translated the New Testament from Aramaic into English. Since Lamsa's New Testament was available through the Aramaic Bible Society, Dr. Wierwille had purchased a copy and was very interested in hearing from its translator. So in February 1957 he wrote to Dr. Lamsa in care of the Aramaic Bible Society, inviting him to our home in Van Wert.

Dr. Wierwille explained, "Dr. Lamsa, a native Assyrian and noted scholar, played a great part in my life to the end that I, having studied Greek and being able to read Greek, discovered there were still words in the New Testament Greek texts that were not Greek. They came from an older language. As I worked this, Dr. Lamsa took me back to show me that Aramaic was the language in which the original scriptures were written."

A scripture verse that Dr. Lamsa was particularly instrumental in explaining to us was Mark 15:34. Before meeting Dr. Lamsa, Dr. Wierwille would not preach on this verse because it didn't make sense to him; it didn't fit with the rest of the Word: "And at the ninth hour Jesus cried with a loud voice, saying, Eloi, Eloi, lama sabachthani? which is, being interpreted, My God, my God, why hast thou forsaken me?"

So many years when Dr. Wierwille was asked to teach on this verse at our citywide three-hour Good Friday services, he would ask one of the other ministers to trade topics with him. But Dr. Lamsa's translation from Aramaic fits just so beautifully; it expresses what other scriptures also say. "And at the ninth hour, Jesus cried out with a loud voice, saying Eli, Eli, lemana, shabakthani! which means, My God, my God, for this I was spared!" It was a cry of triumph, as Jesus Christ saw he was fulfilling the purpose that God had set before him to do—giving his life for our redemption and wholeness. It was such a thrill to our hearts to understand that great truth. You know how much progress you've made in your believing when you've gotten the truth of that Word.

Dr. Lamsa spent a couple of weeks with us in April 1957, at which time he completed proofreading galley proofs of his English translation of the Aramaic text of the Old Testament. He had printed a special leather edition of this Bible of which he later gave us copy #36 with the inscription, "To Dr. and Mrs. Victor Paul Wierwille with God's blessing and my sincere thanks for your interest. October 1957.
George M. Lamsa."

In late August and early September 1957 Dr. Lamsa was again with us for one week of meetings. Dr. Wierwille stated, "Dr. George M. Lamsa really helped me put things together, including the first Aramaic syllabus. I still have the original grammar we all started with in summer school. Then as the years have gone by, scholars started to realize the seriousness of 'Syriac' [as Aramaic is commonly called]. Dr. Lamsa's contribution to The Way Ministry and the world by giving us greater understanding of the Bible because of his Aramaic background has been immeasurable."

The first Way "logo," designed in early 1957

In May of 1957 another lovely daughter, Sara Kathryn, was born. And so all our five children had been born before we left the church in Van Wert.

Our family's 1957 holiday card

213

International Outreach

June 16–30, 1957, we held our first international PFAL class in Van Wert with three men from England: Ronald Hooley, Herbert Stott, and Donald Bailey. There were two from India among the students: Joan Williams and Benjamin McWan. Our Mary also was now old enough to be in the class. This class concluded with a three-day international convention. Then immediately following, July 1–12, Dr. Wierwille taught the Advanced Class to twenty-three new students, including the three from England, two from India, and one from Australia, Rev. Eric Watson. In August Benjamin McWan from India was appointed as director of the Eastern Division International. Earlier in 1957, Eric Watson had been appointed as director of the Western Division International.

Our first international PFAL class

In August Dr. Wierwille submitted his letter of resignation from St. Peter's Church to go into the full-time research, teaching, and fellowship ministry of The Way as of December 1957. Of course, there was also a pressured undercurrent from the hierarchy of the denomination to do so since the publishing of *The Dilemma of Foreign Missions in India*.

The following is Dr. Wierwille's letter of resignation to the St. Peter's congregation:

St. Peter's Evangelical and Reformed Church
Corner of Main and Harrison Streets
Van Wert, Ohio

Victor Paul Wierwille, Th. D., Pastor
109 South Harrison Street

August 7, 1957

To the Consistory of The
St. Peter's E. & R. Church
            and to
The Congregation:

    Greetings to you in the precious Name of our Lord and Saviour Jesus Christ!

    Because I believe God would have me devote more and more time to the non-sectarian, interdenominational work of The Way, Inc., International; to writing and teaching, and thus I would have to be gone from the local Congregation for weeks and even months at a time, therefore, after all these years of service in your midst, I lovingly tender my resignation as your Pastor at this time.

    Never has a minister appreciated His Congregation and people more nor has a minister had more joy in serving a people. I shall forever be indebted to Almighty God and you for His bringing us together and for your accepting us and my ministry. It has been your love, prayer and understanding that has allowed me the freedom to have the hours and years of the disciplined study of His Word, which is responsible for the ministry in The Word which God has seen fit to extend to us by His mercy and grace. I have spoken of you to people the world over and I shall continue to tell them of you. You have been to us a wonderful congregation and it has been in your midst that our present ministry on The Word of God has unfolded and come into fruition. May God's continued blessing be on you now, and may His reward be abundant to each of you when we shall all appear before Him in the Resurrection.

    Naturally we love you with a great love after these many years with you, and we pray that you will send us forth with your love and prayers, that our lives may be a blessing to His children around the world.

                                        Sincerely,
                                      In His Service,
VPW/rb   Victor Paul Wierwille

P.S. Accepted by unanimous vote of the Consistory, August 7, 1957. The Consistory furthermore accepted December 8, 1957 or anytime previous to this which would be most convenient to Dr. Wierwille as his final Sunday in our Congregation.

While we were preparing for this major transition in our lives from our lifelong involvement in the denomination to going independent into The Way Ministry, Joan Williams, the daughter of our dear Indian friends, was developing a serious romantic relationship with a young man in her second year at Defiance College. Just before he left to go home for the December holidays, the young man broke off the relationship. Because of her great disappointment and her cultural background, she became very despondent and ended her life. This came as very shocking, very sad news to us on Christmas Eve, 1957. The Williams family were most understanding of the situation but also very grieved. We buried her body in the cemetery in Defiance according to their wishes.

Dr. Wierwille said, "Those years in Van Wert [in the church there] I was just beginning to put things together, little by little, beginning to see the greatness of it. I just can't put it into words."

He added, "In the early days of our ministry many Christians magnified sin beyond redemption. We need to see what we have in Christ Jesus.

"There were people around and events. God brought people to me, led me places and showed me things in those years in Van Wert. It was an exciting time, a learning time. God just kept leading me and encouraging me."

In the Van Wert church we had people who worked with us and people who worked against us because some would not accept the extent of the Word Dr. Wierwille was teaching. As Dr. Wierwille said, "They all believed in being born again, no trouble about that; but that is the only part they wanted to know. It's like what the Apostle Paul said: he could speak nothing among them except Christ and him crucified." When we moved away from the local church, it was not a great pressure, not a great deal of hurt feelings. Our local congregation would have loved for us to stay, but it was time to move on.

Pastoral Register from the Evangelical and Reformed Church, Van Wert, Ohio:

Name	Pastorate Commenced	Pastorate Ended
Victor Paul Wierwille	June 1, 1944	December 8, 1957

Before we left the church in Van Wert, Dr. Wierwille had asked twelve people to support, work, and pray with us for one year. Not all twelve were members of the church. Dr. Wierwille later reflected, "Now if I had to do it again, I would do what Paul did—take all my people with me across the street, 'to the school of Tyrannus,' or whatever, and teach the Word to anyone who wanted to hear. But at that time I didn't want to hurt anybody's feelings in my denomination, even though they cared little about hurting mine."

Dr. Wierwille expressed himself further. "We did not allow them [the denominational synod] to control our lives; that's why I had to resign from the denomination. The only way I could have stayed would have been to give the denomination control over what I taught, what I spoke, and what I did." I thought about what Glenn Clark's daughter had shared about her father: "Strains of new ideas other than those of the churches were admitted [to Glenn Clark's work]. My father was not a minister, so he neither had to defend the existing church nor was he called on to defend a falling away of the church." Just as Glenn Clark took a stand, Dr. Wierwille was taking a stand. Dr. Wierwille knew, "It's when people take a stand that things get done." It was this conviction that prompted Dr. Wierwille to leave his pastorate and, as an act of believing, launch independently into the full-time Way Ministry. "If you're going to build anything, it takes stick-to-itiveness. The same in moving God's Word. You have to stay faithful. It's the one great requirement of a steward," Dr. Wierwille exhorted.

The last Sunday at St. Peter's Evangelical and Reformed Church was December 8, 1957. After so many years and so many profound experiences with that congregation, this was an emotion-filled day in our lives— concluding thirteen jam-packed years.

After reading the Scripture lesson from Ephesians 2:1-21, Dr. Wierwille prayed:

Our Heavenly Father, unto whom every heart is open and unto whom each and every desire is known, we Thy people have gathered before Thee this hour with thanksgiving in our hearts that Thou has called us out of darkness into the marvelous light of the gospel of redemption and salvation. We thank Thee our Heavenly Father that down through the years Thou hast taught us Thy Word, Thy Word which is a lamp unto our feet and a light unto our pathway. We thank Thee our Father that Thou art the great, good shepherd and that in Jesus Christ we live and move and have our being and that he is closer to us than hands or feet or the air we are breathing. We thank Thee this day our Father for Thy constant protection and care and guidance and love. I thank Thee that even at times when we were far away from Thee, wandered from the sheepfold, Thou did constantly by Thy love, call us back to forgive us of our sin and cleanse from all unrighteousness and to again reestablish our fellowship with Thee. Thank you, Father.

Thoughts he expressed early in the service were, "On a morning like this, human words seem frail and inadequate to express what a person has deep within his heart." Dr. Wierwille expressed that he was thankful for the gospel's being taught boldly in Van Wert and stressed faithfulness to God and the Word.

Dr. Wierwille talked about the Apostle Paul, who wrote to people as his children because he had led them into salvation. He never took anything that didn't belong to him, nor did he ever ask anything they could not give. And his testimony was his walk among them.

After the offertory prayer, our son Don sang "The Stranger of Galilee" before the teaching entitled "If I Only Had One Sermon to Preach," a title Dr. Wierwille borrowed from a book of compiled sermons from all over the world which he had read years before and which held great significance to him.

The following are some of the contents of Dr. Wierwille's final sermon at St. Peter's Church:

Most believers do not know what they have in Christ. . . that's the reason believers are still seeking.

A man must be born again of God's Spirit (I Corinthians 2:12).

So then faith cometh by hearing, and hearing by the word of God (Romans 10:17).

The Word of God liveth and abideth forever.

It is the Word of God that builds believing—only the Word.

Now (right now) are we ambassadors for Christ (II Corinthians 5:20).

Ephesians 2:1, Colossians 1:11—past tense.

Sonship rights.

Sin makes cowards of us all. Are we still sin conscious, knowing our sonship rights?

You and I are what God says we are, and we have what He says we have.

May God bless you.

Before the final, short prayer Dr. Wierwille announced, "There are a lot of out-of-town guests. Mrs. Wierwille and I will be eating lunch at The Whitehall Inn a little later. We'd be delighted to have you join us."

A New Headquarters

While we were preparing to leave the Van Wert pastorate, we had found new housing for our family, as well as for The Way Ministry, at 649 South Washington Street, still in Van Wert. This house was an outstanding example of the Queen Anne style of architecture, with its three-story round tower, fretted windows, elaborate bay window, and distinctive pillared and balustered front porch. And we had all the room we needed.

Parking space was readily available along one side of the street, as well as in our large backyard. The location and house were perfectly suited to use as our family home, Dr. Wierwille's and Rhoda's offices, and a meeting place for the many Way activities.

Although this house was for sale the entire three years we rented it, from December 1957 through January 1961, the house didn't sell until just after we moved in February 1961. God answered our prayers so that we could keep it as long as we needed it. Dr. Wierwille always credited this fact to the believing of Uncle Harry and me.

Our spacious home in Van Wert after moving from the parsonage

We moved into this home the week after the final Sunday service at St. Peter's. Dr. Wierwille was now free from all denominational responsibilities and pressure.

Uncle Harry said, "The in-depth teaching really got going in 1957 when he [Dr. Wierwille] resigned from the organized church. It wasn't a surprise, but then, really it was. I became vitally interested in his work at that point. I wanted him to succeed in his venture."

We began our independent undertaking by having meetings in this Washington Street home on Thursday evenings and late Sunday afternoons. The first Thursday evening fellowship was held on December 19, and the first Sunday meeting, on December 29, 1957. When Dr. Wierwille was away teaching Power for Abundant Living classes, someone else from our fellowship was responsible to lead the meeting and teach.

Our fellowships were small at first. On weeknights we may have had only three or four persons including Rhoda and me—enough for manifestations. On Sundays, Eddie and Donna Doersam with a carload of other believers came from Columbus, Ohio. They were very faithful the entire three years we lived there. Some local people were also: Mal and Jan George, Dorothy Owens (Ermal Owens was traveling much of the time), Rhoda Becker, Dan and Marilyn Friedly, Dick and Dee Fischbach, and Ivor and Evelyn Jones, all of whom to this day remain active in the work of The Way Ministry, except the latter two who have both fallen asleep.

Mr. H. E. Wierwille and Mr. Ermal Owens, our two original Trustees, were faithful with us as long as they had breath. They were so supportive in helping Dr. Wierwille carry this ministry through this crucial, transitional period of time during the late 1950s. It was an act of believing on the part of all of us to get this ministry to take root as an entity independent of the organized denomination.

We prayed about and discussed at length how to get The Way Ministry outreach into every nation. Some of our most fervent supporters and faithful believers from the other branches, such as Dad Wierwille and Dr. E. E. Higgins, had recently fallen asleep, which was costly to the Lord and to us. Dr. Higgins had been a great mainstay for God and this ministry in Chicago. During her lifetime she had inherited a farm which she in turn willed to Dr. Wierwille. She hadn't realized that the will which conferred that farm to her contained a clause stating that in case she had no offspring, the farm would revert to the family. So although Dr. Wierwille could not inherit the farm, he appreciated Dr. Higgins's loving thoughts in this gesture.

Nurturing Growth

Dr. Wierwille kept sending studies out with letters to our leadership so that more of the Word could get to the home fellowships. As of January 13, 1958, the following people were leading fellowships in the various areas:

VAN WERT OH
Mal and Jan George
Sharon Swoveland
Lloyd and Evelyn Ulrey

NEW LYME OH
Ray and Vera Kaderly
Ruth Rose

COLUMBUS OH
Al Waibel
Ed and Donna Doersam

TROY OH
Lawrence Dale
Franklin Shroyer, Jr.
Louise Shroyer

COVINGTON OH
Paul Filbrun
Charles Perrine
Mrs. Max Wolfe

ARCADIA FL
Dick and Dee Fischbach

The head Presbyters were Ronald Hooley in England and J. S. Williams in India.

Foreign students studying in America were Benjamin McWan and Irene Anson from India and Drumond Thom from South Africa.

On May 22, 1958, five months after leaving his pastorate at St. Peter's Church, Dr. Wierwille's name was erased from the roll of ministers of the Evangelical and Reformed denomination, the usual procedure.

When Dr. Wierwille had resigned from the denomination, Uncle Harry decided to put forth his greatest effort to see his brother succeed in his new venture of the work of The Way Ministry research, teaching, and fellowship. On June 9, 1958, H. E. Wierwille sent out the following letter.

Don was our first child to graduate from high school. The class of 1958, of which he was president, had 107 students.

Dear Grads of Power for Abundant Living:

I would love to have come up to see you personally and talk to you about what I am going to write, but since I am in the midst of having an auction sale to dispose of the greater part of my furniture so I may be able to put in about 5 days weekly in the advancement of the Lord's work, it is therefore impossible to see you personally at this time.

As you no doubt already know, the next class on "Power for Abundant Living" starts Sunday, June 15th, at the Grange Hall, Van Wert County Fair Grounds at 7 P.M.

I have been part time in many of these classes for the past three years but I want to tell you that every time V.P. teaches a class that it gets better and better and these Bible truths that he shows us from the Word of God become more astounding than ever.

There are many other truths that God has revealed to him since the original class and he has added them to the other teachings. Such as: What part of the Bible is FOR our learning and what part is specifically TO us today. When the Word of God is rightly divided without anyone's private interpretation then it really becomes more wonderful as a person reads the Word and believes it. A person really must read the Word of God daily and believe it to greatly benefit from the Word and the great Power that is available.

For your own benefit I sincerely hope that you will attend every session, as this is the only class that will be taught in Van Wert this year and it could easily be the last one in Van Wert as there are so many places in the U.S.A., Canada and other foreign countries where they are calling for the teaching on the truth of the Word of God without any private interpretation. The Word of God is so dynamic that the human mind can not grasp it but the people that are filled with the Power from on High can grasp it and act upon it, if they so will.

Sincerely hope to see you frequently at these sessions and may we all become more closely associated so we may be able to help advance these great truths on the power of God so other people over the nation and the world may also enjoy these truths.

"ONLY ONE LIFE, TWILL SOON BE PAST, ONLY WHAT IS DONE FOR CHRIST WILL LAST."

Bless you real good!

Sincerely in Him,
H. E. Wierwille
3 John 2.

    Our Board of Directors worked so faithfully with our Trustees, seeing the Word of God taught and benefiting God's people by their believing action.
    The Trustees, Ermal Owens, H. E. Wierwille, and Dr. Wierwille, made a concerted effort to make known what was then available in this independent work of the ministry to interested students. The following excerpts are from a letter the Trustees wrote "Followers of The Way" that June.

> . . . The summer sessions on PFAL will soon be starting. Give yourself a refresher by attending the class in Van Wert, June 15–27. If you were one who took it a few years ago you should by all means take it again. Dr. Wierwille has added so much to the lectures and you would really be blessed. Also you ought to get at least one other person to come to the class. Our grads are our only recruiting agency. . . .
>
> The Advanced Class on PFAL will this year be held in Troy, Ohio, June 30–July 12. Requirements are a bold determination to learn the Word in order to do the Word, the will and work of God. We want no shirkers but workers, so as to be able to help others also. . . .
>
> Sincerely,
> In His Service,
> The Board of Trustees

At this June 15, 1958, Board of Directors' meeting the question of whether we should join The National Association of Evangelicals was brought up by the President, Dr. Wierwille. He thought that being affiliated with a group might be stimulating. Associating with a large group could possibly also add credibility. It was suggested that the matter be tabled until we knew more details and were able to study the constitution and bylaws of that organization. At the October 19, 1958, meeting the issue was again brought up as a part of "old business." Ermal Owens made a motion to again table the matter until the next meeting and that literature about the association should be sent to all of the members of the board so each one could become informed on the issue.

The teaching of Power for Abundant Living classes was discussed in detail at the June meeting. The Board of Trustees suggested teaching the foundational information up to receiving the holy spirit and then, within a limited period of time, possibly two or three weeks, teach an advanced class on receiving the holy spirit and the nine manifestations. After they tossed that idea around for a while, they concluded that the Power for Abundant Living class should include the receiving of holy spirit and, if necessary, keep the third week open for more teaching on holy spirit, depending on how fast a class was able to receive the information.

At this meeting Dr. Wierwille again stressed the importance of "the undershepherding plan" to help students after they finished the Foundational Class. There had been so much taught in the class that such a plan would assist a new student in making the class material a part of his or her life. He also brought up the subject of *The Way Magazine* as well as our mimeographed studies and monthly newsletters. The magazine format required a lot of time in our already busy schedule. He wondered if we were doing an effective job sending out the studies and letters or if we should go entirely to the magazine format. With so many things such as classes going on, it was voted to publish *The Way Magazine* quarterly and *The Way Newsletter* during the intervening months.

In late July of 1958 the Reverend Vernon Opperman fell asleep. Vernon, whom I mentioned earlier, was the lifelong friend of Dr. Wierwille's. They had gone to public school, college, and seminary together, and were ordained to the Christian ministry on the same occasion. Dr. Wierwille was honored that the Opperman family asked him to assist in Vernon's memorial service, and Dr. Wierwille gave Rev. Opperman's widow his own reserved cemetery plot in Pilger Ruhe Cemetery at New Knoxville for the burial of Vernon's body.

Eric Watson, The Way Ministry's Western Division leader, had been in Hawaii, Fiji, and Samoa; and in September 1958, he was ministering the great power of God in New Zealand. Dr. Wierwille had Eric minister in these places because these were Eric's areas of concern, interest, and need. It was not unusual in these countries to see supernatural power at work because frequently fire walkers were the religious leaders. Dr. Wierwille had taught well to discern by which spirit such workings were accomplished. The rule is given in I Corinthians 12:7: "But the manifestation of the Spirit is given to every man to profit withal." What profit is there in fire walking? In God's Word it is a very detestable act attributed to our spiritual adversary.

At this time Dr. Wierwille organized Sunday morning evangelistic teams, under the direction of Maurice Williman of Van Wert, to go door-to-door witnessing in the cities of Dayton and Columbus, Ohio. The teams were designed to spread information about the Bible and to let people know that they could learn about it in the Power for Abundant Living class. With this type of outreach, these two local areas could get Way fellowships started. This was another one of Dr. Wierwille's many ideas to expand the ministry.

Dr. Wierwille endured some trying times. He wrote a personal letter to "My Dear Friend," the believers. "We must of necessity pull together talking the Biblical accuracy and The Way Ministry. We are beset on every hand by the adversary, but perhaps none greater than the material defeats." Dr. Wierwille was very aware of the passing of time. The inherited farm was demanding some of his time so the farm could be maintained and not become run-down. So while much work was needed at the farm, he felt pulled because he wanted more time to work in God's Word. Others would have to come forward to do the physical labor.

Dr. Wierwille's weekly newspaper column, "The Way I See It," August 1963

In the month of September we made the following offer in our publications: For a donation of ten dollars to the ministry, a person would be sent a free copy of Kenyon's great book *The Father and His Family*, if requested; for a gift of twenty-five dollars one could request the book by E. W. Bullinger, *How to Enjoy the Bible*.

At the October 1958 Board of Directors' meeting all the members felt that it would be a good move to have Dr. Wierwille write a weekly article in the *Van Wert Times Bulletin*, a daily newspaper, and then gradually try to syndicate these to other newspapers.

The board again discussed the possibility of having a seven-day Way Family Camp the next summer. Most of the board members thought it was a good idea, but again we were in uncharted waters and needed more time to think through the details. So the matter was tabled until a later date.

Regarding the starting of The Way Biblical Seminary, Dr. Wierwille announced that he had set up a planning meeting in the New Lyme, Ohio, area for December 7 and 8. He invited Dr. Lamsa to be our guest at that meeting.

At this New Lyme meeting, Dr. Wierwille pointed out that each presiding elder of The Way branches should encourage the people of his area to save their Ohio sales tax stamps and send them in to The Way Headquarters. At this time, nonprofit organizations could get a certain percentage return when cashing them in.

An Ohio sales tax stamp

Two issues we discussed pertained to the fee for PFAL and how Dr. Wierwille could best spend his time. Some of the members of the board recommended charging a registration fee for the class plus a class fee. Others of the members felt that Dr. Wierwille was spending too much time traveling and teaching PFAL classes and that it might be a better use of Dr. Wierwille's time if he stayed at the South Washington Street Headquarters and got some of his writings into printed form as well as worked on new material. Ermal Owens suggested that the Board of Directors should have a meeting the following month so some of these matters could be decided after everyone had time to think and pray about them.

On November 5, 1958, Dr. Wierwille sent out the following letter to our entire mailing list, addressing it to "Dear Follower of The Way." A point of particular interest is that this letter contains the first written reference to Dr. Wierwille's research on what happens after believers die. His study was first published under the title "Do the Dead Live Before the Resurrection?"

In another letter, also dated November 5, 1958, Dr. Wierwille wrote to the people living closer to our home. The two letters follow.

THE WAY, INC., INTERNATIONAL
649 S. Washington Street
Van Wert, Ohio

Dr. Victor Paul Wierwille, President

November 5, 1958

Dear Follower of The Way:

Truth is forever on the scaffold. It is much easier for the rank and file to believe a lie and a half-truth (which is no truth) can be much more easily propagated than genuine truth. Reason? Satan will not tend to interfer with a lie or half-truth and people will keep many more of their so called friends.

The Way is dedicated, by those of us its leaders, to THE TRUTH as it is presented in the Word of God without favor to anyone or any group. To be true followers of The Way not only requires dedication but persistence in faithfulness.

So many people "blow hot" for a little while and then they "cool off." Reason? The Word's greatness is not genuinely real to them. They hold the truth but the truth does not hold them. There are few who believe the greatness of God's Word. That of all His works it is the greatest and that we will be judged by The Word, therefore, surely we must continue to "Study to show thyself approved unto God, a workman that needeth not to be ashamed, rightly dividing the word of truth."

In Jeremiah 15:16 we read "THY WORDS were found,...and THY WORD was unto me the joy and rejoicing of mine heart:..." In John 17:8,14 we read "For I have given unto them the WORDS which thou gavest me;...I have given them thy WORD:..." and then we read "...and the world hath hated them." Those who follow THE WAY and whose hearts, joy and rejoice in God's Word will quickly be caused to come to a shocking fact, namely that they will be in isolated positions, and even hated by those who formerly acted friendly. But, if all forsake us, He and His Word will remain faithful. Such must have been Paul's experience also according to II Timothy 1:15.

Philip said to the Ethiopian "...UNDERSTANDEST THOU WHAT THOU READEST?"

The Ethiopian said "HOW CAN I EXCEPT SOME MAN SHOULD GUIDE ME?..." Many years ago and even today at times I ask myself, who taught me to believe this? Where did I get that idea? And what a shock it is to realize how much we have imbibed from man and tradition, and how LITTLE we have really received directly from The Word of God. I am thankful in my soul and willing always to give up any idea or thought or concept I may hold, which is contradictory to the Word. I give it up gladly with thanksgiving in my soul, that God is so patient, and I have learned beyond question that "sincerity is no guarantee for truth."

I have written frankly and searched the scriptures deeply hour upon hour in endless labor to be able to share with you the past months of work regarding "Do the Dead Live Before the Resurrection." Your faithful and accurate study and readying thereof will be a blessing to your soul. Please advise me of any inaccuracy in any way for we are praying that very soon someone or some group of loved ones will make available its publication in booklet form.

May you have a wonderful Thanksgiving, being thankful above all for your salvation, for being filled with the holy spirit and for the greatness of God's Word. I thank God for those who are faithful to the ministry of The Word, and try to be very good especially unto those of the "Household of faith." Galatians 6:10.

With Thanksgiving,
In His Service,
Victor Paul Wierwille

VPW/rb

November 5, 1958

Dear Friend in Christ:

Greetings to you from Headquarters in the Name of Jesus Christ. I thank God for the ministry of The Word and after all these past months here at The Way Center from which this work is spearheaded I believe that people need beyond anything a more detailed teaching and understanding of The Word, ministering to one another, praying for people and situations and learning to effectively use the manifestation of the spirit. This should continue to be our chief concern.

As you may know I have for years now, off and on, been working on a "free and literal translation according to usage" of certain sections of The Word. I may soon begin to share these things on Sunday Night. We may start with Ephesians.

From November 18th to 25th I will be with B.G. [Leonard] in Canada for a Missionary Convention. Eric Watson will be back from his 7 months afield and the big news is he is getting married to Mona Nelson, one of B.G.'s Congregation. Enroute to Calgary I will stop at Denver to meet with Dr. Stemme of Burton College and Seminary to discuss with him The Way Biblical Seminary.

Thanksgiving is on Thursday, November 27th. I will be back for Thanksgiving and I was wondering if you would like to have a special Thanksgiving Service that night at Headquarters?

If we could get another 6 families interested in our local group meetings who would join with us week after week in fellowship as well as the giving of their tithes for this work and ministry we would have a greater group than we have even now. Although I sure thank God for your faithfulness and you know I have to teach whenever and wherever God opens doors. Some weeks and months our people are gone a great deal, but I know I do, and others do the same, even when we are out teaching we arrange for our tithe to be in every Sunday night.

When it comes to our expenses to operate Headquarters I have complained only about the light bill from Ohio Power. They charge us commercial rates which is morally not fair as far as I am concerned but they are a utility monopoly and they have legal rights backed by the Utilities Commission of Ohio so what can we do.

I have also been thinking about putting the Wierwille family back on an $80.00 a week schedule, but to be real truthful to try to run our family of 7 of us on much less than a hundred and to maintain the dignity that we as leaders of The Way must have, because of the nature of our position, it would be real difficult. We as a family apparently have many obligations which a similar sized family would not necessarily have.

Well we have no complaints only thanksgiving. I have never felt better in my life, in the work of Christ than I feel now. We are free, we can walk in love and in unity with those who want to love us and walk with us. We are free to change when God's Word shows us where we must change. Oh what a joy to be free and to walk in liberty.

Another thing I know is true that if we would have our Bible teaching fellowship on Sunday Morning instead of Sunday Night we would have many more in attendance. Having a family I know what a chore it is to get the children out and ready on Sunday Night when they should be put to bed early. But, we are a pioneering group and as such we may at times have to push ourselves to do certain things that the more or less nominal Christians would not do.

Well God bless you for your prayers and help for The Way ministry and the whole cause of Christ.

Sincerely,
In His Service,
Victor Paul Wierwille

At the November 16 meeting of the Board of Directors we voted to have a one-week camp the next summer from August 1–8, 1959, and that Mal and Jan George were to be in charge. The Georges were prepared and gave a detailed presentation of their tentative plan for the camp.

Lawrence Dale spoke of the value of getting a radio ministry started, another issue which had been on the back burner for a while. Lawrence was also interested in personally paying for advertising PFAL classes in *Christian Life* magazine, this publication being the best-known and widely circulated Christian magazine at that time. We were considering the effectiveness of advertising in several Christian periodicals, Dr. Wierwille having in hand information on the cost for some of these.

It was also on Dr. Wierwille's agenda to discuss making tape recordings of the Power for Abundant Living class available to those who could not attend every class session. The board suggested that it would be a good idea to have a graduate of PFAL accompany the recordings to help clarify the teaching and to answer any questions on these makeup sessions.

The Way Board of Directors suggested that a committee of publications should be appointed by the Trustees. This committee would keep track of our supply of books and reprints needed and also find a way to pay for new printings.

The Columbus branch agreed soon after the board meeting to pay for one thousand copies of *The Joy of His Fellowship*.

Our New Year's retreat started on Friday night, January 2, 1959, with Bishop Pillai joining Dr. Wierwille as a resource leader. We held this time of fellowship and fun at the Mote Recreation Center in Piqua, Ohio, continuing all day Saturday and closing on Sunday morning. Sleeping accommodations in a nearby hotel were available, or some of us could commute from our homes. The local believers furnished food for the leadership, and the other people brought their own food or ate at restaurants.

The cover of The Joy of His Fellowship

Foundational Classes on Power for Abundant Living
1958
(taught by Dr. Wierwille unless noted otherwise)

January	Fort Myers, Florida
February	Arcadia, Florida
	Fort Myers, Florida
April	Columbus, Ohio
May	Troy, Ohio
June	Van Wert, Ohio
August	New Lyme, Ohio
	Kitchener, Ontario, Canada—Mal George
	Covington, Ohio
	Piqua, Ohio
September	Dayton, Ohio
October	Columbus, Ohio
	Urbana, Ohio—Mal George taught during the days; Dr. Wierwille taught during the nights
November	Jamaica, New York

By September 1958 we had the following established groups:

Abroad—in England and India; also in Canada

The United States—in Arcadia and Fort Myers, Florida; Columbus, Troy, Covington, Celina, St. Marys, Piqua, Lima, New Lyme, Van Wert, and Dayton, Ohio; Monroe, Indiana

---

From June 30 to July 11 in Troy, Ohio, Dr. Wierwille taught an advanced class on Power for Abundant Living. Then in August, for the first time, we had two PFAL classes being taught simultaneously: one in New Lyme, Ohio, taught by Dr. Wierwille, and one in Kitchener, Ontario, Canada, taught by Mal George.

A class at Troy, Ohio, starting on January 4, 1959, included five people from Calgary, Alberta, Canada. Dr. Wierwille announced at the New Year's retreat that he believed this class would be "the best ever." He went on to say, "Do yourself a favor—attend this class. It will be instructed beyond any class I have ever taught. Some of you have not sat in the class since before my world tour. You especially should come. Your heart would be thrilled. It is far beyond anything I taught for four or five years.... God's power is in this class and, praise the Lord, His hand is on this ministry."

A Permanent Headquarters

Dr. Wierwille called a special meeting of the Board of Directors on April 5, 1959, "to consider what can best be done to facilitate growth of the spiritual program of The Way." While he was always open to and welcomed suggestions, the people who were working with him knew that their suggestions had to be spiritually sound.

At this board meeting the first item of discussion was The Way's joining The National Association of Evangelicals, an issue tabled at a 1958 board meeting. We had made a full study of this organization and found that their very basic doctrinal statement included the belief in the deity of our Lord Jesus Christ. By this time in the ministry, we knew that this was not Biblically accurate, so we voted not to join.

The President, Dr. Wierwille, then gave his report about the work which had been accomplished since the November 16, 1958, meeting:

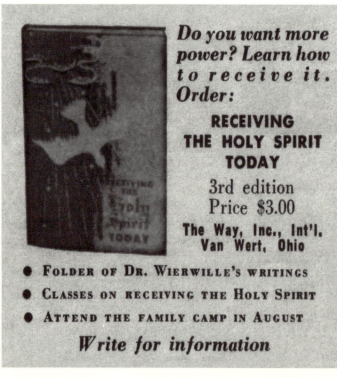

A magazine ad for Receiving the Holy Spirit Today

1. Planning had been done toward the starting of The Way Biblical Seminary. This seminary was always uppermost in Dr. Wierwille's mind so that he might have students to train, committing God's Word to "faithful men, who shall be able to teach others also." We needed physical facilities to do so. Dr. Wierwille stated that when the students had graduated we would not send them out ourselves, but that they would have to find their own place of ministry.

2. Advertising the Power for Abundant Living classes and the book *Receiving the Holy Spirit Today* was under way. We had advertisements in *Christian Life* magazine and *The Sermon Builder* magazine. Through the great interest which Dr. David du Plessis, a leader in the Pentecostal churches, had shown in the book, requests were coming in from all over the world.

Dr. Wierwille explained at this special board meeting, "It is important that we keep our mind on the Word so that we can move the teaching of the Word. A number of people have come to members of the Board of Trustees requesting that this meeting be called in order to see what can be done to move this ministry and help spread it."

When we rented our South Washington Street home in Van Wert, we didn't know how temporary this location would be, as we were very focused on getting the ministry up and running, self-supporting, and growing. Now it was becoming very apparent to us that a larger and more permanent headquarters for The Way needed to be established. So the representatives of the Board of Directors from the various branches looked around their areas for potential headquarters sites. Some of these people were eager to have the headquarters established in the localities where they lived, such as in Troy, Ohio, Fort Myers, Florida, and Chicago, Illinois. In one case where a property was found, the Board of Trustees thought the site didn't have enough acreage so they decided not to pursue that location any further. But some of the members of the Board of Directors became so upset with this decision that they left the ministry. Dr. Wierwille stated that we must have lost thirty people because they thought he was totally wrong in his decision to reject that site. And the loss of thirty followers was a major blow to us in those transitional years. But the Trustees had made a prayerful, logical decision, and we had to live with people's responses.

The following sets forth some thoughts Dr. Wierwille had expressed early in April in letters addressed to "Dear Friends."

> My job is clearly set before me including praying for others and seeing in them even more than they see in themselves even to the end of believing in them no matter what the outward appearance may be at the moment.
>
> It thrills my soul to help people to become aware of the heavenly potentialities within themselves when Christ lives within.

Dr. Wierwille then turned the meeting over to Lawrence Dale of Troy, Ohio, chairman of the Board of Directors, thinking people might speak more freely if he were not presiding. However, he stayed in the background to hear what was going on. A period of free discussion ensued on questions which had arisen concerning the administration of The Way and how we could best get the Word to God's people.

Since the November 16, 1958, meeting, believers had again worked on plans for starting The Way Biblical Seminary. One proposed location for the seminary was the Wierwille farm. The solicitation of funds to begin work on the seminary found resistance at a meeting of the Miami Valley Group. The Way branch in Troy, Ohio, said that they wanted the farm of The Way in New Knoxville to be kept separate from the spiritual arm of the ministry. They wanted to be sure that their money was going to help spread the work of the ministry and not to help pay off the mortgage at the farm or for the business of the farm. They wanted a seminary to be started, but at a location other than the Wierwille farm.

In responding to this concern, H. E. Wierwille gave a detailed report on how the farm had been given to The Way by his brother Victor and himself. None of the money from any graduates of the Power for Abundant Living classes had been used thus far in work done at the farm or for business related to the farm.

Both Eddie and Donna Doersam stated that they and the Columbus branch gave their money to be used in the Lord's work for The Way Ministry wherever needed. Issues kept coming up, and underlying doubts and distrust from certain members of the board surfaced. The pros and cons were discussed about whether The Way should be engaged in any secular business such as farming or the raising of nutria (fur-bearing animals). Dr. Wierwille said that the farm had been given to the Lord's work and that the business side and spiritual side of the ministry of The Way couldn't be separated because we had to have money to operate with. One of the members of the board observed that if anyone other than the Wierwilles had given a farm, she felt it would have been gratefully received.

Several board members thought that the people who give money would like to have a report on where their money went, how it was being used. H.E. then said that an annual financial statement had always been available to the board and to those who requested copies. But to allay people's concerns, Ermal Owens suggested that the financial records of the past be audited. Dr. Wierwille agreed that Ermal Owens's suggestion was good since there was an apparent doubt about the integrity of the

Secretary-Treasurer and suggested that a committee be appointed by the board to hire an independent auditor and have the books audited for the annual meeting scheduled for June.

H. E. Wierwille stated that the books had long been set up and all monies contributed for specific accounts were recorded and spent accordingly. He agreed that according to the bylaws an independent auditor be hired to audit for the fiscal year of June 1, 1958, to May 31, 1959.

Some of the people asked about what was going to be done at the farm and who would be living there. Donna Doersam and Evelyn Jones both expressed that Dr. Wierwille and his family should move to the farm and have the house remodeled so "it will be a comfortable and a respectable place to live and to start teaching from."

Mal George made a motion that The Way farm be the headquarters for the President of The Way, which motion carried.

The President estimated that the whole remodeling job of the house could be done for around thirty thousand dollars. (Later, when the farmhouse had been remodeled, we worked on grading the surrounding land, including the creek bank, which brought the cost up from the original figure.) We needed ten thousand to fifteen thousand dollars on hand to begin work and maybe the balance of the cost could be taken in the form of a construction loan, the amount of which would be made up by monthly contributions in the form of predated checks, if possible. Mal also made a motion that a committee of three be appointed to determine the President's dwelling, whether the old farmhouse should be remodeled or a new house built. The President of the board appointed to that committee Daniel Friedly as chairman, plus Eldo Cupp and Ray Wiley.

Dr. Wierwille asked the Board of Directors if there was any reason not to have The Way Headquarters at the farm. He indicated he would like to have it there and to move there as soon as possible.

Paul and Carol Kuck stated that they were one hundred percent in favor of reconstructing the present houses (the main house and the summer kitchen, the latter to become the Bible Center) to make them presentable and useful in the ministry.

One member of the Board of Directors said that love must prevail in

A glimpse of the summer kitchen in the background; the smokehouse is in the foreground.

any ministry which is to succeed. At this point Dr. Wierwille brought out how important it was that our eyes be stayed on the Lord Jesus Christ and that when people get out of fellowship, to love them and pray for them. He again thanked the board members for what they did to prosper the ministry.

Other items of business were covered, such as "The Way Good-will Service," which was organized by Dick and Dee Fischbach in order to help the Florida branch following the destruction of Hurricane Donna. They requested that we send them our used clothing to meet families' needs there.

Dr. Wierwille then exhorted the new and the ongoing members of the Board of Directors about their responsibilities:

1. Be faithful in the ministry of The Way and stand upon the truths of the Word which God has so marvelously made known unto us.

2. Be willing to share at least 10 percent of our income with The Way Ministry. Materially we must get to the place where we have The Way Ministry at heart and put forth every effort to move it.

Two weeks after this board meeting, Dr. Wierwille wrote a letter to all board members.

The same day, April 17, Dr. Wierwille also wrote another letter, addressing it to Power for Abundant Living class graduates.

... Inc., International

DR. VICTOR PAUL WIERWILLE, PRESIDENT
BRANCHES: UNITED STATES, ENGLAND, INDIA

649 S. Washington Street
Van Wert, Ohio

... Bible Fellowships
... Biblical Center
... Christian Crusade
... Correspondence Courses
... Abundant Living Classes
... Publications
... Broadcasts
... Magazine

April, 1959

Dear Member of the Board of Directors:

Greetings to you in the precious Name of our living Lord and Saviour Jesus Christ! You will be interested in knowing that we are having good spiritual sessions in the Arcadia Group and next week I hope I can interest the Fort Myers believers in the greatness of this ministry.

Having had a couple of weeks now since the Board Meeting, has given all of us time to think. As Founder and President of The Way I am seriously alarmed at the apparent secret intents and purposes of some which under lay the recent meeting but which did not emerge open and "above board." I am deeply sorry for all of us if such was the case. It sounds and tastes too much like a "church board meeting" with which I have had a well rounded experience. The Way Board of Directors must keep their sights spiritually and ethically higher. Satan is constantly trying to bring to bear his forces of criticism, doubt, questioning the sincerity and honesty of the leaders, etc. If we give satan a toehold he will soon have a foothold, not only in our lives but manifested in the greatness of the ministry of the Word of God.

Spiritually, and in every other way, THE WAY is set up to do a world job of teaching. Our incorporation papers, our constitution and our by-laws, were, I believe, guided by the Lord and are as perfect as is possible for humans to set up. We all know that no organization is better than the people who run it. I can not vouch for The Way and what it may or may not do or be after I am gone; but so long as I live I will do my utmost to keep it running in the fashion in which it will be a glory to God.

Perhaps if I shared with you the reasons and purposes for the Board we could be overcomers in all things. You will recall that "The Way setup" has been handed out in both printed and mimeographed form and a copy or copies have been in your possession. If you have forgotten you may obtain a new copy from Headquarters. It stipulates that the Board of Directors is "a fellowship of all head presbyters of each limb and branch plus such elected directors as the Board of Trustees and International Headquarters deem necessary." Note first of all, it is "a fellowship," meaning all must be in one accord and "of one mind and one opinion" as the Word says -- all in the same boat rowing or sailing the same direction. No one can conscientiously and honestly serve on the Board who would feel or be other wise.

The Board is the vital link in a chain between the individuals and

- 2 -

groups of The Way, bringing with them into each Board Meeting the best of everything from the groups, communities, and sections of the Country and World which they represent. The Board brings to The Way the spiritual enthusiasm of its members everywhere, how best to go on to work out the purposes of The Way. The Board contributes suggestions, plans, programs of procedure, and any other thing they may have which would help the ministry.

The members of the Board of Directors form the representation to and from the people. Every director should be informed as to the interests, purposes, procedures and desires of The Way ministry. The directors in turn enthusiastically invigorate the people in their groups and communities. The directors answer their questions and help them to keep going and growing.

Furthermore, and this is one of the greatest privileges for serving on the Board. Take as an illustration that the trustees have decided on a course of action for a certain task. One man or woman on the Board who is qualified and interested should be given this responsibility for its developement. He could be and should be entitled to choose his fellow workers to get that particular job established and done. In this way, according to our set up, there should be a great activity and cooperation and many things should be accomplished cumulatively though different yet in united activities for the advancement of The Way ministry by the Board of Directors.

On June the 7th will be the Yearly Meeting. We are not interested in the negatives and doubts, but interested in developing the positive and good, so as to be able to do a better work for the Lord in carrying out the ministry whereunto He has called us and wherein He has privileged us to serve.

I think it is a privilege to serve on the Board of this wonderful Bible ministry. I trust you think so too. When we come together for the meeting on the first Sunday in June may you be inspired deeply within yourself to not only represent the people but to represent God in the Board and to bring to bear positive and suggestive materials and information which will help all of us to more effectively and worthily carry out the purposes and intents of The Way ministry world-wide.

The Lord bless you real good!

Sincerely,
In His Service,
Victor Paul Wierwille

VPW/rb

April 1959

"...but Satan hindered..."
I Thessalonians 2:18.

Dear Graduate of Power for Abundant Living Class:

Satan's opposition to the ministry of The Way is strong evidence we must be on the right track.

If you are one interested in The Way ministry and what it teaches and stands for, Satan will do everything in his power to discourage you and prevent you from supporting it regularly and faithfully. He will bring doubt into your mind concerning the honesty and integrity of its leaders, its plans and its works.

The devil knows that you will not only receive the finest academic and biblical training and teaching on the accuracy of God's Word through The Way ministry, but that you will acquire a certainty and assurance in your life you never possessed until after you came in contact with The Way.

The devil knows the worth of a soul saved and filled with the "Power of God," but he wants us to forget that, and to look at the material side, especially the money. That way Satan can keep us giving as little as possible in supporting it and so keep it from spreading.

You are my only contact for spreading this ministry. If you fail me, then in your life time and mine we will have written our own story. Don't let Satan so soon make you forget the spiritual light and power and physical and even material blessings that have come to you because of my ministry.

There is only one question I want you to ask yourself and by your answer you will know and so will I, how much The Way ministry has you as a co-worker. Do you believe in The Way ministry and what it stands for? If your answer is yes, you will not only pray and believe with me, but you will write to me and support my efforts with your tithes and offerings.

I have given my ALL for the sake of ministering the wonderful Word of God. I am glad and happy to minister to you the spiritual food from the Word. Surely you should not begrudge me your material support. We operate the business end of The Way ministry more economically than any Christian organization I know. We have only two salaried employees: my secretary, Rhoda Becker, and my personal assistant, Malvin George. Both are doing twice as much work as should be required of them. I need these two helpers and we should really have two more people on our salaried staff—but Satan hinders.

Here is how your support helps:

1. Not one penny of your money has been used in The Way farm or in the business connected with it.

2. It is used to meet current expenses including the operation of Headquarters, salaries, foreign missions and home missions, necessary, but limited, office equipment and publications.

HERE IS WHAT YOUR ADDED INTEREST WOULD HELP TO DO:

1. Get Malvin George out teaching full time. He is spiritually prepared to teach Classes on Power for Abundant Living. The only reason he isn't out full time is because it takes money and Satan has hindered.

2. Get other people academically ready to teach others. This takes not only a location but the staff to do it. As far as I am concerned I know God has given us the location, all we need is the friends who really are thankful for what they have received and learned and are willing to help us.

3. Help me to keep the financial pressure off of me by meeting our current expenses on time. Today we are $629.30 in the red. This would not be a source of burden to me if Satan did not hinder our people who have received from me. People many times say, "V.P. shouldn't have anything to do with the material end." I assure you I wouldn't have if the necessary material needs were in.

4. Down through the years, from time to time, my children had to draw their savings for their anticipated future education out of the bank to get the current expenses paid. It hurts my personal pride to write this to you, but it's the truth. Don't you really feel that my children should not have to do this? Don't you think I ought to take care of my family? Don't I have even this right? Through the years The Way has helped many young men and women financially through The Way Student Aid Foundation, but not one penny has been offered to my son who is now in college preparing for the ministry, nor will I ever allow my son to receive one cent. But wouldn't you say that the people whose lives have been blessed by my ministry should see to it that my children have their savings restored?

5. The Way needs a permanent place for Headquarters and since we have the farm which is ideally located, from all transportational points of view, I would like to establish our Headquarters there and live there with my family, and start training people in a small way maybe, but at least that way we would get started. After I am gone it may be you or your son who will live there to direct the activities of The Way. I am sorry that Mrs. Bomholt and Mrs. Wiley met with such opposition among some of you among whom I have bled my heart out. I don't want you to do anything you don't want to do. You need not be in favor or financially support the establishing and revamping of the two houses at the farm, you can send your contributions in and "ear mark" it for any purpose you desire for it to go, and for that purpose or purposes it will be used as it has always been used. There are so many needs I have listed a few, if you desire to know other needs The Way is endeavoring to carry out spiritually, write to me and I will give you details. Also any question you may have regarding The Way, its work or ministry, if you will write me or see me I will answer your questions. Don't let your questions or doubts defeat The Way ministry. I need you and God needs you if I am to do the work, in a larger way, to which He has called me.

I thank God for everyone of you who have faithfully stood by me to help and I know God will not only bless you now but reward you in the resurrection. God bless you.

I believe I can say to you what Paul said to the believers in Corinth. Will you please read the first five verses of I Corinthians Chapter 2. These are my words to you and may God have mercy upon us for so soon forgetting what He has done for us in Christ Jesus.

Sincerely,
In His Service,
Victor Paul Wierwille

P.S. Before you go to bed tonight will you write me and then having written me please read I Corinthians 3:4-11 and then pray for me and the ministry of His Word. God loves you and I do and I love to teach and study His Word.

By early June the branches of The Way sent annual reports to Headquarters in anticipation of our annual meeting of the Board of Directors. The reports included whatever advancement had been made in each branch during the year, thankfully noting healings, answers to prayer, meeting the needs of others, and opportunities to witness for the Lord.

At the annual meeting on June 7, 1959, Dr. Wierwille read the constitution and bylaws of The Way, making copies available to everyone. The purpose of the Board of Trustees was also read: To be responsible for all management and business of The Way. The defined purpose of the Board of Directors was read, which said the board was (1) to serve in an advisory capacity, (2) to represent the various branches of The Way, and (3) to accept responsibility to help move the ministry of The Way.

In accordance with a decision made at the special board meeting in April, the independent auditor's report for the fiscal year of June 1, 1958, to May 22, 1959, was submitted by H. E. Wierwille.

The committee that had been appointed at the April 5 meeting to determine whether the President's dwelling could be remodeled or should be built new gave its report.

1. *Each point in this report is the unanimous opinion of the committee.*

2. *One cannot describe a good building program without first describing the expected nature and scope of The Way's activities for many years ahead.*

3. *Had there been revelation, there would have been no need for a committee. We gained information through the senses so we could reach logical conclusions.*

4. *We did not consider questions which board members can answer without on-the-spot study. For example, sentiment was not evaluated. Suitability of the New Knoxville area was not considered.*

5. *The remodeling and expansion plan for converting the summer kitchen into an office, meeting room, and apartment is fairly satisfactory. The building appears sound and suitable for remodeling. However, the suggested plan could be improved considerably.*

6. *The remodeling and expansion plan for the house has so little merit that further consideration is not justified. This plan would not produce a good, suitable building even though it would cost more than a better, more suitable new building would cost. Remodeling would cost more than similar new construction because little of the present structure would be used. The house is not structurally sound enough to justify major expense in remodeling or expansion.*

   The house could be improved at moderate cost with few changes in the basic structure, but the result would not be truly satisfactory as a residence for V.P. plus headquarters for The Way. Moderate changes would preserve sentimental values, but the proposed plan would destroy them.

7. *A comparison of several potential building sites was made.*

   The wooded area east of The Way farm would be almost perfect. The indicated cost is not objectionable. The best site on The Way farm is the woods. Having north rather than south exposure, location of trees, and greater distance from a paved road make it less desirable than the other site.

   The location of the farm buildings would be less satisfactory due to difficulty in financing a house separated on a farm, lack of good large trees, and detraction of farm buildings and activities. Also, building elsewhere would leave the present buildings available for use. The greater difficulty in financing would be due to the fact that such a building program would have little effect on the value of the farm.

A discussion followed of possible sites for building a new house for the President but no conclusion was reached, probably because there was no money to go ahead with the project at that time.

The issue Dr. Wierwille had to resolve was what to do with the existing farmhouse. If we didn't in some way use it, it would be an eyesore and we would have to move it or hold a match to it.

The remodeling of the house was then seriously discussed by the Trustees. In spite of the special committee's conclusion, the Trustees thought remodeling the old farmhouse was the only way to go because there was at least something concrete in the shell of the building to work with.

Dr. Wierwille's schedule in 1959 included teaching classes in Calgary, Alberta, Canada, which meant being gone for six weeks from June 13 to July 27. He wrote about his work there in a letter addressed to The Way Ministry Co-laborers on July 16.

Dear Co-laborer of The Way International:

I send you our Christian love and greetings from Calgary, Alberta, Canada, where we have been since our arrival on June 13th getting the work of The Way International of Canada under way.

God has been wonderfully good, but opening a new territory is always a chore and takes great believing action and boldness. But thank God His Word is His will and it does work.

Mr. E. C. Manning, the Christian Prime Minister of the Province of Alberta, has officially signed all the necessary papers and we now have an official standing with the government of Canada as The Way International of Canada with Headquarters in Ohio. Isn't that a wonderful step forward. I am so thankful for our neighbor, Canada, and especially for our Christian friends, Mr. and Mrs. Peter Luider here in Calgary, who have been so hospitable as to open their hearts and home to us [including Dr. Wierwille and myself with John Paul and Sara]. The Y.M.C.A. here never allows outside groups to conduct classes, but they have opened their doors to us. God was surely in it. Praise His Name!

Fellow-workers of The Way, this is truly the greatest ministry on The Word of God in the world. May we stand faithful in one mind to carry out the work whereunto we have been called of God for this day and hour.

The Way Camp on Power for Abundant Living starting August 1st at Lake Geneva, Wisconsin will be a great and fruitful experience in Christian living. I hope you don't miss it. I give you the Word of the Lord when I say it will be tremendous.

We will continue to minister here in Calgary until July 27th at which time we will leave here to get to Camp in time to see all of you and to have a blessed time in the Lord.

In my first Class here we had a vital Christian lady, Mrs. Myrtle J. Oldaker who wrote the work which I am herewith enclosing as another of our studies in "Understanding the Bible." I have taught you this before, but is it not wonderful that our Christian believers know truth and write it. Just a card to her from you in appreciation for her article would make her very happy. She is a vivacious and enthusiastic Christian. Her address is 536 23rd Avenue, S.W., Calgary, Alberta, Canada.

God bless you—See you at Camp—and do write to Headquarters so I get to hear from you.

Sincerely,
In His Service,
Victor Paul Wierwille

Vesper hour at our first Family Camp

The first Way Family Camp was to be held August 1 to 8 at Camp Aurora, Lake Geneva, Wisconsin, with Mal and Jan George as directors. Since our experiences at Glenn Clark's C.F.O. camps, we had had a great desire to do our own week-long camps. So we, and especially Dr. Wierwille, were very excited to finally see our first one come to pass. There was a special program for children ages three to twelve, for the youth group, and for the adults. Dr. Wierwille and Bishop Pillai were to be our resource leaders. Ever since this first week-long camp venture at Lake Geneva, we incorporated at least one "Way Family Camp" in our annual program until 1994.

The camp daily programs never varied very much.

7:00	Private Devotions and Prayer
7:30	Breakfast
8:45	Devotion with Motion
9:00	Studies in Abundant Living
11:00	Creative Arts (renamed "Expressive Arts")
12:00	Pilot Council Meeting
12:30	Lunch
1:30	Horizontal Hour
2:30	Prayer Workshops (renamed "Hour of Power")
3:30	Recreation
5:30	Supper
7:00	Vesper Hour, songfests, etc. (renamed "Hillside Sing")
7:30	Light Through an Eastern Window (interchangeable with Studies in Abundant Living)
10:00	Quiet

THE WAY CAMP
"Power for Abundant Living"

"Power for Abundant Living", as taught by The Way International, has helped men and women around the world to know as a reality the power of God and to manifest that power in daily living.

The Way International is a fellowship of Christians who believe in the accuracy of God's Word. By applying the principles of The Word, they demonstrate in daily living the power of God through Prayer and Love. The life of every person will be enriched in body, soul and spirit as they fellowship with other Christians living the power of the Abundant Life.

The heartbeat of The Way Camp is the prayer workshop. The individual is taught the accuracy of The Word and the keys to prayer, and as he applies them, his needs are met. As Dr. Victor Paul Wierwille in his class, "Power for Abundant Living" has often said, "Christians need to know what is available today; know how to receive it, and then know what to do with it after they have received what is available".

Courses in "Studies in Abundant Living" and "Light Through an Eastern Window", creative arts, recreation, rest and fellowship combine to make the camp a wonderful experience in Christian living.

A DAY OF FELLOWSHIP

- 7:00— Morning Devotions
- 7:30— Breakfast
- 8:45— "Devotion with Motion"
- 9:00— "Studies in Abundant Living"
- 11:00— Creative Arts and Crafts
- 12:30— Dinner
- 1:30— Horizontal Hour
- 2:00— Prayer Workshops
- 3:30— Recreation
- 5:30— Supper
- 7:00— Vespers, Specials, Songfests
- 7:30— "Light Through an Eastern Window"

A page from the camp brochure

The Way Newsletter was written to keep the believers informed about the activity of The Way.

August 1959
Van Wert, Ohio

Dear Follower of The Way:

Greetings from International Hdqs. The Wierwille family is home, after two classes in Calgary and our first National Way Camp and more than 5745 miles. Hdqs. was a welcome sight, but above all seeing all the gang was best. They are wonderful in "holding the fort" when I am gone. God bless them.

Spiritually the two Canadian classes were a blessing, but one of these times I will have a class up there that really "jells" and then watch out. You will see some real workers come up and out of that group in Calgary. They have the spiritual ability.

As for The Way Camp there is only one word—FABULOUS!...

The enthusiasm for The Way Biblical Seminary is on the way. It looks like it could open real soon. Are you interested?

The Way Camp for 1960. Is there a campgrounds located in your area that could be had? Send us the name or even the particulars if you can.

After my Columbus class we will take a little vacation if you care to call it that, to WORK at The Way Farm, Sept. 11–26. We could use help painting, wiring, cleaning up etc. Do you want to give a day?

So many things happening just now that this letter simply gives you the facts. I trust you will join with us in prayer and work. God is really blessing. This is your opportunity to join in. God has opened every door. Souls are waiting to be set free. God has given the GO SIGN. Your prayers and interest will be greatly blessed of Him. We love you. God bless you and pray and believe with us.

Sincerely,
In His Service,
Victor Paul Wierwille

In October 1959 a group of our women met at Grand Lake St. Marys, where we had rented two cottages for a Women's Retreat. When we arrived, the doors of the cottages were locked. The weather was damp and cold; and after making an access through an unlocked window, we found the cottages frigid inside. So we called Dr. Wierwille, who was at home in Van Wert at the time, and told him our plight. He invited all the women to come to our home to have our retreat. He then proceeded to think of how he could especially bless all of us.

He was getting out the oil lamps and beginning to fill them when he immediately detected the smell of gasoline in the kerosene can. We never found out how this happened, but God certainly spared our home from destruction at this time. God had protected Dr. Wierwille as well as all of us at the retreat. We ladies had an especially good time, probably because we were so grateful not to be in cold, damp cottages and very thankful that our home in Van Wert had remained safe and sound. Everyone enjoyed a wonderful day and a half together.

Remodeling at the Farm

In early November Dr. Wierwille went to Jamaica, Queens, New York, to teach a Power for Abundant Living class. As usual, the members of the class became very blessed at the knowledge they were receiving and bubbled over to tell others about it. Mr. J. A. Shoremount, a tall Swede, seventy-five years old and a lay minister who dearly loved God and His Word, was witnessed to at that time. After hearing about it, he was very eager to take the class. And since the next class was scheduled for February 23 to be taught in Covington, Ohio, "Brother Shoremount" made arrangements to attend it. He stayed with Dr. Wierwille's sister Lydia and her husband, Martin, about forty-five miles from where the class was held, and commuted nightly to the class. By the third session Brother Shoremount was so blessed by the Word of God he was learning that he told Dr. Wierwille he would like to do something special for him. So he volunteered to be the architect for redesigning and remodeling the farmhouse. Dr. Wierwille wholeheartedly and very thankfully accepted his offer. Although I had the know-how to draw a floor plan, we needed an architect to help with structure. God worked this aspect out before we even felt the need. That's our God and Father! When the new house was completed, Brother Shoremount estimated that what we had kept of the old structure, including the slate roof, was worth around seventeen thousand dollars.

On Sunday, January 3, 1960, The Way Board of Directors held a meeting at the home of Mr. and Mrs. Robert Etter in Piqua, Ohio. By this time most of the Board of Directors were in agreement that the Biblical Seminary should be started at The Way farm.

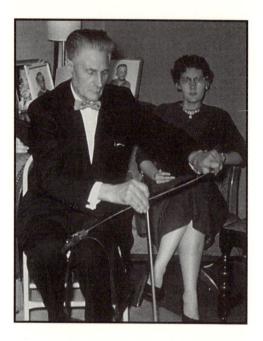

The multitalented Brother Shoremount playing the saw

The year 1959 had been a full schedule of outreach and classes. The following are the foundational classes on Power for Abundant Living taught in 1959 by Dr. Wierwille except for the one noted otherwise.

January	Arcadia, Florida
	Troy, Ohio
February	Arcadia, Florida
March	St. Paris, Ohio—Mal George
May	Piqua, Ohio
June	Piqua, Ohio
June 14–July 26	Calgary, Alberta, Canada (two classes)
August 23–September 4	Columbus, Ohio
October	Troy, Ohio
November	Jamaica, New York

From November 29 to December 11, 1959, Dr. Wierwille taught an Advanced Class in Arcadia, Florida. According to sister Lydia's diary, our regular weekly Bible studies (we now call these fellowships "Twigs") began in January 1959. They were held at various homes of those in the group. The New Knoxville and New Bremen believers met together.

The vision in the early days of 1960 was for the old farmhouse to contain both the living quarters for our family and office space for Dr. Wierwille and Rhoda Becker, his secretary. After much prayer and thought, this decision was made because brother Harry was inspired to personally pay for the project. He knew I had been working on plans for the remodeling of the house and that I was very blessed with them, so he directed me to "plan it as you like; not sparingly, but as you think we need it." That settled it: the headquarters of The Way was to be moved to The Way farm.

Dr. Wierwille observed at the January 1960 board meeting, "Some people may look at our ministry set in the middle of Ohio's farmland and think we should move to a big city. . . . It may take a while before the wisdom and simplicity of this land takes root in your heart, but when it does, you know that the great spiritual nerve center of the ministry just wouldn't be the same without the quiet, rural atmosphere of the surrounding corn and wheat fields. . . ."

The work thus commenced, even while the George family was still living in the farmhouse. The Georges—Mal, Jan, and their four children—had to find another place to live, and God made the right one available to them quickly. Mal has told, "I looked high and low for a place for us to live, and I talked to everybody I knew. I'd see a house for rent, but it never would fit our need. The tendency is to become concerned. One day as I was coming home from looking for a new place to live, Father just said to me, 'Take no thought for it; there'll be a place for you when the time comes.' So, lo and behold, in about another month we passed this house that had already been rented when we looked at it previously. Now the occupants had suddenly moved away, so we rented it and we've lived in that house ever since. When you believe God when He tells you stuff, it's going to happen." And they moved February 13, 1960, out of the farmhouse into a home in New Knoxville that was just perfect for them and their children.

Mal and Jan George with their three oldest children: Susan, Mark, and Paul

Our plans for relocating in New Knoxville moved in stages. First Dr. Wierwille and our family needed housing. So Uncle Harry assumed the financial responsibility to deal with the housing issue while the rest of the Board of Directors continued to think of their commitment to a teaching center, always a paramount issue.

Our plan for remodeling was to finish the basement of the house after the first and second stories had been completed and paid for. However, when we began looking for a meeting place in our vicinity, we couldn't find anything that seemed appropriate. People would be coming to our meetings from distances like Columbus, Toledo, and Bucyrus, so we needed to have hospitality facilities as well as a meeting place for them. Thus it became clear that for the purpose of meetings the basement had to be finished along with the rest of the house. Rest room and kitchen facilities needed to be provided for the convenience of our people as well.

Concerning the remodeling project, Karen relates, "Once the decision was made to remodel the farmhouse, Mother would leave our home in Van Wert early in the mornings and take J.P. and Sara with her. She had to leave early in order to get J.P. to kindergarten in New Knoxville on time, which was a forty-mile drive. My brother Don at that point was in college in Bluffton, Ohio. I was in high school, as was my sister Mary. The school had no cafeteria, so Mary and I would come home at noon and make our own lunch. This was new to us, since before the remodeling of the farmhouse Mother had methodically always been home to make our noon meal and give life to our home."

The Wierwille Home in the process of being remodeled the summer of 1960

The remodeling was quite radical, as parts of the house were at least one hundred years old. We jacked up the entire house and dug a complete basement. We then added the southeast corner on the first floor to become Dr. Wierwille's office with a deck on the second floor. We added ten feet on the north end of the house, two stories with the full basement. This made the size of the house adequate for offices as well as living quarters for our family, which temporarily included Uncle Harry.

Dr. Wierwille's teaching mission for England and Holland came about as planned, with a PFAL class beginning on January 24 in Poynton, Cheshire, England, and another class in Holland beginning on February 6. He wrote, "I was received in England with loving and prayerful arms by our

An advertisement as it appeared in the Haarlems Newspaper (Netherlands) Saturday, February 13, 1960

Interdenominational Evangelical Committee
Special Revival Meeting - Monday 8 o'clock - Begijnhofkapel
The American minister Rev. V. P. Wierville, Ohio
has a message for you this evening (simultaneous translations).
God's plan for this world continues. You may not stand to the side ["you must get involved"], because this is about you.—Reserve this evening!! (Choir service starts at 7:30 o'clock.)

Translation of advertisement

251

friends who came to the U.S. to take my class: Bailey, Hooley, and Stott, plus others who received power from on high through the labors of these men." Later however, the Advanced Class, scheduled to begin on February 21 in England, did not come to pass because the people were not ready for it. Thus, having a couple of extra days, Dr. Wierwille went to Geneva, Switzerland, to visit, after which he returned on February 23 to begin the class in Covington, Ohio.

At the next meeting of the Board of Directors, on February 21, 1960, a few members were absent. And again at the annual meeting in June these same people did not return or care to be members of the board any longer. They did not agree with the decisions of the Board of Trustees concerning having the headquarters on the farm.

Since the President of the Board of Trustees, Dr. Wierwille, was teaching in Europe and Mr. Ray Wiley, chairman of the Board of Directors, was absent, H. E. Wierwille, Secretary-Treasurer of The Way, led the board meeting in February. We focused on planning another building which would be The Way Bible Center. The Board of Directors were in agreement that the Biblical seminary should be started at The Way farm in the simple manner previously proposed. We realized that our first idea to remodel the second little brick house at the farm, known as the summer kitchen, wasn't going to work, as this building would not be large enough to accommodate our needs. H. E. then passed out a listing of the estimates for construction of The Way Bible Center. The Board of Directors were given the following suggestions to contact people who could help get the work rolling:

1. Stimulate interest in The Way Bible Center through personal visitation. Tell the people how wonderful The Way Ministry is and how it is advancing worldwide. Get them inspired for the Lord, but don't use any further pressure.

2. Round up people in the various areas to help with the labor.

Mal George stated how important it was that we be totally sold on the ministry of The Way. "We in The Way must learn to put first things first in our lives and quit putting everything else ahead of the Lord." It was because of this type of attitude that Dr. Wierwille had long ago determined to have Mal make decisions for the ministry when he was out of town.

The work at The Way Headquarters kept progressing, as well as in many other areas of the country. Dr. Wierwille kept his people well-informed and inspired to help, so he also sent out another such letter in April 1960.

649 S. Washington Street
Van Wert, Ohio
April 1960

Dear Christian Friend:

"If you're happy and you know it say Amen," is the title of a song the children sing. This morning, while writing this letter, I too can sing it and say it. I am so happy and I know it because I know what The Word says. I have the more Abundant Life and in Him I am more than a conqueror.

Sometimes when Satan hinders and besets on every hand I get so happy because I know he is a defeated foe and that all he can do even through friends whom I have brought into deliverance and the greatness of God's Word is absolutely nothing as far as the whole picture is concerned....

The more I see Satan raise his head and fight this ministry of the accuracy of His Word the more I realize that the ministry God has given me is so wonderfully great and marvelous, else Satan wouldn't have such a concern. I feel sorry for those whom Satan defeats and gets walking on their sense knowledge, thinking it is revelation. What a counterfeit. But don't blame me, or The Word of God, for neither The Word of God, nor I, one of its teachers, can be held accountable for people's actions. God's Word will stand in spite of man's belief or unbelief. IT IS GOD'S WORD. If there is confusion, the Word says it is of Satan and with it will go every evil work. What is the profit of it all? Outside of love—NOTHING. With love and believing—EVERYTHING.

I thank God for the fruitfulness of our ministry the past month in Florida. On April 7th–10th I was with Dr. Bob Young, the Presbyterian minister and his people at Rochester, Michigan. Had a great unfolding of the Word April 14th, Columbus, Ohio in the home of Mr. and Mrs. Edwin Doersam. April 17th is Easter—Bring a basket lunch and join us in Van Wert at 11 A.M. and Easter Sunday Night at 7:30 P.M. April 19th, Miami Valley Group at the Civic League in Troy. I'd like for every Miami Valley grad who believes in the ministry God has given me and wills to follow my leadership to be present. April 24th, Power for Abundant Living class starting in Napoleon, Ohio. Drive over and give it a good send off.

The Lord's hand on the work at The Way Farm can not be disputed. The Way house remodeling is moving ahead under the direction of Mr. Shoremount with great speed. The Way Biblical Center (HQ) has had a lot of work done on it also. The septic tanks, etc. have all been put in. We now await further help from the Lord to go ahead with pouring of the foundation and putting in the rough plumbing at the remodeling of the old farmhouse. Every Saturday some have joined hands to work at The Way Farm. You are invited. God bless them for their faithfulness according to the promises they made. I wish you a joyous Easter Season but above all that the Word of God may live in you abundantly.

Sincerely,
In His Service,
Victor Paul Wierwille

The Diamond Club

In April 1960 Dr. Wierwille first instituted the Diamond Club. Dr. Wierwille was looking for seventy-five people who would stand with him, support the ministry, and move the Word as a team. He wrote, "An inner circle of true believers could do so much more. I believe if I could have, by the grace of God, seventy-five individuals or families to join me for one year in THE DIAMOND CLUB, we could do what hundreds thus far just have promised and talked about. The Diamond Club will be made up of those who really believe in the ministry of The Way and pledge themselves for one year to pray each day for me and the ministry as well as to share the first tenth (tithe) of their weekly or monthly checks with The Way for its continuation and growth." The Diamond Club never had meetings and received no public attention.

Diamond Club Goals and Objectives

The purpose of the Diamond Club is to develop men and women who will:

1. **MOVE** God's Word over the world.
2. **READ** God's Word daily.
3. **PRAY** perfectly all the time (S.I.T.).
4. **SPEAK** God's Word and witness boldly to all people.
5. **ESTABLISH** a powerful, personal prayer life.
6. **BECOME** the faithful men of II Timothy 2:2 who shall be able to teach others also.

Members of the Diamond Club are committed to:

1. **READ** God's Word every day.
2. **PRAY** for each other every day.
3. **PRAY** for the outreach of the ministry every day.
4. **PRAY** for the spiritual needs of the ministry every day.
5. **DO** all that we can, verbally and spiritually for the work of the ministry.
6. **ABUNDANTLY SHARE** the first fruits of our income with the ministry each week.

THE DIAMOND CLUB

_____ covenant with God to stand faithfully with me in the furtherance of The Way Ministry, national and international. To pray daily and to tithe systematically. I pray that God will in a special way multiply His Abundant Life to you and that you being a co-worker with me will be your most joyous experience as you too see The Way to "go" and "grow."

In His Service,
Victor Paul Wierwille

Rev. Robert Thom, a missionary from South Africa, was invited by Dr. Wierwille to speak at our June 12, 1960, annual Board of Directors' meeting. He said, "The Way is needed in Africa." He told us that Dr. Wierwille's book *Receiving the Holy Spirit Today* had been a source of revival among the Dutch Reformed ministers in South Africa, and many had manifested holy spirit just through reading it. Rev. Thom asked us to help get the book published in at least seven different African languages.

In early June our daughter Karen graduated from high school, earning the distinction of being valedictorian of her class of 145 students.

Following the devotional period and lunch the President reiterated the exhortation concerning the responsibilities of the Board of Directors.

A detailed report of the upcoming camp to be held from August 6 to 13 at the Brethren Retreat Grounds at Lake Shipshewana, Shipshewana, Indiana, was given by our camp director, Mal George. Again we planned a complete program for adults, youth, and children with housing facilities for 140 people. Dr. Wierwille suggested that a newsletter be sent out offering a camp special to parents who registered before July 1. The cost for the camp period for their children six years and under would be $10.00; children six to twelve years of age, $25.00; and children thirteen through high school, $27.50. Scholarships which had been available were already spoken for. Dr. Wierwille told about a man from India who had requested a scholarship. So at the suggestion of a board member, an offering was taken on the spot for this purpose.

THE CAMP STAFF

Malvin L. George	**Camp Director**
C. Janice George	**Youth Director**
Mrs. Vera Kaderly	**Children's Director**
Gilbert Welbaum	**Song Leader**
Mrs. Cordella Adams	**Coordinator, Morning Watch**
Mrs. Max Wolfe	**Camp Secretary**
Mrs. Dorothea Wierwille	**Registered Camp Nurse**
George Jess & Max Wolfe	**Recreation Directors**

Dr. Wierwille announced to the board his plans to teach a class in Arcadia, Florida, July 10–22, and scheduled a retreat for young people before that in New Lyme, Ohio, June 24–26.

Dr. Wierwille opened a discussion of the building project at The Way farm. He stated that H. E. Wierwille had assumed the financial responsibility for the remodeling of the home, believing God to prosper his business so that he could pay off five hundred dollars a month on the home for two years, and at the end of two years pay off the balance.

Dr. Wierwille, as he did at the end of every fiscal year, thanked the members for what they had done to prosper the ministry.

The day after the board meeting Dr. Wierwille wrote a letter to "Followers of The Way." Here are some excerpts.

June 13, 1960

Dear Followers of The Way:

...Yesterday, Sunday, June 12 was a tremendous day at headquarters. God brought together believers for a day of great rejoicing. Rev. Robert Thom, from Southern Africa gave a dynamic message at the 11 o'clock hour.... He would like for us to start a class in Africa on December 27....

All the members of the Board agreed before God to serve and work for the advancement of The Way ministry, and to help people to receive and to manifest the more abundant life. There was only one note of sadness and that was regarding those who have had the light and teaching but are not in one mind or one accord in this tremendous ministry. We prayed for all these as well, being reminded by the Word that, 'We wrestle not against flesh and blood.' We believe God in His love and mercy will give us again all of these....

Work days at the farm are Monday through Saturday. Come when you can. You should see the progress.

A word for our learning. I taught in each class that tongues with interpretation or prophecy does NOT give guidance or revelation. The three worship manifestations are to be used in believers meetings for edification, exhortation and comfort of the WHOLE body.

Whether a prophet or prophetess is of God can be known by two ways: does it agree with the Word and secondly, if it comes to pass. Any prophecy which contradicts the Word could not be of God but is Satan inspired. I also taught everybody never to interpret tongues in their private prayer life. Those who do will 'go off the deep end.' It is contrary to God's Word. I also taught, you cannot force revelation. Never go to someone and say, 'Will you try to get revelation on this or that for me?' That is wrong. Satan will trick you if you do. Furthermore let me remind you that a talebearer is about the lowest of Christians. The tongue can be a mighty weapon for evil. Bridle the tongue and we bridle our lives. Walk with us in one mind, with one spirit and the blessings of God will be upon all of us through Christ Jesus our Lord.

Sincerely,
In His Service,
Victor Paul Wierwille

Dr. Wierwille so very much desired to see the people who had left us come back, though I don't remember one who actually did return to the ministry.

Dr. Wierwille was again very blessed with the second Way Family Camp. The following contains excerpts of the letter I wrote at Dr. Wierwille's request following the camp experience.

August 1960

Dear Followers of The Way:

... The second annual WAY CAMP is history and what a Camp! The Campers who were present both last year and this year said, "Yes, the first Camp was wonderful, but this year's Camp was even better." The highest attendance we had was 119. Mal and Jan George, with the guidance and cooperation of the Pilot Council did a tremendous job of directing the Camp....

Camp Motto: "God first, others second, and I am willing to be third."

Camp Slogan: "We do not have problems, only OPPORTUNITIES!!"...

The impressions of the Camp will become even more deeply imbedded in our souls as we continue to walk worthy of the vocation wherewith we are called and stand with one another in the 'unity of the spirit' which we have in Christ. "He hath blessed us, chosen us, redeemed us, justified us, made us acceptable, abounded toward us in all wisdom, made us meet and delivered us from the power of darkness and translated us into the kingdom of His dear Son."   —Dr. V. P. Wierwille

Sincerely,
In His Service,
Mrs. V. P. Wierwille

Before The Way Family Camp closed, some were asking for the dates of the next camp. They were ready to plan to come the next year.

In the August 1960 issue of *The Four Square Magazine,* Dr. Wierwille's article "Keeping Your Spiritual Deposit Account Alive" appeared. This was another branch of outreach.

Keeping Your
SPIRITUAL DEPOSIT ACCOUNT ALIVE

by Dr. Victor Paul Wierwille
Pastor, Evangelical and Reformed Church of Van Wert, Ohio; Author of the Book "Receiving the Holy Spirit Today"

Timothy was dear to the Apostle Paul. I can understand why Paul's love went out to Timothy. The Christian walk is often a lonesome walk as far as true followers are concerned. There are few who continue to stand faithfully in cooperation and love over the years. When a "man of God" finds even one believer who truly loves him and stands with him in the ministry of the Word, he has found a pearl of inestimable value. He has found another Jonathan. He has a true friend.

Under the mighty ministry of Paul all Asia heard the Word of God in two years and three months as it stemmed out from Ephesus according to Acts 19:8, 10.

"First Love" Faded

God did no ordinary mighty works by the hands of Paul, but extraordinary miracles, according to Acts 19:12. Many believed, were saved, confessed the Lord Jesus Christ, and showed their works openly, even to the end that when they were converted, many who before their salvation operated in the "Black Arts" field, now, after they were saved, brought their "hooky pook" black magic books and burned them publicly in a great revival fire ceremony. When the value of the books burned was tabulated the final inventory indicated a value of 50,000 pieces of silver. "So mightily grew the Word of God and prevailed," in Ephesus and the surrounding country (Acts 19:18-20).

Yet, within a few short years after this great revival Paul writes to Timothy, "This thou knowest, that all they which are in Asia be turned away from me; . . . (II Timothy 1:15). It is little wonder to me, that Paul having found such an one as Timothy who stood and continued to stand with him said, ". . . Timothy, my own son in the faith: . . ." (I Timothy 1:2), "This charge I commit unto thee, son Timothy, . . ." (I Timothy 1:18). ". . . Thou, O man of God, . . . hast professed a good profession before many witnesses." (I Timothy 6:11, 12). ". . . Timothy, my dearly beloved son: . . . I have remembrance of thee in my prayers night and day; Greatly desiring to see thee, . . . that I may be filled with joy; . . . remembering the unadulterated faith that is in thee. . . ." (II Timothy 1:2, 3-5).

Paul's "Right Arm"

No one was more refreshing to Paul than Timothy; which is truly evident, even in the last days of Paul's life here on earth, when he sent to Ephesus and requested Timothy to come with all speed to see him (II Timothy 4:21). He wrote to Timothy saying, "The cloke that I left at Troas with Carpus, when thou comest, bring . . . and the books, . . . especially and parchments." Paul so loved Timothy that he entrusted him with what we call the Word of God, *the written Word*. How touching, how tender, how loving and how human.

"Wherefore I put thee in remembrance that thou stir up the gift of God which is in thee (Timothy) by the putting on of my hands." This gift of God here referred to in Timothy is one or more of the gift ministries listed in Ephesians 4:11 as apostles, prophets, evangelists, pastors and teachers. "By way of (or through the means of) the putting on of my (Paul's) hands" we clearly understand: for when hands are laid on a candidate at the time of ordination prophecy goes forth which will corroborate the ministries within (II Timothy 1:6).

"Be thou not therefore ashamed of the testimony of (witnessing for) our Lord, . . . Who hath saved us, and called us with an holy calling, not according to our works, but according to His own purpose and grace, which was given us in Christ Jesus before the world began" (II Timothy 1:8, 9).

That Paul is here definitely dealing with salvation and its intended spiritual blessings can not be disputed. The New Birth, "Christ in you" is the GREAT SECRET of I Timothy 3:16. ". . . Great is the mystery (secret) of godliness: God was manifested in the flesh, justified in *pneuma*, seen of angels, preached unto the Gentiles, believed on in the world, received up into glory." "This is a great mystery (secret): but I speak of Christ and the church" (Ephesians 5:32). We rejoice in the revelation of this GREAT SECRET which was ". . . kept secret since the world began," ". . . hid in God . . ." until the revelation of it was given to the Apostle Paul (Romans 16:25, 26; Ephesians 3:9).

The "Called Out" Ones

In other ages this great mystery was not made known unto the sons of men (Ephesians 3:5). It had always been ". . . hid from ages and from generations, . . ." (Colossians 1:26).

The GREAT SECRET was not concerning specifically Jews or Gentiles as such, but concerning a peculiar people, taken out from both Jews and Gentiles, and made "fellow-heirs" and members "of the same body." In essence "the one body," the spiritual body of Christ in which there is neither Jew or Greek but a new creation (Ephesians 3:6; Romans 10:12; I Corinthians 12:13; Galatians 3:8; Colossians 3:11).

Thus the transgressors of the Jews and sinners of the Gentiles who confess the Lord Jesus and believe God raised Him from the dead are called out and made a New Body, an Assembly, an *ecclesia*, which is "the church

AUGUST, 1960   7

From a paragraph in the Thanksgiving letter of November 7, 1960, Dr. Wierwille again showed his concern for others as he wrote:

> I wonder if you might not find it in your heart to stand with me at this Thanksgiving time so that The Way ministry can send some financial gifts to genuine Christian men working for the cause of Christ in India. I feel it is the will of God that we should, by all means, send a Christmas check to both Dr. Das and Dr. Williams, to help them in their work. It will make their hearts rejoice to receive a gift and they will bless you for it. I trust the Lord will touch your heart in this matter.

In late December of 1960, as we were within six weeks of moving to the new headquarters at New Knoxville, Dr. Wierwille was inspired to fellowship specifically with our Van Wert folks who had shared with us much in labor and regular fellowships. He wrote the following note of invitation:

> Dec. 14, 1960
>
> Dear Friends:
>
> Usually there are so many out of town guests when we get together that Mrs. Wierwille and I and our family would just like to have our Van Wert folks to join us at The Way headquarters.
>
> On Thursday evening, December 22, at 6:30 we would like you to join us in a pot-luck fellowship dinner. Since this will be our last Christmas together here at Van Wert we would truly be thankful for your fellowship.
>
> Sincerely,
> In His Service,
> Victor Paul Wierwille

In excerpts of a letter to the Diamond Club on December 17, 1960, Dr. Wierwille expressed his heart at that time.

> Every New Year's Eve, for many years now, Mrs. Wierwille and I have hosted in entertaining many of our intimate friends and loved ones. We had fully intended to be nestled in our new home and to open there on New Year's Eve. Since this is impossible we are still planning our New Year's affair to be held here at Headquarters in Van Wert on Saturday night, the 31st, beginning when you arrive and concluding after midnight. As a member of the Diamond Club you are specifically invited this year.
>
> The inside life of The Way ministry is vitalizing. The Springfield class was just 'so, so.' Some 'leg-pulling.' The great hunger and thirst to receive the Holy Spirit was manifested in too few.
>
> A remarkable thing happened on Sunday evening, December 4, in the class. I spoke a few minutes on the urgency of getting this ministry on the greatness and accuracy of God's Word to the people around the world. Several wonderful letters with checks enclosed came in during that week, with a note knowing how important this ministry is....
>
> God bless you, as I said in my Christmas letter to you, but may I say it again that you may always remember my appreciation, love and prayers for you, because you believed especially to join me in the Diamond Club.

The year 1960 was filled with Dr. Wierwille's working with his hands as well as teaching classes and having many other meetings. Always the exhortation was "Let's keep our hands joined in 'one mind with one spirit.'"

The following is the listing of Foundational Classes in 1960, all taught by Dr. Wierwille:

January	Poynton, Cheshire, England
February	The Netherlands
	Covington, Ohio
May	Napoleon, Ohio
July	Arcadia, Florida
September	Grand Rapids, Ohio
October	McClure, Ohio
November	Springfield, Ohio

In November, Dr. Wierwille also taught an Advanced Class in Troy, Ohio.

The New Year's Retreat on January 1 to 3, 1961, was again held at Mote Park Recreation Center, Piqua, Ohio, with David du Plessis as our guest. Having just returned from a meeting of Pentecostals in Geneva, Switzerland, Brother du Plessis could give accounts of the mighty moving of God's spirit worldwide.

At the January 22, 1961, meeting of the Board of Directors held at Columbus, Ohio, Dr. Wierwille led a discussion about the Ecumenical Bible Center, as we were now calling the seminary, and how it could be built. In discussing the finances, the consensus of the board was that we should get started and believe that finances would fall in line. Dr. Wierwille also told about how helpful the Diamond Club had been to the ministry.

Dr. Wierwille read letters from various grads telling of how God had blessed them financially, physically, and spiritually since they had taken the Power for Abundant Living class. He also read the following findings concerning an adult human's memory, which concept became more deeply rooted in his teaching techniques.

It is a fact that for any given impression which the minds of one hundred people receive, twenty-five forget at the end of twenty-four hours, fifty have forgotten at the end of the second day, and only fifteen remember it four days later, and in sixteen days, practically everyone has forgotten it. Sixty-two percent of the acceptance of all ideas comes after the sixth time they are presented; so it takes repetition, repetition, and repetition.

The following letter was to again keep our people informed of the activity of the ministry, pointing out the spiritual program being carried on as well as a very great step in the physical realm. On January 24, 1961, Dr. Wierwille sent this letter, which demonstrates how much was going on while we were packing up in Van Wert, getting ready for our permanent move to New Knoxville.

the Way ...International

VICTOR PAUL WIERWILLE, FOUNDER
BRANCHES: UNITED STATES, ENGLAND, INDIA

...Bible Fellowships
...Biblical Seminary
...Christian Crusade
...Correspondence Courses
...Abundant Living Classes
...Publications
...Broadcasts
...Magazine

649 S. Washington Street
Van Wert, Ohio

January 24, 1961

Dear Friend of The Way

Greetings to you in the Name of Jesus Christ. The Way ministry is on the move. People are being saved, filled with Holy Spirit, delivered and growing in the Word. Please read this letter carefully and note things on your calendar.

Week of January 29th, Monday through Thursday, we will welcome your help at The Way Farm to get the basement completed for as little retardment in continuing our work as possible. We will be at the Farm every morning by 9 A.M. Bring paint brushes and rollers and any other tools you think you might need.

Moving date to The Way Farm, February 1st and 2nd.

Mailing address for The Way, Inc. after February 1st is New Knoxville, Ohio. Phone: 4545.

Note this important announcement carefully. Due to the fact we could not move early enough, our guest John Noble, a prisoner in the Russian slave camp, will present his hair raising message according to the following schedule:

Saturday, February 4th, 8 P.M., American Legion Hall, W. Main St.,
   Van Wert, Ohio.
Sunday, February 5th, 3 P.M., American Legion Hall.
Sunday, February 5th, 8 P.M., Miami Valley. Contact Mr. and Mrs.
   Kenneth Grubbs, Troy, Ohio. Phone: FE-2-4364.

Sunday, February 12th, 7:30 P.M., first Fellowship and Teaching service at our new International Headquarters of The Way. One mile South and half mile West of New Knoxville, Ohio, on Route 29. We will be looking for you at the John Noble meetings and you won't want to miss the first Sunday Night Fellowship at the farm. Bless you good!

Hurriedly, but
In His Service,
Victor Paul Wierwille

VPW/rb

Again, it was brother Harry who had met John Noble and learned of the tremendous experience of God's deliverance in his life. Harry then introduced John to Dr. Wierwille. The Noble family had had a camera manufacturing business in Dresden, Germany, prior to World War II. Having been taken by Russia as slave labor at the end of the war, John and his father had been in various prisons from 1945 to 1955: Dresden, Muehlberg, Buchenwald, and others, and finally, in Vorkuta in Siberia. John was miraculously released through the personal intervention of President Eisenhower. He described his release: "No radio was on; the 'Nun Danket,' 'Now Thank We All Our God,' was playing louder than ever in my heart." Every Wednesday night, people who knew of his situation had prayed faithfully for his release, and those prayers were indeed answered.

John related, "Many times during my long imprisonment, I thought of Job. In his famous pledge he declared, 'All the while my breath *is* in me, and the spirit of God *is* in my nostrils; My lips shall not speak wickedness, nor my tongue utter deceit' " (Job 27:3 and 4). His message was indeed inspiring to our audiences in showing God's love and care for His children. The *International Association of Panoramic Photographers* magazine of December 1992 noted that when the Berlin wall fell in 1989, the Noble family reclaimed their camera factory and the family home. Praise God! What a miracle!

Moving Day

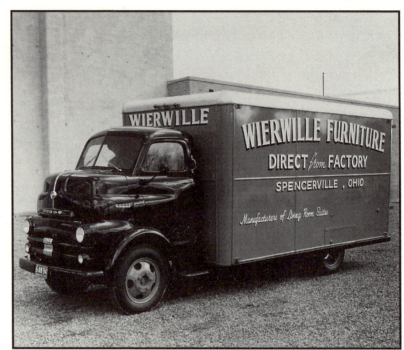

Moving day arrived. It was now Thursday, February 2, 1961, a very blustery, frigid winter day. The temperature reached ten degrees with blizzard conditions. Some of our lady workers arrived early at our remodeled home to get an idea of which rooms the boxes and furniture were to be delivered to as they arrived from Van Wert. The ladies lit the living room and basement fireplaces to help the furnace in heating the house.

At 1:30 P.M. the Wierwille Upholstery Company trucks arrived with the first loads of our furniture and household goods. The easiest way to move the furniture and boxed things was through the four-foot sliding glass doors off the east porch. The brisk wind also forced through the house each time the door glided open. What a day!

That evening we had our first fellowship in the living room in that new home. There still was no carpet on the floor, and the chairs had not yet been delivered, so the next best thing to sit on were boxes, the stairs, and pillows on the floor. Those present were ladies and children: Rhoda, Miney Shroyer, Jan George and her children (Susan, Mark, Paul, Tim, and David), Evelyn Jones, Mary Wierwille (Reuben's wife), and myself with J. P. and Sara. The men were still out with the moving trucks, which were hauling the last loads of furniture. They arrived at 10:00 and 10:30 P.M.

Dr. Wierwille, myself, and our family had spent over sixteen years in Van Wert. For Dr. Wierwille these years were filled with many hours of research in God's Word as well as many miles of travel in search of the truth. That had also been Dr. Wierwille's time of pastoring the congregation of his church with sermons, radio broadcasts, choir rehearsals, women's guild meetings, weddings, confirmations, counseling, and other church-related activities. Dr. Wierwille was busy learning about people and the practical application of the Word he was researching. This was his life-style in Van Wert. From the following letter you will see that his vision, his goal to reach people with God's rightly divided Word had not changed.

THE WAY, INC.
NEW KNOXVILLE, OHIO

February 20, 1961

Dear Follower of The Way:

We are moved! Praise God—not only for our new headquarters home, but for those who prayed and believed and for everyone who helped us to get moved in. What a task, considering both offices, etc. Our address is New Knoxville, Ohio. Phone: 4545.

We opened officially on Sunday night (Lincoln's Birthday) February 12th with a great song service and an inspirational fellowship culminating in an alive and vital communion service. The spirit of fellowship was the sweetest this side of Heaven and how I wish all of my friends could have been blessed with us. Representative Martin Feigert from Van Wert supplied our Ohio State flag and State seal and U.S. Representative Walter Moeller has volunteered to send us the U.S. flag flying over our National Capitol on Washington's Birthday, the founder of our country. Isn't that wonderful!

Open House for everybody on Saturday afternoon and evening, March 25th.

We have a wonderful teaching fellowship each and every Sunday Night at 7:30 at Headquarters and we invite you to join us whenever possible. Thursday, at 8 P.M. each week is our local prayer group joining with other prayer groups across our Nation. We maintain a 24 hour a day telephone line open for prayer. Call 4545, New Knoxville any hour any day, we are at your service in His behalf.

Ministers and wives, missionaries, full time Christian workers: Class on Power for Abundant Living, Y.M.C.A., Xenia, Ohio. Contact Headquarters or write Rev. Paul Crockett, R.D.#3, Xenia, Ohio. Phone: Drake 2-5274. The class will meet in the mornings only at 8:30 A.M. I will pay you to get your minister and his wife into this class. Perhaps you have a minister or missionary friend you could bring in. This may be the most outstanding class The Way has ever offered.

Sincerely,
In His Service,
Victor Paul Wierwille

In moving from Van Wert to The Way farm, life kept forging ahead. Dr. Wierwille seemed to have a fountain of plans for serving God's people. As he many times said, by keeping our hands joined in "one mind with one spirit" we would together move God's Word.

We had made the transition from the Van Wert pastorate to giving our full-time believing efforts to The Way Ministry. With our move to Dr. Wierwille's childhood land, we continued to be challenged to depend upon God to open doors of utterance. We were doing everything we knew to spread the dynamic knowledge of His Word, the Word we had been given and which we were so eager to share.

Books by
Victor Paul Wierwille

Receiving the Holy Spirit Today

Are the Dead Alive Now?

Studies in Abundant Living Series

    Volume I, *The Bible Tells Me So*
    Volume II, *The New, Dynamic Church*
    Volume III, *The Word's Way*
    Volume IV, *God's Magnified Word*
    Volume V, *Order My Steps in Thy Word*

Jesus Christ Is Not God

Jesus Christ Our Passover

Jesus Christ Our Promised Seed

About the Author

Seldom does a wife write a biography of her husband. But Mrs. Victor Paul Wierwille is a unique person and acted courageously in undertaking the work of chronicling Dr. Wierwille's life. Because both of them were reared in the same rural, German-American community in western Ohio in the mid-1910 to 1930s, Mrs. Wierwille is intimately familiar with the times and culture of their lives from the very beginning.

The only years Victor and Dorothea experienced differently were the three years the future Mrs. Wierwille spent in nurses' training in Cincinnati, Ohio, and her future husband was in college near Sheboygan, Wisconsin. They married in July 1937, and as a team, they began their lifelong pursuit of learning and ministering God's Word to God's people.

Mrs. Wierwille, a multicapable person, brings to us the history of her husband's life from 1916 to 1961. She writes with accuracy, color, humor, and sensitivity. *Born Again to Serve* makes a special contribution to the faithful followers of The Way Ministry, showing the life of our Founding President and father in the Word, a man who clearly heard God's call and then followed it to serve.